CRITICAL HUMANISMS

Critical Humanisms

Humanist/Anti-Humanist Dialogues

MARTIN HALLIWELL
and ANDY MOUSLEY

EDINBURGH UNIVERSITY PRESS

© Martin Halliwell and Andy Mousley, 2003

Edinburgh University Press Ltd
22 George Square, Edinburgh

Typeset in Fournier by
Koinonia, Manchester, and
printed and bound in Great Britain by
Antony Rowe Ltd, Chippenham, Wilts

A CIP record for this book is available from the British Library

ISBN 0 7486 1504 0 (hardback)
ISBN 0 7486 1505 9 (paperback)

Frontispiece: George Grosz, 'Travelling People'
('Fahrendes Volk', 1918)
Henry Boxer Gallery, Richmond, Surrey
www.henryboxergallery.com © DACS 2003

Contents

Acknowledgements

We would like to express our gratitude to the University of Leicester and De Montfort University for granting us study leave at the same time in Autumn 2002 to complete this book. Warm thanks also to Jane Dowson, who has been an ongoing source of guidance, friendship and wisdom, to Jackie Jones at Edinburgh University Press for her enthusiasm, advice and efficiency, to Henry Boxer for his kind loan of the image, and to the Hammer & Pincers in Wymeswold for the spontaneity it encouraged. The expertise and supportive response of Paul Hegarty, Richard King, George Lewis, Janet Lewison, Makiko Minow-Pinkney, Michael O'Brien, Tom Olsen, Joe Phelan, Bernard Sharratt, Phil Shaw and the late Nicholas Zurbrugg have also been greatly appreciated. To Laraine, Debbie and Dan we give heartfelt thanks for both the calculable and incalculable ways in which they have informed our thinking. Versions of some chapters have been presented as papers at the University of Leeds (November 2001), Loughborough University (April 2002), De Montfort University, Leicester (September 2002), University of Paris X, Nanterre (June 2003) and Senate House, University of London (July 2003).

Towards a Critical Humanism

During its euphoric heyday in the late 1970s to the mid-1980s, critical theory told a grand and dramatic narrative about itself, and this despite the suspicion from some theoretical quarters of grand narratives. The narrative pivoted around the idea that the advent of modern theory constituted a climactic turning point, a moment of complete rupture, a clean and decisive break from the past. Critical theory, ran the narrative, was the brave new world, and all that went before it old, bad, usually bourgeois and most often humanist. This is more or less the story told by Terence Hawkes in the general editorial preface to the *New Accents* series that began in the 1970s and contributed to the mission to package and popularise theory:

> In various parts of the world, new methods of analysis have been developed whose conclusions reveal the limitations of the Anglo-American outlook we inherit. New concepts of literary forms and modes have been proposed; new notions of the nature of literature itself, and of how it communicates are current; new views of literature's role in relation to society flourish.[1]

In this version of the seductive narrative that critical theory constructed about itself during its high period, dominated by the French thought of Baudrillard, Derrida, Foucault, Kristeva, Lacan and Lyotard, theory represents the good new days which will supersede the bad old days of 'baggy' humanism represented by such influential figures as Matthew Arnold, F. R. Leavis and T. S. Eliot. The uncritical, vaguely defined Anglo-American humanism of these thinkers was banished as 'fragmented, self-contradictory, confused and flawed' in favour of nuanced, self-reflexive and more rigorous theory.[2]

The first section of this Introduction will show how critical theory made humanism less baggy. While we do not want to resurrect such a humanism, there is a certain eclecticism about our own approach, which is reflected both in the angular distortions and graphic free play of George Grosz's dadaist image *Travelling People* (see frontispiece), and in the plural humanisms (rather than singular humanism) of the title. The human, from this perspective, is too amorphous to be easily defined, and to try to name it in a prescriptive way is paradoxically to be anti-humanist, because it denies individuals the role of interpreting for themselves what being human means. Rather than a given entity, this perspective takes the human to be an open-ended and mutable process. Baggy humanism can thus be recast as a post-foundationalist view of the human: a view, that is, which accepts the postmodern suspicion of essentialist categories. At the same time, however, we do not want the human in this book to become so lacking in foundations that it disappears. Too ungrounded and the human loses its critical edge, because everything from totalitarianism to raking gravel can be thought of as an expression of the human. An ethically and politically grounded humanism is surely necessary, for we have to have some sense of what a human being is to know when he or she is being degraded and what human agency is when it is denied. But too tightly defined, on the other hand, and the human is in danger of becoming a reified and prescriptive category. These questions, and others closely related to them, will be more fully elaborated later in the Introduction. First, we will turn to the attempt by critical theory in the 1970s and 1980s to make humanism less baggy.

From Baggy to Streamlined Humanism

The phrase which best identifies the baggy nature of mid-nineteenth- to mid-twentieth-century Anglo-American humanism is 'criticism of life'. Used by Matthew Arnold in the nineteenth century in his claim that poetry 'is at bottom a criticism of life; that the greatness of a poet lies in his powerful and beautiful application of ideas to life – to the question: How to live', the phrase reappears in the work of F. R. Leavis and the American critic Lionel Trilling. In the mid-1960s, before the moment of high theory, Trilling appropriated Arnold's phrase to promote the idea that literature makes 'a declaration about the qualities of life that life should have, about the qualities life does not have but should have'.[3] The use of the phrase performs two operations at once: first, it constructs literature as an affirming and enriching counter-language to those forces in the world, such as science, technology, utilitarianism, mass culture and commerce, which are perceived to be a threat to, or an impoverishment of, the human; and second, the phrase 'criticism of life' maintains an oppositional role for literature (and other forms of high culture), by resisting the tendencies within certain strands of formalism and modernism to remove literature from any intimate contact with 'life'. By opposing art to science, culture to commerce, and life to technology in the name of threatened human values, this form of humanism did have a critical edge, but was less searchingly critical of its own founding presuppositions. For example, as René Wellek observed in 1937, Leavis' appeal to 'the possibilities of life' is gloriously nebulous.[4] While such appeals often performed the critical function of resisting the capitalist and technocratic tendency to quantify everything and thus close down 'the possibilities of life', they are susceptible to the charge of being blind to their own assumptions.

The critical theory of the 1970s and 1980s made the humanism of the Anglo-American tradition much less amorphous, by identifying what was perceived to be its underlying premises, and by eliding it with a longer history of humanism, that is often thought to have originated with Renaissance scholarship and to have gained momentum through the Enlightenment. In 1980, at the high point of the popularised version of critical theory, Catherine Belsey located the essence of humanism in its inflated assumption that '"man" is the origin and source of meaning, of action, and of history'.[5] This essentialist account of humanism is still current, although there is increasing recognition that humanism is not reducible to it. Iain Chambers' *Culture After Humanism* (2001) is an example of this revisionism. He characterises the humanism which has become dominant as 'an inherited sense of the world in which the human subject is considered sovereign, language the transparent medium of its agency, and truth the representation of its rationalism'.[6] However, instead of adopting a staunchly anti-humanist stance, Chambers veers via the thought of the German philosopher Martin Heidegger towards a looser or post-foundational humanism by suggesting that: 'Being in the world does not add up, it never arrives at the complete picture, the conclusive verdict. There is always something more that exceeds the frame we desire to impose.'[7] Chambers' succinct definition has become the dominant way of thinking about humanism in the 1990s and clearly identifies those interrelated aspects of an ideology which anti-humanists persistently identified in order to challenge. A baggy, half-theorised humanism was difficult to attack because its suppositions were unclear and implicit, but a humanism with a clear agenda and clear assumptions was a humanism that could be questioned.

We are not simply suggesting that critical theory's version of humanism is a pure invention, but that humanism has been tidied up, packaged and streamlined by some anti-humanists in such as a way as to negate its actual diversity. It is possible, of course, to choose a route through intellectual and cultural history that substantiates this streamlined definition. If the protagonists are taken from the tradition of specialist philosophical enquiry, rather than from the less systematic logics of humanist literary criticism – if, in other words, the protagonists are Descartes, Locke and Kant rather than Arnold, Eliot and Leavis – then the history of humanism looks a rather less messy affair. Because some influential versions of critical theory in the 1970s and 1980s were intent on being more rigorous and scientific than their 'baggier' forebears, it is not surprising that their version of humanism and its history reflected this scientism.

But what, precisely, are the premises of the humanism which theory identified and attacked? Chambers specifies three important and interrelated characteristics of what this book will subsequently call 'classical' or occasionally 'liberal' humanism: the sovereignty of the subject (a key feature of liberal humanism); the transparency of language; and rationalism. Each of these was persistently questioned during the high period of critical theory's anti-humanism. Thus the supposed sovereignty and independence of the individual were questioned by asserting the primacy of language and society in profoundly shaping our identities. The notion of language as a transparent medium of expression of that human individuality and independence was challenged by the poststructuralist insistence that not only does language 'speak us' as much as we 'speak it', but also that language is an opaque medium which frustrates our efforts to ground meaning and identity. To take two examples: the French critic Paul Ricoeur is one among many thinkers who has argued that subjectivity is 'opaque' and 'expresses itself through the detour of countless mediations – signs, symbols, texts and human praxis itself',[8] and, on the subject of moral theory, the sociologist Zygmunt Bauman contrasts a coherent system of ethics based on firm foundations to an '"ethically un-founded morality" in which moral questions are put together piecemeal while we construct ourselves'.[9] These expressions of post-foundationalism (in which no grounds for subjectivity or morality can be established) have serious implications for a humanism taken to be irredeemably foundationalist. The third characteristic identified by Chambers, that 'truth' is the representation of the independent subject's 'rationalism', rests upon an Enlightenment view of human reason and understanding as perfectible. Enlightenment thought is more fully examined in Chapter 4, but one important 'motto of enlightenment' for Immanuel Kant was to 'have courage to use your *own* understanding'.[10] Such is Kant's Enlightenment faith in human reason that he believes the independent use of one's reason will lead to an undistorted understanding of reality. Faith in the march of human reason towards perfection is itself not the only way of characterising Enlightenment thought, but it has contributed towards the idea of humanism established by a largely French and post-structuralist canon of critical theory that it is a belief-system with an inflated and uncritical view of human capacities. As the French anthropologist Claude Lévi-Strauss described it in the French newspaper *Le Monde* in 1979:

> What I have struggled against, and what I feel is very harmful, is the sort of unbridled humanism that has grown out of the Judeo-Christian tradition on the one hand, and on the other hand, closer to home, out of the Renaissance and out of Cartesianism, which makes man a master, an absolute lord of creation.[11]

If unbridled humanism is the only kind of humanism that has ever existed, then anti-humanists are right to attack it. This book, however, offers a more complex account of humanism and its perceived opposite anti-humanism.

Three Phases of Anti-Humanism

It would be misleading to privilege the 1970s and 1980s as anti-humanism's only key period, for it was itself shaped by, as well as transformative of, the work of previous thinkers. A tradition of anti-humanist thought can thus be invoked, but with two important qualifications: first, that just as humanist thought is not monolithic, so, likewise, anti-humanism has taken different forms; and second, that proto-modern thinkers like Marx and Nietzsche have often been recruited to the anti-humanist 'cause', and seen only in this light, when it is possible to identify currents of humanism in their work. We shall discuss later in the Introduction the idea that perceived anti-humanists may actually be read otherwise. For now, we will survey some of those aspects of earlier thinkers' work that have encouraged recent theorists to construct them in their own anti-humanist image.

Three phases within a tradition of anti-humanist thought can be identified. To the first phase, which stretches from the mid-nineteenth to the early twentieth century, belong Darwin, Freud, Marx, Nietzsche, Saussure and Weber. Encouraging a broad engagement with the processes of modernity, these thinkers can be thought of as germinal figures so far as subsequent anti-humanist thinkers are concerned. In most, although not all, of these cases the characteristic most conducive to anti-humanism is their privileging of impersonal systems over human agency and individuality. Marx, Darwin, Saussure and Weber offer panoramic views of movements and systems so vast or impersonal in scale that flesh-and-blood human beings seem to pale into insignificance. As in Greek tragedy, human beings appear to be at the mercy of forces beyond both their control and understanding. Whether the forces in question are economic (Marx), evolutionary (Darwin), linguistic (Saussure), or social (Weber), humanity is understood to be the mere effect of causes which are located elsewhere, and penetrable, it seems, largely retrospectively and then only by experts. The anti-humanist aspects of Freud's and Nietzsche's thought are slightly different. Freud concentrates more upon the individual psyche and its complex formation than upon social, economic or evolutionary systems, but he nevertheless made a scientific system out of the psyche, and one which is furthermore only partly penetrable because of the unconscious forces running amok within it. Meanwhile, Nietzsche showed considerable disdain for what he saw as the boring and bogus rationality of human beings committed to *passé* Enlightenment ideas of truth and progress. Such, then, are the differently inflected anti-humanist elements of the thinkers who have become foundational for second and third wave anti-humanists.

To the second phase of the late 1960s belong the French thinkers Barthes, Baudrillard, Deleuze, Derrida, Foucault and Guattari. The germinal texts of this second phase (discussed in the following chapters) are Foucault's *The Order of Things* (1966) and *The Archaeology of Knowledge* (1969); Derrida's *Of Grammatology* (1967) and his essay 'The Ends of Man' (1969); Barthes's essay 'The Death of the Author' (1968); Baudrillard's *The System of Objects* (1968); and Deleuze and Guattari's *Anti-Oedipus* (1972). These texts also formed the basis of the reception and transmission of French theory during the 1970s and 1980s. This latter phase, which coincided with the emergence of postmodern theory, is the third movement of the anti-humanist tradition. Such British and American popularisers and translators of French theory as Catherine Belsey, Geoffrey Bennington, Terence Hawkes and Christopher Norris (in Britain) and Peggy Kamuf, J. Hillis Miller and Paul Rabinow (in America) helped to shape the complex strands of French poststructuralist thought into a narrative that treated logocentrism, phallocentrism and humanism as the cardinal sins of Western metaphysics. In the version of modern critical theory which unfolded under the auspices of this third phase of anti-humanism, terms like 'experience', 'consciousness', 'testimony', 'life', 'individual' and 'human' were not just endangered concepts, but perceived to be endangering to the refinement of theory. In order to distance themselves further from baggy humanism, critical theorists tend to reject these terms in favour of 'structure', 'system', 'discourse' and 'inscription'. The precise nature of the shift in vocabulary is exemplified in the displacement of the humanist term 'influence' by the concept of 'intertextuality' (meaning that no text exists in isolation from other texts). Although these two terms are comparable, where influence suggests interpersonal contact between people, intertextuality rewrites influence as an impersonally linguistic phenomenon that happens independently of human agents.

This loss of agency did not just derive from the crisis of New Left politics following the 1960s, but also from the dismantling of subjectivity as a meaningful metaphor for discussing identity. For example, in the perceived anti-humanist text *The Ecstasy of Communication* (1987), Jean Baudrillard argued that 'the religious, metaphysical or philosophical definition of being [has] given way to an operational definition in terms of the genetic code (DNA) and cerebral organization ... We are in a system where there is no more soul, no more metaphor of the body.'[12] If, in Baudrillard's terms, the metaphors of 'body' and 'soul' have lost their potency to describe the parameters of selfhood, then there can be 'no more individuals, but only potential mutants'.[13] Instead of using modernist tropes of exile and alienation, Baudrillard writes in terms of 'metastasis' as 'a deprivation of meaning and territory' and as an expression of the interminable spreading of disease, a malignant cancer that rends the core of the humanist self and for which there is no treatment.[14] Emptied of its own substance, the human can no longer form the basis of appeals to alienation or dehumanisation, since these latter concepts presuppose the recognition of basic human characteristics against which alienated versions of the self might be measured.

The essentialist conception of the self that Baudrillard declares redundant has come to typify classical humanism. However, even if this one part of the humanist tradition were taken to represent the whole, there are still different ways of inflecting it. For example, essentialism can be taken as arrogant, as well as limiting, when it posits a fixed, transcendent subject as the source of society, history and language: 'man' as 'the origin ... of meaning, of action, and of history', as Catherine Belsey puts it. But it can equally be thought of as a more humble attempt to salvage the limits and givens of the human in situations where such limits are perceived to be eroded. These two possibilities explain the coexistence in certain writers, such as Baudrillard, of the moods of euphoria and mourning, celebration and loss. The death of the humanist 'self' or 'soul' is at once cause for celebration because it transgresses a limit, and the occasion for mourning because of the loss of foundations. Either way, however, humanism is understood primarily as a foundationalist discourse, and language, history, society and technology as impersonal forces that threaten the humanist project. The 'human' emotions of euphoria and mourning may still be residually present in a writer like Baudrillard, but they are often muted in the work of other anti-humanist writers because of their association with a discredited and outdated humanism whereby each and every reference to the human becomes tarred with the same foundationalist brush. While it is possible, as we suggested earlier, to recast thinkers within the anti-humanist canon as humanists, this can only be accomplished with the help of an expanded understanding of humanist thought.

Critical Humanisms

Against the popular image of humanism as monolithic, this book identifies a diverse tradition, by discussing the varied contributions to humanism that have been made by a range of thinkers drawn from philosophy, literature, science, theology, sociology, cultural studies and critical theory. That humanism is generally conceived as a Western discourse is made clear by the concentration of thinkers from Europe and North America. However, while Edward Said argues that humanism often sustains its coherence by means of 'the unexamined prestige of culture (as in France) or by science (as in the Anglo-Saxon world)' and so eliminates 'the possibility of a valuable kind of radical self-criticism', it is precisely this 'radical self-criticism' in which this book is interested.[15] The inclusion of figures like Frantz Fanon, Martin Luther King, Stuart Hall and Mikhail Bakhtin helps to rethink the parameters of Western humanism when it is brought into sometimes reluctant dialogue with other cultural, national and ideological traditions. This book does not offer a comprehensive postcolonial critique of humanism, but it absorbs the spirit of what Said calls the critical humanist enterprise of making 'connections between things' and addresses the implications of Said's claim that 'we cannot discuss the non-Western world as disjunct from developments in the West'.[16]

The diversity of humanist thought is also reflected in the way we consider humanism under the categories of Romantic, existential, dialogic, civic, spiritual, pagan, pragmatic and technological humanisms. Each of these categories is represented by three thinkers, who have been chosen carefully because their perspectives both overlap and diverge. Although some sets of thinkers contribute to a coherent tradition of thought (notably Chapters 2 and 7), often the thinkers chosen to represent a given category are from very different cultural, national, historical and intellectual backgrounds. To give an example: Chapter 5 on spiritual humanism discusses the work of the German Jewish philosopher, Walter Benjamin, the African-American civil rights activist Martin Luther King and the French practitioner and theorist of psychoanalysis Julia Kristeva. Some of these figures might have been discussed alongside other thinkers examined in the book under more obvious headings: for example, Benjamin might have been discussed alongside Marx under the category of Marxist humanism; King might have been discussed with Frantz Fanon and Stuart Hall under postcolonial humanism; and Kristeva with Hélène Cixous and Luce Irigaray as French feminist humanists. Although these modes of thought can be accessed across the categories that are actually used, we have tried to avoid familiar groupings in order to construct an alternative taxonomy of humanist thought. The historiographical issues raised by the taxonomy we use will be discussed in more detail below, but one of the reasons for the sometimes far-flung comparisons and contrasts is to explore the historically diverse ways in which particular humanist motifs, such as the spiritual, have been inflected. If humanism is not a monolith, then, likewise, neither are any of the categories, such as spiritual humanism, discussed in this book. Spiritual humanism has itself taken markedly different forms, and this diversity is demonstrated by focusing on figures whose influential perspectives on the spiritual are historically diverse.

Thus instead of a single humanism, we have constructed eight categories of humanism, each of which is inflected in three significantly different ways. This tendency towards proliferation bears out the point made at the beginning of the Introduction about the book's eclecticism. A post-foundationalist concept of the human will be loose to some extent, but the looseness can be more or less explained as, and more or less the basis of, a critical humanism. It is one thing to say that human life is messy and complicated, but another to spell out the critical implications of that messiness, and to refuse to define the human as a result of those implications.

So what are the critical implications of a post-foundationalist humanism that refuses to define the human? First, there is the point that to define the human may be damagingly and unethically prescriptive. Given the 'many crimes', writes Alain Finkielkraut in *In the Name of Humanity* (1996), that have been 'committed in the name of higher values – in particular, humanity', any humanism which constructs itself as a norm may be highly questionable.[17] One glaring example is the colonialist construction of Western civilisation as the beacon of enlightened humanity, and non-European cultures as primitive and savage. Such a construction is based on a highly prescriptive, normative and very often racist humanism. It is against this humanism that Fanon in *Black Skins, White Masks* (1952; discussed further in Chapter 2) argues for a 'new' humanist ethic of reciprocity, which instead of defining the self and the human against a dehumanised other, restores 'to the other, through mediation and recognition, his human reality'.[18]

A second reason for not defining the human follows on from the first, and has to do with the abstract nature of a humanism which identifies human attributes outside their particular embodiment in one or another specific cultural and linguistic context. On this view, the categories 'man' and 'woman' are mere abstractions, removed from living human beings, and insufficiently attentive to actual human diversity. While abstract humanisms may themselves be the product of particular times and places, their normative and prescriptive power is based upon their perceived ability to transcend time and place. To restore a sense of context to otherwise abstract definitions is thus another of the aims of a critical humanism committed to the idea that people are primarily socially embodied and culturally situated beings. To abstract the human from historical embodiment is paradoxically to alienate human beings from a sense of situation, context and locality. If this sounds like a definition of the human, then it is a definition that takes us towards historical and cultural differences rather than away from them.

A third, again related, point is that definitions of the human may end up commodifying, quantifying and reductively demystifying the human. To make a list of the 'ten things everyone needs to know about human beings' is to reify human beings and to deny the openness of the human to interpretation and reinterpretation. It is also to deny that other all-too-human attribute of unpredictability. To render the human transparent and quantifiable additionally reflects the dubious rhetoric of mission statements, business plans, audit culture, and psychological profiling. In *Minima Moralia* (1951) Theodor Adorno blamed 'organized culture', and particularly the popularisation of 'depth-psychology', for cutting off 'people's last possibility of experiencing themselves'.[19] Since the 1940s and 1950s, when Adorno was writing, the further penetration of the inner world by technocracy, science and popular psychology reinforces the need for a post-foundationalist resistance to the tyranny of naming and quantifying the human. This position is also bound up with the recent reorientation to modes of thought that had in the 1960s and 1970s been branded repressive. For example, in 1993 the poststructuralist and postcolonial thinker Gayatri Spivak suggested a turn away from a straightforward critique of 'Western ethics', moving from a 'critical phase into a more affirmative phase, into areas where agencies can come'.[20]

These are some of the reasons for not defining the human, and for keeping humanism loose, but with the important qualification that the looseness is explained and justified in such a way that it becomes critical of tendencies to reduce, reify or prescribe the human. What we aim to do in the following chapters is not to prescribe but to explore, not to close down but to open up what being human has meant, means now and might mean in the future. The 'critical' in *Critical Humanisms* thus involves being critical of various premature closures whereby one version of humanism is taken to be representative of the whole, whereby humanisms (plural) cannot be in critical dialogue with one another because there seems to be only one version on offer, and whereby the human itself is taken to be a given, rather than contestable and criticisable. This pluralist perspective, however, constitutes only one half of the story that *Critical Humanisms* will tell, for as we also indicated at the beginning of the Introduction, too much openness may lead to a complete loss of the human. So having presented reasons for not defining the human, let us now consider reasons for grounding it. We shall then show how a dialectic between foundationalist and post-foundationalist concepts is written into the structure of the book, into its historical methodology and into the approach taken in individual chapters.

One reason for a grounded humanism is that if the human does not operate as some kind of given, then words like alienation, depersonalisation and degradation lose their evaluative and ethical force; as we suggested earlier, it is surely necessary to have some sense of what a human being is in order to know when he or she is being degraded. The second, connected justification for a foundationalism is that it puts into question the notion of the endless plasticity and pliability of the human, on the basis that such a notion is tantamount to suggesting that human beings can live under any conditions whatsoever. Given a rapacious capitalist system that restlessly refashions human desires in order to keep itself going, do we not need to rescue a notion of what people 'really' need? Moreover, to claim that there are no limits to the human, and that we can endlessly refashion ourselves, smacks of hubris. A third reason for a foundation is that it counteracts the tendency of intellectual work in general, and of highly theorised intellectual work in particular, towards what might be called infinite regression. In the Dutch Renaissance scholar Desiderius

Erasmus' *Praise of Folly* (1509), itself a species of humanist text, the narrator Folly ridicules medieval scholastics for their supersubtle intellectualism which results in over-interpretation of the Bible. The satire on their 'subtle refinement of subtleties' depends upon the recognition that the theologians' professional over-concern with technicalities has taken them further and further away from the spirit of the Bible and its perceived relevance to human experience.[21] Erasmus wants a Bible which is accessible and which speaks to people's need, as he sees it, for meaning, purpose and sustenance. He has little use for a Bible as the exclusive property of professional critics. Erasmus wants theologians to come out of their ivory towers (or monastic equivalent) and proselytise, as a way of reversing the tendency for ideas to become so specialised that they cannot be transported beyond the realm of professional interpreters.

Perhaps there are lessons here for us. High theory continues to be attacked for its impenetrability, but high theory is perhaps only symptomatic of the supersubtle gymnastics that intellectual work can often perform for the benefit of other gymnasts. Academic writing generally favours thicker descriptions and fuller pictures of phenomena than have hitherto existed. Whether the phenomenon in question is a historical period (such as the Renaissance), or a cultural/aesthetic movement (such as Romanticism or modernism), or a concept (such as humanism), the former signposts which presented themselves as reliable are usually substituted for more complex and sophisticated cognitive maps. Thus of modernism, for example, Peter Brooker writes:

> A fuller picture would only confirm the plurality of modernisms, across their several divergent and contrary formations. The proper approach therefore must be one which reveals and questions hegemonic structures by bringing marginalised figures and movements into a fuller dialogue, in a fuller and more argumentative artistic and cultural history.[22]

At what point does a fuller picture, a picture which includes previously excluded perspectives, begin to accumulate rather than to integrate perspectives as part of what Brooker refers to as a fuller dialogue? At what point does a productive dialogue end and implosion begin? Can a phenomenon, like humanism, be over-interpreted, to the point where it can no longer operate as a ground for ethics, politics, agency and dissent?

Dialogue, rather than proliferation, is the aim of this book: dialogue *within* each of the chosen categories of Romantic, existential, dialogic, civic, spiritual, pagan, pragmatic and technological; dialogue *between* these categories; and dialogue also *between* foundationalist and post-foundationalist perspectives. We prefer the term dialogue to debate, because whereas debate suggests an irresolvable antagonism between entrenched positions, dialogue implies the possibility of finding value as well as common ground in another's viewpoint.

Conceived in this way, dialogue involves the search for a common cause which is never complete, but which does not implode.

Structuring and Historicising Humanism

The plurality that this book embraces is a structured plurality. Where the emphasis on diverse humanisms disassembles the monolith of classical humanism, the structuring of this plurality suggests a way of reassembling humanism. It suggests a way, that is, of maintaining limits and critical dialogue in the face of extreme post-foundationalism, which might suggest that the 'human' is a completely open-ended signifier, subject to endlessly different interpretations. The book's structure is such that the eight categories under which we discuss various humanisms can be paired off as follows: Romantic/existential; dialogic/civic; spiritual/pagan; pragmatic/technological. Each pair is in turn part of a larger dialectic between those humanisms which generally speaking look inwards towards the self and subjectivity as sources of human value and meaning, and those whose more outer-oriented outlook lead them to examine the human in relation to others and to society in general. Thus the movement of the book is from the inner-oriented Romantic/existential to the outer-oriented dialogic/civic, and this movement is then differently inflected in the progression from spiritual/pagan to pragmatic/technological. Of course, this structure is too neat, for in the hands of some of the thinkers we examine, the 'inner' and the 'outer' are not mutually exclusive categories. This dialectic is nevertheless one of the structuring principles of the book and reinforces the notion that the plurality of humanisms we examine can at the same time be thought about in terms of certain persistent orientations. Read together, as they can be without over-disturbing the continuity of the book, the chapters on dialogic, civic, pragmatic and technological humanisms suggest the worldly orientation of human beings and their need for social goods of various kinds. That need is variously expressed as a need for others (dialogic humanism), for citizenship (civic humanism), for practical social action (pragmatic humanism), and for the enhancement of social life through technoscience (technological humanism). Meanwhile, the chapters on Romantic, existential, spiritual and pagan humanisms point to the various ways in which humanism has been inwardly inflected, sometimes, though by no means always, at the expense of a worldly orientation.

As for the general historical methodology of the book, we have tried to respect the different historical, intellectual, national and trans-national contexts that shape the work of the various figures discussed. The introductory sections of each chapter also place the thinkers we examine in broader contexts by locating their similarities to and differences from other influential thinkers. Thus shadowing the featured figures are a series of thinkers and writers who have also shaped, reshaped or attacked the various categories of humanist thought we examine. Amongst these are Plato, Aristotle, Erasmus, Descartes, Newton, Kant, Darwin, Kierkegaard, Peirce, Heidegger, Buber, Derrida and Nussbaum, as well as Lyotard, Chomsky, Fukuyama, Deleuze and Guattari discussed in the Conclusion. Reference to the work of these figures fleshes out the intellectual and cultural history of humanist and anti-humanist thought that this book aims to provide. We have also made reference to particular cultural forms like film, art and photography and to literary figures such as Philip Sidney, John Keats, Albert Camus, Richard Wright, Alice Walker and Don DeLillo, not only to exemplify certain points and to thicken the cultural and historical texture of the book, but because of the important contribution of the arts to humanist dialogue.

We have also respected and made use of the usual markers of historical, cultural and artistic periods, such as the Renaissance, the Enlightenment, Romanticism, modernism and postmodernism. However, we have chosen not to pursue a chronological narrative of humanism of the kind provided by, for example, Tony Davies' *Humanism* (1997). Such a narrative can be extracted from the book, by reading across thinkers and strategically reconstructing the chapters, but it is not its main focus. Neither have we chosen to examine in depth and detail a specific historical period, such as the Renaissance or Enlightenment, for its humanist ideas. Entire books, such as *The Cambridge Companion to Renaissance Humanism* (ed. J. Kraye, 1996) and Mike Pincombe's *Elizabethan Humanism* (2001), have been devoted to such periodised treatments of humanism.[23] Instead we privilege the persistence across time of our chosen humanist categories, while also charting some of the various historical inflections of those categories. Thus the spiritual, for example, might be taken as one (amongst several other) human 'needs' or aspirations, but it is a need that has been expressed in different ways in different times and places. Once again, a dialectic between foundationalist and post-foundationalist perspectives is evident, this time in the historicising of categories which at the same time can be seen as outliving their historical specificity. Where a linear, chronological narrative might see one form of humanism as being neatly superseded by another (Romanticism following the Enlightenment), this book traces continuities between thinkers and periods, while also staging dialogues between them that reflect their different historical situations. Thus we enable the eighteenth-century Enlightenment thinker Mary Wollstonecraft, the twentieth-century neo-Enlightenment theorist Jürgen Habermas, and the post-Enlightenment practitioner and theorist of cultural studies Stuart Hall, to 'talk to each other' both beyond and within the historical differences concerning the human value and importance of citizenship. Against the temptation to fetishise historical difference, by suggesting that past mind-sets can never be fully recouped by present mind-sets because of the unbridgeable gulf separating them, we practise a way of doing intellectual history which respects difference, but which also traces deeper continuities.

Humanism/Anti-Humanism

A historical method that identifies continuities and discontinuities, together with a humanism that is expanded beyond the popular conception of it, can also be used to question the anti-humanist narrative which claims to have superseded humanism. Has 'man' been 'erased', like 'a face drawn in sand at the edge of the sea', as Foucault eloquently writes in the final sentence of *The Order of Things?*[24] Or is it the case, as Kate Soper suggests, that 'anti-humanist argument' often tends 'to secrete humanist rhetoric'?[25] It may be difficult to detect such humanist secretions, especially given the more iconoclastic anti-humanist pronouncements of the 1970s and 1980s, which decentred the human subject in the name of structuralist science or the absolute primacy of language and society. But even alongside these pronouncements, other inflections of theory prevailed which did not so much destroy the human subject, as return him or her to language. A subjectivity conceived along classical humanist lines as preceding language is a subjectivity that is arguably alienated from, and lacking a meaningful relationship to, language. And, conversely, language that is devoid of any trace of a human subject will tend to be thought of as an impersonal system of codes and discourses. This depersonalisation of language is reflected in the widely anthologised essay 'The Death of the Author' by French theorist Roland Barthes, in which he describes the literary text as a 'tissue of quotations drawn from the innumerable centres of culture'.[26] But even in this forceful and influential anti-humanist text, a humanist rhetoric can be detected in the way that Barthes views the text as staging a crisis of subjectivity. 'Writing', he claims, 'is the destruction of every voice, of every point of origin. Writing is that neutral, composite, oblique space where our subject slips away, the negative where all identity is lost.'[27] The self as a core that precedes language is lost, but loss is seen in terms of a subjectivity which is now threatened, troubled and put into process by language. Finkielkraut makes a similar point when he suggests that anti-humanism is still humanist because it unsettles 'the self-confident subject to the very core of his being, to make man anxious in order to make him more human'.[28] This unsettling of the subject is based on putting him or her inside rather than outside a troubling relationship with language. Language paradoxically becomes more rather than less expressive of subjectivity, because subjectivity is not statically prior to language.

Read as a pure anti-humanist text, then, we might say of Barthes's essay that it replaces the essentialist self with the impersonal codes of language. But read as a closet humanist text which avoids the essentialism so often associated with humanism, we might say that it merely replaces one kind of subject (as core) with another (as linguistic/social process). This second concept of identity has been widely embraced in critical theory. Its roots are arguably as much in Romantic humanist notions of a dynamic and mysterious self, as they are in anti-humanist traditions. The loneliness of the Romantic wanderer, alone with thoughts and feelings that cannot easily be expressed, is radically transformed by the linguistic turn taken by structuralism and poststructuralism, but the dynamism and the mystery are still present in Barthes's invocation of language and the subject in language as opaque and in flux.

This last point leads to a further consideration of the points of intersection between humanist and anti-humanist rhetorics. It seems as though anti-humanist critical theory cannot do without one or another notion of excess. In the case of Barthes and other poststructuralists, the source of excess is language and the notion that concepts are never completely themselves because they are haunted by the spectre of past and present inflections of them.[29] Although this excess is often taken to undermine the classical humanist beliefs in stable subjectivity and perfectible knowledge, there are ways of 'humanising' excess, in the way that Anglo-American critics humanised 'bagginess'. This book will explore the different ways that excess has been humanised. To refer back to our description of the book's structure, excess can be broadly understood as an inward or outward movement. Thus excess can be internalised via the Romantic concept of an unfathomable interiority, or the spiritual concept of a soul, or the pagan appeal to wild impulse, or the existentialist notion that individuality can never be defined in advance of existence. Outwardly inflected, excess may be the excessiveness of other people to one's own consciousness (see Chapter 3), or the fragility of community and citizenship in a world that appears to exceed them (Chapter 4), or the threatening excess of technology (Chapter 8), or the irreducibility of human experience to metaphysical precepts (Chapter 7). Again it is important to stress that these inward and outward manifestations of excess are not mutually exclusive. Neither is it the case that all of the thinkers embrace one or another principle of excess. And where they do, they do not necessarily embrace it unequivocally, for excess may be seen as threatening to a foundationalist humanism or as the friend of a humanism which finds the concept of foundations limiting. As we indicated earlier, the appeal to foundations may well look like an anti-humanism from the point of view a non-prescriptive humanism. Thus if anti-humanist argument, according to Soper, often tends 'to secrete humanist rhetoric', then the opposite is also true, that humanism secretes, or can be perceived as secreting, anti-humanist ideas. The most prevalent of the range of recent seemingly anti-humanist terms – inhuman, posthuman and transhuman – will be discussed in detail in the

Conclusion, where we argue that they actually point to the existence of further critical moments within the discourse of humanism: moments, that is, when humanist appeals may paradoxically suggest a movement beyond or against humanism itself. The perception of humanism as anti-humanist and vice versa, all depends, of course, on what is meant by the human. The temptation to conclude that the human and anti-human are therefore in the eye of the beholder is the product of the crisis to which humanism has been brought in the last third of the twentieth century.

Crises, however, can be productive because they oblige us to pause and re-evaluate. The outcome of the crisis to which humanism has been brought by anti-humanist declarations of the end of humanism has been, not to abandon it, but to reanimate its relevance for dealing with contemporary issues. Evidence of a renewed sense of the, often problematic, relevance of humanist thought to contemporary issues are the recent publications by two premier intellectuals that focus on the Balkan conflict in Eastern Europe: Noam Chomsky's *The New Military Humanism: Lessons from Kosovo* (1999) and Michael Ignatieff's *Virtual War: Kosovo and Beyond* (2000). Meanwhile, the French theorist Tzvetan Todorov, in *On Human Diversity* (1993) himself calls for a new '*critical humanism*' that may 'avoid the traps into which the doctrine that goes by the same name has sometimes fallen over the centuries'.[30] By the term 'doctrine' he means the unbridled, as well as prescriptively universalising humanism often seen by anti-humanists of the 1970s and 1980s as the only form of humanism to have existed. In his most recent book, *The Imperfect Garden: The Legacy of Humanism* (2002), Todorov retrieves a complex and nuanced French humanist tradition which tries to avoid the ever-present dangers of human hubris and the excesses of individualism, on the one hand, and determinism, on the other. In *Culture After Humanism*, Iain Chambers likewise takes 'critical leave' as he puts it, 'from the history of possessive subjectivism, and its self-confirming knowledge', but warns that this 'need not mean to abandon "use-value" and the "human" to the fetishisation and alienation of modernity'.[31] *Critical Humanisms* takes its place alongside these other revisionist texts as a timely intervention in debates on the demise of humanist discourse in the late twentieth and early twenty-first centuries. We will show humanism to be both a pluralistic and a self-critical tradition that folds in and over itself, provoking a series of questions and problems rather than necessarily providing consolation or edification for individuals when faced with intractable economic, political and social pressures. The emphasis on plurality, however, also contains within it a recognition of the need and desirability of grounds from which to denounce human degradation, alienation and oppression. *Critical Humanisms* also implies that what is crucial to the development of critical theory as a coherent field of study is a reorientation of itself to humanist ideas.

Slightly off-centre and very easy to miss in the image by Grosz used as a frontispiece to this book is a heart. We have used the term 'critical' in several ways in the Introduction to suggest how a rehabilitated humanism might be productively critical of contemporary social values; to suggest that humanism itself is a self-critical tradition; and to point to the crisis out of which a critical re-evaluation of humanism can take place. However, a book that only turned humanism into an object of critical enquiry might be thought of as heartless. But for the heart near its centre, Grosz's image might similarly be thought of in terms of a certain modernist impersonality, for the 'travelling people' he represents do not seem to have much to do with one another. Where they do, there are suggestions of violence. A coldly critical enquiry into humanism might itself do a kind of violence to its subject if it did not integrate into its rationalist discourse an awareness of the importance of human emotions. It is for this reason that Chapter 1 focuses on the central place that feeling occupies in Romantic humanism.

CHAPTER I

Romantic Humanism

(Shakespeare – Marx – Cixous)

In a letter of 1818, the English Romantic poet John Keats wrote that 'axioms in philosophy are not axioms until they are proved upon our pulses'.[1] Whatever truths exist independently of the individual, for Keats as for other Romantic writers, these truths have to be inwardly experienced before they can be accepted as true. Central to this inward experiencing of truth is feeling. Axioms, so Keats implies, need to touch us, they need to resonate with our emotional lives, if they are to avoid being coldly and inhumanly external to us. The ideas of the German Romantic philosopher August Wilhelm Schlegel in *On Dramatic Art and Literature* (1809–11) are pertinent here, and especially Schlegel's distinction between organic and mechanical form. According to Schlegel, 'form is mechanical when, through external force, it is imparted to any material without reference to its quality', whereas 'organical form … is innate; it unfolds from within'.[2] Keats's claim about the need for philosophical axioms to be experienced 'on our pulses' implies an organicist concept of the human, for 'true' axioms would be those in sympathy with the emotional and mental propensities of human beings. On this model, human self-realisation is an organic process which counteracts the external moulding of subjects by such dehumanising phenomena as science and rationality. In the same letter, Keats draws a distinction between John Milton, who is seen as the poet of reason, and William Wordsworth, the poet of emotion.[3] Distinctions of this kind have contributed to the perception that Romantic writers reacted passionately against Enlightenment science and rationality.[4] While Keats does not totally oppose reason, he sees reason as being incomplete without feeling, for feeling is thought by Romantic writers like Keats to have more immediate relevance to what being human means. Before we consider from a Romantic humanist perspective the shortcomings of reason, it is useful to explore the opposite perspective, namely the shortcomings (from the perspective of reason) of that aspect of Romantic humanism which extols feeling.

As we shall see in Chapter 4, reason has often been associated with emancipation from feeling and instinct. Feelings may seem natural, but a sceptically inclined reason may question their naturalness, especially when they are seen, as by the Enlightenment thinker Mary Wollstonecraft, to reinforce cultural stereotypes of women as innately emotional. If some human beings are encouraged by their culture to be more emotional than others, then does this mean that feelings are always the product of nurture rather than nature? Should we therefore be suspicious of universalist appeals, such as Keats's, to 'the human heart'?[5] Keats is not totally hostile to reason, nor is Wollstonecraft to feeling. Nevertheless Wollstonecraft inclines at times towards an anti-sentimental rationalism, which treats feeling as its 'unthinking' opposite. Feelings, from the perspective of such a rationalism, are a form of superstition in that they belong to the realm of unquestioned belief. If we resist the temptation to caricature Enlightenment rationalism in terms of an over-confident belief in its own objectivity, then it is possible to see a degree of continuity between an Enlightenment thinker like Wollstonecraft and certain strands of anti-humanism. The continuity is based on the scepticism, rather than the supposed objectivity, to which reason gives rise. Objectivity is in other words one face of reason, but sceptical enquiry is another, and it is misleading to think that all Enlightenment thinkers can be characterised only in terms of the former category. For example, in *Enlightenment* (2000), Roy Porter claims that 'there never was a monolithic "Enlightenment project"' and that Enlightenment thinkers 'espoused pluralism, their register was ironic rather than dogmatic'.[6] Anti-humanist scepticism may go further in terms of its disturbance of all grounding narratives of the human, but it owes at least something of its spirit of enquiry to the Enlightenment.

Anti-humanist scepticism has thus itself led to a questioning, not only of human reason as the key to truth and enlightenment, but also of feeling as an alternative ground. In 'Nietzsche, Genealogy, History' (1971), for example, Foucault writes:

> We believe that feelings are immutable, but every sentiment, particularly the noblest and most disinterested, has a history. We believe in the dull constancy of instinctual life and imagine that it continues to exert its force indiscriminately in the present as it did in the past. But a knowledge of history easily disintegrates this unity.[7]

To write history and difference back into feeling is not necessarily to spurn feeling, for a historical perspective can inject feelings with a dynamism that is lacking when they are treated as 'immutable'. By questioning the supposed objectivity of reason, anti-humanist scepticism can also unearth, as Nietzsche does, passions in modes of knowledge such as science which have conventionally designated themselves as neutral and passionless (see Chapter 6). This is the point at which anti-humanist attacks on the supposed objectivity of human reason may find some affinity with the Romantic humanist rehabilitation of feeling, but with the Foucauldian qualification that affairs of the heart are as subject to historical change as affairs of the head.

However, concentration on the historicity of feelings may still lead to a certain alienation from them, for once feelings are no longer considered to be universal, they may be drained of their own substance. In 1982, at the height of the most recent wave of anti-humanism, Arthur Marotti wrote an influential essay for Renaissance studies called '"Love is not love": Elizabethan Sonnet Sequences and the Social Order'. Reversing what he saw as the formalist fallacy of removing texts from their social contexts, Marotti restored the public dimension of putatively private poems and treated 'love' as the medium through which Elizabethan socioeconomic circumstances reveal themselves. 'Love lyrics' writes Marotti, 'could express figuratively the realities of suit, service and recompense with which ambitious men were insistently concerned as well as the frustrations and disappointments experienced in socially competitive environments'.[8] Love is thus treated by Marotti less as a phenomenon in its own right than an epiphenomenon, a secondary symptom of a cause located elsewhere, in the struggle for employment at court.[9] Marotti thus displaces the love theme of sonnet sequences with what he considers to be the 'real' subject of the sonnets, namely courtiership and power. Published two years after Stephen Greenblatt's *Renaissance Self-Fashioning* (1980), Marotti did for Elizabethan poetry what Greenblatt had done for Renaissance studies in general, which was to undermine the notion of a pure, unfettered, private subjectivity set apart from the public operations of power. For all the advantages of returning a sense of socioeconomic context to Renaissance love poetry, there are some problems with this approach. It is tempting, for example, to suggest that the displacement of love by court politics indicates a level of embarrassment, on the part of critics like Marotti, about love *per se*. To speak of love is to court the risk of becoming sloppy and sentimental. Better, then, to treat love as a metaphor for something else, in this case the 'hard', public, masculine world of competitive courtiership.

For Keats, philosophical axioms that are not inwardly felt are coldly impersonal. Likewise, anti-humanist cultural criticism of the kind practised by Marotti, may seem heartless, especially for a reader who might have been expecting love poetry to be about love. The effect of such anti-humanist cultural criticism is comparable with what the twentieth-century German playwright Bertolt Brecht called an 'alienation effect' (*Verfremdungseffekt*). Brecht did not want his audiences to become so emotionally absorbed in his dramatic characters and situations that they lost their capacity to reflect upon the historicity and transformability of 'human feelings, opinions and attitudes'.[10] For a Marxist playwright writing in Nazi Germany, total emotional identification was one step on the way to an audience becoming duped as 'a cowed, credulous, hypnotized mass'.[11] The thinking, questioning consciousness that Brecht encouraged in his audiences, and which Marotti uses to unsettle our assumptions about love, are both manifestations of Enlightenment reason in its sceptical rather than objective mode. What characterises both of these modes, however, is a certain emotional disengagement. Writing of the various elements, including rationalism, which have contributed to the formation of the modern self, Charles Taylor suggests that the disengagement of various forms of rationalism from Descartes to the present day 'demands that we stop simply living in the body or within our traditions or habits and, by making them objects for us, subject them to radical scrutiny and remaking'.[12] Taylor's account is comparable with the analysis of modernity given by Jürgen Habermas (see Chapter 4). What is crucial to recognise for the purposes of both this chapter and for *Critical Humanisms* as a whole, however, is that to some extent this book itself follows on in the tradition of disengaged rationality as described by Taylor, by turning the human into an object of rational enquiry and critical debate. For all the Brechtian advantages of such an enquiry, it may appear at times as though the human as a source of immediate emotional identification has been lost. To paraphrase Keats: 'humanisms are not humanisms until they have been proved upon our pulses'. Thus at the same time as a rational enquiry is conducted, we do not want to lose sight of the desire for emotional identification with the human. Romantic humanism is one of the names we can give to that desire.

The three writers discussed in this chapter are the sixteenth-century English playwright William Shakespeare (1564–1616), the nineteenth-century German economic and social philosopher Karl Marx (1818–83), and the contemporary French feminist Hélène Cixous (1937–). Examined together, the three thinkers advance the aim of the book to present dialogues between historically diverse figures about various perceived aspects of 'the human'. In the case of this chapter, historical difference is accompanied by the generic diversity represented by drama (Shakespeare), social and economic theory (Marx), and feminism (Cixous). However, there are other, related reasons for this particular combination of thinkers. Shakespeare has been chosen first, because as a Renaissance humanist, he represents what has often been taken in modern history to be a founding moment of humanism; second, because Romantic writers often viewed him in their own image, as a poet of the emotions rather than as a dramatist; third, because as a dramatist he stages conflicting humanisms, whilst at the same time bearing out the Romantic view of him; and fourth, because he powerfully dramatises how feeling as a public phenomenon is at risk from extreme forms of disengaged rationality and how, as a result, public and private, outward and inward selves threaten to split apart. Marx has been chosen as an Enlightenment rationalist who, like other Enlightenment rationalists such as Wollstonecraft, appeals at the same time to the emotions, by showing how the possibility of immediate emotional identification with human suffering is stunted by capitalism. Like Shakespeare, Marx also presents feeling as both bounded and unbounded, existing sometimes within but also sometimes beyond the orbit of reason and understanding. Finally, Cixous has been selected for her questioning of male rationality from the point of view of a feminist form of Romantic humanism which celebrates human creativity as the expression of the richness of the individual's emotional life.[13]

None of the thinkers discussed here is an obvious Romantic in the sense of belonging to the 'Romantic period'. But Romantic humanism is not specific to Romanticism 'proper'. It travels because, to look at matters from within the perspective of Romantic humanism, human feeling persists, even as it is threatened and mutable. One important, historically based movement examined in this chapter is the movement between broadly functionalist and anti-functionalist theories of the emotions. By 'functionalist', we mean useful and comprehensible. Thus according to functionalist models of the emotions, which can be traced back to Aristotle, emotions are purposeful, whereas, according to an anti-functionalist model, which can be traced back to the Greek thinker Longinus, emotions are too grandly mysterious to be purposeful. Both models are present in the work of the thinkers considered in this chapter, though to varying degrees and with different emphases.

William Shakespeare

The Renaissance humanism which shaped and was itself shaped by Shakespeare is as diverse as humanism is in general. The term *umanisiti* refers to the fifteenth-century Italian scholars and pedagogues who were responsible for the renaissance of classical values and learning, but it is difficult to pinpoint the precise content of those ideas and values.[14] The idea that scholars should be worldly and that classical authors could teach worldly skills through the mastery of the practical art of communication, known as rhetoric, informs one version of Renaissance humanism, which bears comparison with the civic and pragmatic humanisms discussed in subsequent chapters. But rhetoric, to identify one aspect of Renaissance humanism, points in more than one direction as far as its conception of the human is concerned. It could itself lead, for example, to an extreme form of emotional disengagement. According to Stephen Greenblatt in *Renaissance Self-Fashioning* the rhetorical handbooks which were popular in the Renaissance were 'essentially compilations of verbal strategies' which offered their users 'the power to shape their worlds, calculate the probabilities, and master the contingent'. They also implied, he continues, 'that human character itself could be similarly fashioned, with an eye to audience and effect'.[15] Greenblatt's description of the rhetorical self as a strategically constructed, malleable entity implies that feelings themselves might be performed for effect, or that they might be subordinated to the calculations of an entrepreneurial rationality. However, if Renaissance rhetoric was put to the use described by Greenblatt, then it also gave rise, through its emphasis on debate and argumentation, to the kind of rationally oriented dialogism which also informs the methodology of this book. As the art of persuasion, which encouraged those trained in it to argue either side of a case, rhetoric belonged to the realm of probable rather than certain knowledge. In relation to ideas about human existence, different arguments could thereby be constructed as to the place of human beings in the grand scheme of things. One famous example is the disquisition which takes place in Shakespeare's *Hamlet* (1600) on the nature of 'man'. Seen on the one hand by Hamlet, as 'noble in reason' and 'in apprehension ... like a god', 'man' is, on the other hand, 'the quintessence of dust'.[16] Hamlet's deliberations on where humans fit into the scheme of things supply more questions than answers to the dilemma of what 'being human' means: are human beings gods or animals, angels or dust? Is human life purposeful because God made it so, or purposeless?

These and still further options are explored in a play in which rationality is a notoriously slippery affair involving Hamlet arguing his way in and out of a number of possible situations. As Hamlet himself puts it: 'there is nothing good or bad but thinking makes it so'.[17] Part of Hamlet's attempt to restore foundations to a dialogism that has exceeded itself is to restore feelings to public legibility in a world which is experienced by Hamlet as bereft of authentic emotion. To his mother Gertrude's question about why his grief over the death of his father 'seems so particular with thee', Hamlet responds:

> Seems, madam? Nay, it is. I know not 'seems'.
> 'Tis not alone my inky cloak, good mother,
> Nor customary suits of solemn black,
> Nor windy suspiration of forc'd breath,
> No, nor the fruitful river in the eye,
> Nor the dejected haviour of the visage,
> Together with all the forms, moods, shapes of grief,
> That can denote me truly. These indeed seem,
> For they are actions that a man might play,
> But I have that within which passes show,
> These but the trappings and the suits of woe.[18]

This speech points in two directions at once. Hamlet's initial response, 'Seems, madam? Nay it is,' suggests that the outward manifestation of his grief does 'denote ... truly' the way he is feeling. Here, being and seeming coincide. The rest of the speech, however, sees a rift between signs and psyche, public and private, outer and inner worlds. Outward signs thereby become inexpressive, and Hamlet turns away from these inauthentic exteriors into an interior world

which is only partly accessible to others. Hamlet's recoil from the visible world
is one of many examples in the Renaissance of the dissociation of feeling from
public life. Religious reformers, for instance, made their own, different contribution to the 'silencing' of external phenomena, by downgrading the Catholic
doctrine of justification by works and upgrading justification by faith. Works
were thereby rendered less expressive than the faith that came from within.[19]

In *Inwardness and Theater in the English Renaissance* (1995), Katharine Maus
suggests that the 'alienation or potential alienation of surface from depth' in
Hamlet and Renaissance culture often presented itself in the form of the
sceptical question 'of how to know what [other minds] are thinking'.[20]
Emotions are also obviously at stake here. Given Hamlet's appeal to an
inaccessible interiority, is it possible to imagine feeling what he feels? Is his
grief so 'particular' to him that no one else can possibly imagine experiencing
the same emotion? When Keats writes of the need for 'axioms in philosophy'
to be 'proved upon our pulses', he is appealing to a shared vocabulary of
feeling. But there is also in Romantic writers' insistence upon intensely felt
personal experience a strong sense of particularity. Both tendencies are present
in the proto-Romantic Hamlet's public exhibition of a grief that is at the same
time hidden. While feeling remains part of public ritual and expression, it is to
some extent decipherable. Thus it is possible to argue that the public exhibition
that Hamlet makes of his grief is an expression of human neediness. In
Upheavals of Thought: The Intelligence of the Emotions (2001), a book itself
partly devoted to restoring public legibility to the emotions, Martha Nussbaum
characterises feelings in general 'as complex object relations'.[21] By this she
means that they are intimately linked to 'our urgent need for and attachment to
things outside ourselves that we do not control'.[22] Emotions may be messy,
complex and directed at uncontrollable objects, but they are nevertheless
partly knowable as a result of the truth they reveal about our incompleteness.
To say that Hamlet is acutely sad because a part of him has died does not do
justice to the depth of emotion he experiences, but the trauma which bereave-
ment entails is nonetheless recognisable. We can complicate matters by
suggesting, with Nussbaum, that grief may also be accompanied by feelings of
resentment because the object of affection is uncontrollable as far as death is
concerned, or by feelings of guilt because we do not always treat well the
people who matter to us. We may even want to complicate these emotional
matters still further by adopting Freud's perspective in *The Interpretation of
Dreams* (1900) that Hamlet cannot take vengeance on his father's murderer,
Claudius, because Claudius 'shows him the repressed wishes of his own
childhood', namely to keep his mother for himself.[23] The complexity of
Hamlet's emotions is exacerbated because of the inward turn he takes, but the
basis of emotion rooted in human need remains legible.

Shakespeare characteristically invites us, in play after play, to reach to the bottom of emotional states, even as he teases us with the possibility that, to appropriate a phrase from Bottom in *A Midsummer Night's Dream* (1595), the emotional state in question 'hath no bottom'.[24] *Macbeth* (1606), for example, encourages us to fathom the emotional states which underlie otherwise external phenomena. The dagger, for instance, is the 'thing' whose origin in human emotions the play seeks to disclose, even as Macbeth contributes towards its reification. It is all too tempting for Macbeth to alienate from himself and all human motives the murder he is about to commit and treat the dagger as though it represented a purely external compulsion. 'Thou marshall'st me', Macbeth says to the dagger as though it has nothing to do with him – only to admit in the next breath that it is signposting 'the way that I was going'.[25] The socio-historical explanation that murder is the product of the culture of violence in which the Macbeths exist is important, but does not fully explain their fantasies of omnipotence. Murder is the ultimate denial of the other, and killing the king, the head of the social order, gives rise to feelings in the Macbeths of unbridled power: 'What cannot you and I perform', asks Lady Macbeth of her husband, 'upon/Th'unguarded Duncan?'[26] However, this feeling of unbridled power is short-lived and ultimately isolating, as the heavily eroticised dependency between the partners in crime is overwhelmed by feelings of shame and emptiness:

> Life's but a walking shadow; a poor player,
> That struts and frets his hour upon the stage,
> And then is heard no more: it is a tale
> Told by an idiot, full of sound and fury,
> Signifying nothing.[27]

This is unbearably bleak and tells us something about the emotional void to which narcissism leads. In political terms, the play could be read as a warning from the point of view of hierarchy and authority against the evils of individualism. But Shakespeare the Romantic humanist never dissociates politics and society from the deeper human and emotional questions that underlie them. Alan Sinfield has suggested that modern theoretical approaches to *Macbeth* in particular and to literature in general challenge the assumption of older criticism that 'the characters are actual people', by treating them instead as 'textual arrangements which involve ideas about people'.[28] Anti-humanist criticism, as represented here, tells us not to get too emotionally involved. It tells us to be dispassionate and disengaged, lest we make the humanist error of mistaking ideology (that which societies naturalise as the 'truth' about humans) for the human itself. Characteristically the insistence is upon the social construction of reality and the priority of 'textual arrangements' over people: 'people' come second because people are the effect of social construc-tions. We do not want to deny the importance of placing texts in their ideological contexts; neither do we want to disregard the social and historical uses to which appeals to the human have been put. However, from a Romantic humanist perspective, the hierarchical relationship between 'textual arrange-ments' and 'people' needs to be reversed or considered more dialectically. For what if 'textual arrangements' were the product of 'people' who then somehow lost sight of the fact that these textual arrangements have their origins in human emotions? One of the outcomes of this loss of symbiotic relationship between creator and creation would be to call the alienated creation something like a 'textual arrangement'. We create, but we forget why we created and thus our creations seem alien and inhuman. One of the names Shakespeare gives to this kind of forgetfulness is Iago.

Othello (1604) dramatises the further impetus towards the alienation of feeling from public life, through the rationally disengaged attitude adopted by that supreme rhetorical self-fashioner, Iago. Throughout the play, Iago ventriloquises a variety of languages: the language of the tavern, of advice to rulers, of masculine homosocial bonding, of feudal service, and of love. How-ever, none of these discourses leaves any emotional trace on a body and mind wilfully purged of all passionate entanglements. When Iago announces in Act I that 'for necessity of present life,/I must show out a flag, and sign of love,/Which is indeed but sign', he is in effect announcing the existence of a self from whom signs have become totally disengaged.[29] It is for others to be moved and seduced by language and the images of the human represented in language. A nomadic traveller between tongues, Iago remains an aloof, unfeeling observer of his own and others' verbal performances. Signs thus become instruments for manipulation for Iago, by virtue of being systematically drained of any emotional content. Where recent theoretical conjunctions of linguistics and psychoanalysis have encouraged us to locate language acquisition as the traumatic site of loss (see the section on Julia Kristeva in Chapter 5), the project of *Othello*'s most conspicuous rhetorician is to drive wedges between signs and psyche, language and emotion. Casual about motivation, to the point of regarding motivation itself as yet another conveniently manipulable sign – 'I hate the Moor,/And it is thought abroad, that 'twixt my sheets/He's done my office; I know not if't be true …/Yet I, for mere suspicion in that kind,/Will do, as if for surety' – Iago consigns one linguistic domain after another to the market-place of disposable cultural capital now liberated from the angst of psychic investment.[30] Communication thereby becomes totally instrumentalised.

Iago exemplifies a supreme form of rational disengagement. We earlier described reason as having two faces, those of objectivity and scepticism. In the light of Iago, we can add a third, namely cynicism. As a stager of humanist dialogues which encourage critical reflection rather than emotional absorption, Shakespeare is himself partly complicit with the disengagement of Iago. Feeling is itself often subjected by Shakespeare to rational scrutiny: Hamlet, for example, wonders whether revenge is a natural passion or part of the script which is given to actors in the kind of situation in which he finds himself. However, as an antidote to a world in which human beings coldly observe their own and others' affairs with an eye only to calculation, Shakespeare persistently attempts to resuscitate feeling and maintain, through the public form of drama, its public status. Given Hamlet's appeal to the unseen depths of the self – 'I have that within which passes show' – feeling may not always be amenable to public expression or understanding. But Shakespeare continues to explore, as well as paradoxically to intensify, the sense of hidden depths in the hope of shedding light on them. At the close of *King Lear* (1605), Edgar says to the surviving characters of the tragedy:

> The weight of this sad time we must obey;
> Speak what we feel, not what we ought to say.[31]

These words resonate across the entire Shakespearean canon. Tongues and hearts are so often alienated from one another that the task of putting them back together seems as urgent as it seems monumental. How can the heart and tongue, the private and the public come together, once the public world has been drained of emotion and the inner world has become opaque? A Romantic humanist psychology partly premised upon the existence of an agonised, or more positively, a richly creative inner emotional life may be brought to light only with difficulty, but needs to be in some sort of dialogic relation to the rational self if the human is to be more than an 'object' of critical enquiry or cynical manipulation. Rather than drain roles of emotional content in such a way as to render them inauthentically 'external', Hamlet wants to bring something of himself to the roles he plays. At the same time, he refuses to be totally identified by any one role, as this would empty him of a Romantic sense of further possibility. Shakespeare thus attempts to return emotion to the public world, at the same time as he intensifies the sense of the rich interiorised life of the emotions. Such is the Romantic humanist drama of the emotions which takes place in Shakespeare.

Karl Marx

As we suggested in the Introduction, Marx has often been viewed as an anti-humanist thinker because he privileges impersonal systems and historical forces over human beings who are seen merely as their effects. It is nevertheless possible to rescue from Marx a humanist account of people's needs. A basic feature of Marxist humanism is the conviction that capitalism will have to be superseded if the world is to be a better place for people to inhabit. For Marxism to think like this, it has to have some notion of what 'people' and their needs are like.[32] On the whole it assumes that people desire not to be hungry, lonely, uncared for, or oppressed. If such human needs seem so basic as to be incontrovertible, then this speaks to that important aspect of Marxism which concerns itself with such humdrum but necessary basics. Adapting Marx's concepts of use and exchange values, we might say that these basics should not be subject to the capitalist law of exchange which dictates that nothing is ever so completely itself that it cannot be traded for something else. A human being is not the equivalent of a sum of money, and yet the buying and selling of human beings, as slaves, for example, suggests just such an equivalence. Capitalism flattens all values to an economic level, and Marx (and most versions of non-vulgar Marxism) think that human life should not be reduced in this way. A concern with certain irreducible basics of human life makes Marxism an unfashionably normative discourse, for whereas the tendency of contemporary critical discourses is to celebrate difference, Marxism tempers its own embrace of heterogeneity with a normative notion of human need. This affirmation of human need means that Marx's concept of human nature and emotion are not particularly mysterious. Unlike Hamlet's 'that within which passes show', the human heart is mostly legible as far as Marx is concerned. At the same time, however, Marx is drawn to that other aspect of Romantic humanism which sees feeling as volatile, anti-rational and unbounded.

As a rationalist demystifier of capitalist society, Marx does not examine or explore feeling in the way that Shakespeare does. Nevertheless, by Marx's concept of 'consciousness' we should understand a holistic conception of the human, which refuses to separate out feeling and reason. The prospect of living in a mindless and emotionless state in which 'things' hold sway over human existence is at the heart of the key categories in Marx's thought of alienation, reification and abstraction. It will therefore be useful to focus primarily on these concepts. In *Capital* (1867), Marx writes of the way capitalism renders human values and processes indecipherable because of the way the capitalist system reifies 'value' by attaching it to things rather than people. Consumers in capitalist economies buy jars of coffee from super-markets but such is the distance between the points of production and consumption that they have no immediate consciousness of the human conditions under which the coffee was produced. Things thus appear to exist independently of the human beings who labour to create them. 'Value', writes Marx, 'does not have its description branded on its forehead; it rather transforms every product of labour into a social hieroglyphic.' He continues:

Later on, men try to decipher the hieroglyphic, to get behind the secret of their own social product: for the characteristic which objects of utility have of being values is as much men's social product as is their language. The belated scientific discovery that the products of labour, in so far as they are values, are merely the material expressions of the human labour expended to produce them ... by no means banishes the semblance of objectivity possessed by the social characteristics of labour.[33]

We belatedly become aware that commodities are the product of human labour and social arrangements even as the capitalist system still feels precisely like an impersonal system impervious to human realities. Capitalism still appears, to use Marx's term, 'objective' (meaning, in this instance, thing-like), rather than subjective (in touch with emotions, values and choices). Products are thus indecipherable as human products; as with the dagger in *Macbeth*, objects are set over against subjects; creations are alienated from their creators.

The capitalist obfuscation of immediate by highly mediated knowledge that is abstracted from human relations is echoed by Marx's own highly theoretical, rationalist analysis of commodity production. If capitalist production disengages itself from human processes, then Marx meets one kind of abstraction with another by privileging systemic analyses over the lives of actual people. Moreover, because human history, for Marx, is the grand procession of one economic system after another, human beings do sometimes appear as mere effects of these systems. However, Marx criticises as much as he practises abstraction, and in *Capital* he writes at length about the actual lives and working conditions of those at the sharp end of capitalism. Marx thus attempts to capture the sense of the human cost, at once mental, physical and emotional, of wage labour. 'Capital', he writes,

> takes no account of the health and the length of life of the worker, unless society forces it to do so. Its answer to the outcry about physical and mental degradation, the premature death, the torture of over-work, is this: Should that pain trouble us, since it increases our pleasure (profit)?[34]

Marx is working both with and against abstractions here. 'Capital', abstracted as 'it', might not care about the human cost, but 'society', another abstraction, might make capital care. Amidst these abstractions, however, there is a 'somebody', namely Marx, who does definitely care, even as that care is translated into the 'hard' language of rationalist demystification. Thus Marx tentatively puts emotion back into a system from which it has been banished. In Keats's terms, he proves his philosophical axioms on his own pulse and makes them resonate with the readers' own emotions.

Alienation and abstraction are also present in the domination of exchange over use values. 'The exchange relation of commodities', writes Marx, 'is characterized precisely by its abstraction from their use-values'.[35] What is meant by this, as indicated earlier, is that commodities are stripped of their use value because in capitalist society buying and selling establishes a momentum of its own, irrespective of the usefulness of things. Marx's insight here is prescient, on two counts: first, the food mountains in the late twentieth century are one gross example of the way that capitalism deems objects expendable unless they can be sold; and second, given the conspicuous consumption encouraged in capitalist economies particularly since the 1950s, the notion, to which Marx himself is partially drawn, that capitalism can service 'real' human needs seems increasingly dubious. More apposite is the notion that capitalism creates and recreates desires which in masking themselves as needs alienate us from a sense of what 'really matters'. While such matters are debatable, because from a historical perspective the needs of human beings change over time, human debate is short-circuited by the reign of objects and by the equation of their consumption with happiness.

In *Capital*, however, human needs are not perceived to be so historically changeful as to become indecipherable, and neither are emotions construed as being so beyond language that they cannot be accommodated within Marx's rationalist analysis. Emotions, in *Capital*, are neither sub-rational or supra-rational. They are themselves rational, eloquent and intelligent. When Marx moves from abstract analysis to concrete situation and describes, with the help of officially commissioned reports, mid-nineteenth-century working conditions in Britain, he writes with considerable emotion. The life of adults and children working in the match industry, for example, is described by Marx as follows:

> The manufacture of matches, on account of its unhealthiness and unpleasant-ness, has such a bad reputation that only the most miserable part of the working class, half-starved widows and so forth, deliver up their children to it, their 'ragged, half-starved, untaught children' … With a working day ranging from 12 to 14 or 15 hours, night-labour, irregular meal-times, and meals mostly taken in the workrooms themselves, pestilent with phosphorous, Dante would have found the worst horrors in his Inferno surpassed in this industry.[36]

Occasionally, the reports cited by Marx give brief testimonies from the workers themselves; for example, the nine-year-old William Wood who worked in the Staffordshire pottery industry: 'I work till 9 o'clock at night six days in the week. I have done so for the last seven or eight weeks.'[37] The boy's voice is mediated by another official report, which is in turn mediated by Marx. This sequence of mediations mirrors the fate of the commodity within capitalism that gets further and further removed from its human origins. Marx's attempt to restore immediacy and presence to the experiences of exploited workers is based on his emotional identification with them. For such identification to take place, some basic sense of what it must have felt like to be a nine-year-old in a match factory in the mid-nineteenth century has to be assumed. While it would be arrogant for Marx to think that he can climb inside the heart and mind of such a child, his horrified reaction is comprehensible because the emotions that he reads into the experience of child labour are themselves legible. His emotional intelligence – call it intuition – tells him that something is wrong here. Emotions, then, are not irrational, but all too rational. To put it in terms of Marx's concept of use-value, emotions are rational because they provide useful knowledge about the needs of human beings. The solid immediacy of emotions thus counters the abstract principle of exchange built into the capitalist system.

Marx's concept of use- and exchange-value is partly derived from Aristotle.[38] The functionalist theory of the emotions which Aristotle offers in *The Poetics* is also relevant to Marx's concept of use-value, for it proposes that the emotional power of tragedy serves an educative purpose.[39] Marx, in the more emotional passages of *Capital*, can be seen as assuming a broadly Aristotelian under-standing of the emotions as purposeful. Martha Nussbaum's books, *Love's Knowledge* (1990) and *Upheavals of Thought*, also stand in this tradition (even as they ask questions of it), and, likewise, Romanticism works variations on it in its emphasis upon feeling as a mode of special insight. However, there is another important aspect of Romantic humanism, which, to use Marx's langu-age again, is less tied to foundationalist concepts of the human use-value of emotions and more interested in the mysterious possibilities of the emotions.

In *The Communist Manifesto* (1848), written with Friedrich Engels, Marx characterises capitalism as a restlessly energetic force which is in a permanent state of revolution and which corrodes all previous human ties and certainties. 'The bourgeoisie', they write, 'has put an end to all feudal, patriarchal, idyllic relations'; it has 'drowned the most heavenly ecstasies of religious fervour, of chivalrous enthusiasm, of philistine sentimentalism, in the icy water of egotistical calculation'.[40] Such is the constant 'revolutionizing' of 'the instru-ments of production, and thereby the relations of production, and with them the whole relations of society', that 'all fixed, fast-frozen relations ... are swept away ... all that is solid melts into air'.[41] According to Marx and Engels the forces unleashed by capitalism will eventually lead to its destruction, for a 'society that has conjured up such gigantic means of production and of exchange, is like the sorcerer, who is no longer able to control the nether world whom he has called up by his spells'.[42] The paradoxical outcome of capitalism is therefore communism, for communism takes one step further the revolu-tionary fervour of capitalism. It is the heady spirit of revolution and the prospect of bringing into being things as yet unborn that characterise *The Communist Manifesto*. Instead of countering the principle of exchange-value with that of use-value, *The Communist Manifesto* anticipates that communism will outstrip the Promethean unboundedness of capital. Where the Romantic poet Percy Shelley claimed that poetry 'purges from our inward sight the film of familiarity which obscures from us the wonder of our being', in *The Communist Manifesto* Marx similarly embraces that soaring Romantic principle of the sublime.[43] Kant theorised the sublime by proposing that the contemplation of such awesome natural phenomena as 'shapeless mountain masses towering one above the other in wild disorder' is an example of a sublime moment when our capacity to reason is called to rise to the challenge of the extraordinary and 'employ itself upon ideas involving higher finality'.[44] A sense of the infinite and the unknowable may be conveyed through poetry (Shelley), Nature (Kant), or through the revolutionary fervour which capitalism bequeaths to communism (Marx), but what is common to all of them is a sense of passionate excess.[45] If the 'philistine sentimentalism' referred to by Marx and Engels in *The Communist Manifesto* is based on a nostalgic attachment to the reassuringly familiar, then the concept of the sublime makes of the human heart an altogether more awesome and mysterious affair.

In *The Eighteenth Brumaire of Louis Bonaparte* (1852), the sublime aspect of Marx's Romantic humanism is also present. Despite the fact that Marx in his youth wrote poetry, his treatment of art and culture is fairly thin. However, in his use of aesthetic categories to characterise the bourgeois revolutions of the seventeenth and eighteenth centuries, Marx appeals to a concept of art as a form of human self-magnification. The heightened sense of the human projected by tragic drama, for example, feeds into Marx's Romanticised concept of revolution as the release of hitherto unrealised human powers. However stolid bourgeois life may be in reality, bourgeois revolution, according to Marx, pretends to the status of high human drama:

> [U]nheroic as bourgeois society is, it nevertheless took heroism, sacrifice, terror, civil war and battles of peoples to bring it into being. And in the classically austere traditions of the Roman republic its gladiators found the ideals and the art forms, the self-deceptions that they needed in order to conceal from themselves the bourgeois limitations of the content of their struggles and to keep their enthusiasm on the high plane of the great historical tragedy.[46]

According to this claim, unlike bourgeois revolution which draws 'its poetry from the past', proletarian revolution must be genuinely new and draw its poetry 'only from the future'.[47] Nevertheless, what both forms of revolution share in common, as far as Marx is concerned, is the creativity, imaginative power and heightened emotions often associated with Romantic poetry.

Hélène Cixous

The French feminist and poststructuralist Hélène Cixous persistently invokes the idea of a subversive female excess which undermines the man-made linguistic order. 'You can't talk', Cixous writes in 'The Laugh of the Medusa' (1975), 'about *a* female sexuality, uniform, homogenous, classifiable into codes – any more than you can talk about one unconscious resembling another. Women's imaginary is inexhaustible, like music, painting, writing: their stream of phantasms is incredible.' She continues:

> I have been amazed … by a description a woman gave me of a world all her own which she had been secretly haunting since early childhood. A world of searching, the elaboration of a knowledge, on the basis of a systematic experimentation with the bodily functions, a passionate and precise interrogation of her erotogeneity. This practice … is prolonged or accompanied by a production of forms, a veritable aesthetic activity, each stage of rapture inscribing a resonant vision, a composition, something beautiful … I wished that that woman would write and proclaim this unique empire so that other women, other unacknowledged sovereigns, might exclaim: I, too, overflow; my desires have invented new desires, my body knows unheard-of songs.[48]

Such words and phrases as 'rich and inventive', 'rapture', 'overflow', 'new desires', 'unheard-of songs' recall the sublime version of Romantic humanism of both Shakespeare and Marx, but with the difference that Cixous places far more emphasis on the body as a source of inspiration. The sublime Romantic humanist in Hamlet says to Horatio 'There are more things in heaven and earth, Horatio,/Than are dreamt of in your philosophy' and Marx's feel for Romantic excess spurs him to imagine a future when untapped and as yet unseen human resources will be unleashed.[49] Likewise, it is the Romantic sense of unboundedness in Cixous that gives rise to her claim that 'I, too, overflow; my desires have invented new desires, my body knows unheard-of songs.'

To a limited extent, Cixous retains a broadly Aristotelian theory of the emotions as functional and educative, for the feminist point made by Cixous is that by getting in touch with the full panoply of her senses 'woman' will regain access to 'her goods, her pleasures, her organs, her immense bodily territories' that have been 'kept under seal' in the patriarchal culture in which she has been obliged to exist.[50] For Cixous, the passionate life, the life which is also open to experience and experimentation, is a life worth living, not just for oneself but for the receptivity to others to which such a life naturally gives rise. Cixous thus embraces emotions partly from the point of view of the passionate and compassionate ethics which they engender. Emotions show us the way to a more fulfilled and humane existence. Such is the 'intelligence', as the subtitle of Nussbaum's book has it, of the emotions. In 'Sorties: Out and Out: Attacks/

Ways Out/Forays' (1975), Cixous reinforces this message about the emotions by contrasting the masculine culture of thrifty self-interest and self-aggrand-isement – 'a man is always proving something; he has to "show off", show up the others' – with the receptivity and giving 'without self-interest' of women.[51] Cixous is aware of the way 'History' has exploited 'feminine reception': 'a woman', she writes, 'by her opening up, is open to being "possessed", which is to say, dispossessed of herself'.[52] But she nevertheless retains a conception of empathic femininity in which self and other are in loving rather than destructive relationship:

> I am speaking here of femininity as keeping alive the other that is confided to her, that visits her, that she can love as other. The loving to be other, another, without its necessarily going the rout of abasing what is same, herself.[53]

Clearly, the lessons to be learned from the emotions are different in the case of Shakespeare, Marx and Cixous, but not so different as to prohibit recognition of a certain family resemblance. Hamlet's neediness following the death of his father, the Macbeths' eroticised dependency as partners in crime, Marx's com-passion for the plight of child labourers, and Cixous' emphasis upon giving are all variations upon a sentimental truth. Even the cold-hearted Iago's denial of need can be recouped from the sentimental perspective that he over-protests his self-sufficiency. Emotions, then, can tell stories of a general kind about who we are: in Nussbaum's terms, they are intelligent; in Marxist language, they have a use-value; in Aristotelian terms, they serve educational and social purposes. As such, they are also compatible with the perfectionist principles of the Enlightenment discussed in the next chapter on existential humanism.

However, as with the other thinkers discussed in this chapter, Cixous also reserves an important place for excess. As a thinker who leans towards post-structuralism, she often locates excess in terms of language. In 'Sorties', for example, she privileges writing and particularly feminine writing (*écriture féminine*) as the source of excess. Rather than giving sober, thrifty expression to a self that is thought to precede language, feminine writing is 'where writing, freed from law, unencumbered by moderation, exceeds phallic authority, and where the subjectivity inscribing its effects becomes feminine'.[54] Language, for poststructuralists, is indeterminate, and it is the flow of meaning that for Cixous is exemplified by feminine writing because women are thought to be more multiple than men. To some extent, therefore, Cixous 'externalises' excess by thinking about it less in terms of the unseen depths of the self, than in terms of language and its effects. However, a Romantic sense of an unnam-eable and overflowing interiority is still present in Cixous' writing. The sexu-ality and emotional repertoire of 'woman' are seen by Cixous as inexhaustible and hitherto untapped inner resources to which feminine writing gives voice:

Her libido is cosmic, just as her unconscious is worldwide. Her writing can only keep going, without ever inscribing or discerning contours, daring to make these vertiginous crossings of the other(s) ephemeral and passionate sojourns in him, her, them, whom she inhabits long enough to look at from the point closest to their unconscious from the moment they awaken, to love them at the point closest to their drives; and then further, impregnated through and through with these brief, identificatory embraces, she goes and passes into infinity.[55]

Here and elsewhere, Cixous contrasts a finite with an infinite subjectivity, based on bodily passions and emotions which pass beyond functionalist theories of the emotions as useful to concepts of human need. Indeed, Cixous at times scorns the idea of utility. 'The logic of [masculine] communication', she suggests, 'requires an economy both of signs ... and of subjectivity. The orator is asked to unwind a thin thread, dry and taut.' Women, by contrast, 'like uneasiness, questioning. There is waste in what we say. We need that waste. To write is always to make allowances for superabundance and uselessness.'[56] Waste is explicitly identified by Cixous as emotional effluence: writing 'is good' she claims, because it lets 'the tongue try itself out – as one attempts a caress, taking the time a phrase or a thought needs to make oneself loved, to make oneself reverberate'.[57] Whereas (masculine) reason is driven by such utilitarian goals as the will to truth or power, (feminine) emotion is spendthrift. This represents Cixous' anti-functionalist view of the emotions, although it is hard to sidestep the functionalist retort that the desire to caress serves some human purpose. However, for the Romantic humanist Cixous to think about emotions too much in terms of their use-value would be to corroborate what she describes in 'Castration or Decapitation' (1981) as 'the pervasive masculine urge to judge, diagnose, digest, name'.[58] This is similar to the perspective of the other influential French feminists, Luce Irigaray and Julia Kristeva (discussed in Chapters 3 and 5). Naming for these writers tends to be seen as a masculine tyranny, which applied to the passions would empty them of their subversive otherness.

The mystery of the emotions is pursued further by Cixous in *Rootprints: Memory and Life Writing* (1994), written with Mireille Calle-Gruber. Of crying, for example, Cixous writes: 'the shedding of tears is a mystery throughout all our lives. We do not know why we cry, when we cry, how much we cry. Tears are not in a direct relation with the apparent cause.'[59] But crying is not totally beyond understanding either, for 'I have the feeling', she continues, 'that I am understanding something in flashes, in dazzles', even if these momentary insights fade.[60] Cixous' meditations on the mystery of the emotions forms part of an anthropology of the human itself. 'We must absolutely not let go of the word "human",' she writes, and as a Romantic humanist who places feeling near the centre of her humanism, she makes the sentimental claim that what we all have in common is 'the heart'.[61] However, the heart is 'the most mysterious organ there is'.[62] Her notion of what she calls the 'more human' or 'better human', which she offsets against the prescriptively norm-ative character of classical humanism, is in keeping with this insistence upon the mystery of the emotions. Referring to her novel *Neutre* of 1972, she writes:

> One of the roots of *Neutre* was a reflection on the destiny of the 'human' mystery – a mystery that is settled violently most of the time. Because ordinary human beings do not like mystery since you cannot put a bridle on it, and therefore, in general they exclude it, they repress it, they eliminate it – and it's *settled*. But if on the contrary one remains open and susceptible to all the phenomena of overflowing, beginning with natural phenemona, one discovers the immense landscape of the *trans-*, of the passage.[63]

Can, or should, such a humanism be politically effective? A Romantic humanism which takes emotion to be complex but ultimately useful with regard to human need is likely to be more outward looking and practical than its sublime counterpart. To hold the view that emotions tell us things about ourselves is compatible with those humanisms, such as civic humanism, which seek to define the human in some identifiable way with a view to making a practical difference to the way we live. Shakespeare, Marx and Cixous all retain this quasi-Aristotelian view of the emotions as a source of enlightenment. But they also veer, and Cixous more than the other two thinkers, towards a view of the emotions (and consequently of the human) as unsettled and 'overflowing', as Cixous expresses it in the above quotation. The sublime Romantic humanist is likely to belong nowhere, is likely to resist having a 'local habitation and a name', because human emotions are beyond what can be represented or socially accommodated.[64] Hamlet's 'that within which passes show' and Cixous' own appeal to 'our incalculable interior richness' do not easily lend themselves to a practical, everyday, communicable politics.[65] The tension between political and social engagement, on the one hand, and a complex sense of interiority, on the other, will be pursued further in the next chapter on existential humanism. Cixous herself appears to be aware of this tension when she says that the state of being '*trans-*' does not mean that 'everything will be adrift' in terms of 'our thinking' and 'our choices'.[66] As a way of tempering Romantic mystery and making it serve a practical, critical and political function, she invokes a form of citizenship based on 'the necessity of only being the citizen of an extremely inappropriable, unmasterable country or ground'.[67] Like Shakespeare and Marx, then, Cixous presents emotion as a source of human richness and possibility. But each of these thinkers also retains a notion of the use-value of emotion, the difference being that Cixous ultimately tries to put the incommunicable itself at the centre of a politics.

Primary Texts

William Shakespeare

Hamlet [1600], ed. Harold Jenkins (London: Methuen, 1982).
Othello [1604], ed. M. R. Ridley (London: Methuen, 1958).
King Lear [1605], ed. Kenneth Muir (London: Methuen, 1972).
Macbeth [1606], ed. Kenneth Muir (London: Methuen, 1951).

Karl Marx

(with Friedrich Engels) *The Communist Manifesto* [1848], trans. Samuel Moore (Harmonds-worth: Penguin, 1967).
The Eighteenth Brumaire of Louis Bonaparte [1852] (Moscow: Progress Publishers, 1934).
Capital: A Critique of Political Economy, Volume 1 [1867], trans. Ben Fowkes (London: Penguin, 1976), p. 167.

Hélène Cixous

'The Laugh of the Medusa' [1975], in *Feminisms: An Anthology of Literary Theory and Criticism*, ed. Robyn Warhol and Diane Herndl (New Brunswick: Rutgers University Press, 1991).
(with Catherine Clément) *The Newly Born Woman* [1975], trans. Betsy Wing (Manchester: Manchester University Press, 1987), particularly 'Sorties: Out and Out: Attacks/Ways Out/Forays'.
'Castration or Decapitation?' [1981], trans. Annette Kuhn, in *Feminist Literary Theory: A Reader*, 2nd edn, ed. Mary Eagleton (Oxford: Blackwell, 1996).
(with Mireille Calle-Gruber) *Rootprints: Memory and Life Writing* [1994], trans. Eric Prenowitz (London: Routledge, 1997).

CHAPTER 2

Existential Humanism
(Sartre – Arendt – Fanon)

In his 1969 essay on the demise of humanism 'The Ends of Man', Jacques Derrida targets what he sees as the perfectionist principles of Enlightenment philosophy, a perfectionist impulse that we have shown is also evident in certain strains of Romantic thought. Derrida queries the suppositions that led to the theory of 'perfect constitution' toward which human beings and civil society were thought to be moving in eighteenth-century Europe. He sees the 'question "of man"' as not only the cornerstone of Enlightenment ideology, but central to the whole tradition of French philosophy from Descartes's *cogito* in *Discourse on Method* (1637), through Jean-Jacques Rousseau's proto-Romantic theory of the 'savage man' in his *Discourse on Inequality* (1755), to existentialist thought in the mid-twentieth century.[1] Early in the essay Derrida singles out Jean-Paul Sartre for criticism among modern thinkers for defining existentialism in explicitly humanist terms in his 1945 lecture *Existentialism and Humanism* and for making 'human-reality' the 'irreducible horizon and origin' of his study.[2] Derrida is critical of Sartre for not going far enough in his speculations as to what constitutes the human, but applauds his attempt 'to suspend all the presuppositions which had always constituted the concept of the unity of man' and start with a clean state. This notion of a 'clean slate' reflects the British philosopher John Locke's theory in *The Essay on Human Understanding* (1690) that human life begins as a *tabula rasa* and is only given shape through experience. While Locke's ideas fed into the Enlightenment belief in the sovereign individual and the supreme value of knowledge, this image of a 'clean slate' is also echoed in modern existentialist thought as a way of stripping away the masks that often prevent the individual from having a clear view of him or herself.

We will come back to Derrida's particular criticisms of Sartre later, but this chapter focuses more broadly on the humanist implications of existentialist thought. Humanism is a central term for the three thinkers featured here: the French philosopher and writer Jean-Paul Sartre (1905–80), the German thinker Hannah Arendt (1906–75) who became one of the most provocative and wide-ranging thinkers in the mid-twentieth century after she emigrated to America, and the Martinique psychiatrist Frantz Fanon (1925–61) who is generally

accepted as 'the founding father of modern colonial critique'.[3] The emergence
of existentialism as an identifiable discourse is usually located in the mid-
nineteenth century (although it was not given a name until much later) in the
religious humanism of Søren Kierkegaard. In refusing to accept traditional
assumptions about the relation between 'the human' and 'the divine',
Kierkegaard took nothing at face value and resolved to test out experience
even if it meant risking his identity. For example, in *The Sickness Unto Death*
(1849) rather than seeing the individual as an indivisible self, Kierkegaard
describes humans as 'a synthesis of the infinite and the finite, of the temporal
and the eternal, of freedom and necessity, in short, a synthesis. A synthesis is a
relation between two. Considered in this way, a human being is still not a self.'[4]
His theory of a self in the process of 'becoming' and his challenge to live
intensely at all costs are the reasons why he was rescued from relative obscurity
in the 1930s and lionised as one of the precursors of modern existentialism.

Kierkegaard's refusal to invest in Enlightenment confidence in human
knowledge and rejection of the notion of a perfectible self were inspirations for
Martin Heidegger and Karl Jaspars in Germany and for Sartre and Albert
Camus in France. Despite personal antagonisms – Heidegger dismissed Sartre's
reading of his work as wrongheaded, Camus and Sartre famously fell out in
1952, Arendt was scornful of Sartre and turned away from Heidegger with his
political allegiance to the Far Right, and Fanon was critical of Sartre for his
Eurocentrism – these thinkers rejected the values of classical humanism for its
failure to criticise its founding suppositions and to examine what Derrida calls
the 'history of the concept of man'.[5] While religious existentialism had its
advocates in twentieth-century thinkers like Gabriel Marcel, Martin Buber and
Emmanuel Levinas (see Chapter 3), its most common manifestation was as an
atheist or agnostic strain of thought that addressed secular conditions and
worldly concerns. Rather than focusing on Kierkegaard's need to justify religious faith, Sartre, Arendt and Fanon each used existentialist ideas to address
ideological, ethical and social problems. All three were critical of the pretensions of classical humanism in its optimistic Enlightenment guise of
perfectibility: Sartre critiqued liberal humanism in his novel *Nausea* (1938),
Arendt avoided using the term for its suggestion of a blind optimism in human
progress, and Fanon attacked European humanism so vehemently that Neil
Badmington has recently claimed him as a posthumanist thinker.[6] However, as
with many of the other figures in this book, although they wished to jettison
humanist elements, Sartre, Arendt and Fanon can each be more profitably
shown to develop a 'new humanism' in their attempts to critically redefine its
parameters.

The popular conception of existentialism (and also of Romantic thought),
begins with the notion of the isolated individual, separated from others because

once all the layers of social relatedness such as family, work relations and national identity are stripped away, little, if anything, remains to bind individuals together. For example, the anti-heroes Antoine Roquentin in Sartre's *Nausea* and Patrice Meursault in Camus's novella *The Outsider* (1942) are isolated in chaotic worlds in which their actions are precarious and often lead to adverse consequences. On this theme, in his major philosophical work *Being and Nothingness* (1943), Sartre claimed that the universe is absurd because it does not make sense and cannot be made to cohere by pursuing a particular scientific or religious methodology: rather, it is a dense, inchoate and contradictory fact with which the individual must contend. This position seems to echo Descartes's proposition that if we doubt everything else in existence, then the only thing that remains indubitably is the mind itself. However, Sartre takes a step beyond Descartes in questioning even the basis for this knowledge because it suggests something 'essentially' human that cannot be doubted: in this case, a mind that thinks. Sartre rejects this notion of 'essence' and replaces it with the notion of 'existence' that precedes thought and cannot be fully expressed in any form of language. As the following section on Sartre discusses, this theoretical move is contentious (and was criticised by Heidegger), but it does provide a starting point for dealing with what existentialist thinkers deem to be the most basic parameters of human existence. Instead of constituting the grounds of 'human nature' as something definable, the existentialist starts with primordial experience – what Sartre calls that 'which exists before it can be defined by any conception of it' – and then attempts to fashion an identity out of the absurd chaos in which one finds oneself, just as an artist would begin with a blank canvas and make a painting out of a complex mixture of impulse, design, chance and craft.[7] The critic may retrospectively impose a standard of beauty, harmony, vitality or accuracy on the painting, but from an existentialist perspective whatever is created on the canvas is authentic for the artist as long as it is done with sincerity. Instead of trusting to scientific or religious verities, the existentialist authenticates the self by taking nothing for granted and by believing in nothing except the possibility of self-invention.

As with the Romantic insistence that axioms need to be felt on the pulse, the three thinkers discussed here develop different strains of existentialist thought to tackle theoretical problems on an experiential level. Sartre's reputation derived largely from his being the first thinker to fully articulate existentialist ideas, even though his major work *Being and Nothingness* was written in the shadow of Heidegger's 1927 treatise *Being and Time* (and although Heidegger did not like the label of existentialist). The questions Sartre addresses are appropriately basic: what does it mean to say 'existence' precedes 'essence'? How does one contend with an absurd and disorderly universe? How does one deal with the freedom that such absurdity brings? And, how can one act responsibly in the face of meaninglessness? All these questions have humanist implications in respect of those values which are retained after others have been rejected as worthless. Although Sartre was critical of Enlightenment ideas, there are elements of his work that revive some of the nodal points of classical French philosophy. Hannah Arendt offers a useful counterpoint to Sartre in her development of German existentialist thought that owes much more to Heidegger than to Parisian existentialism. She also deals with the 'human condition' in basic terms but, rather than addressing abstract problems of choice and responsibility, Arendt dealt with tangible issues of agency and power in the face of injustice, inequality, racism and social evil. Her transatlantic perspective helped her to contrast the totalitarian politics that drove her out of Germany in the 1930s with the ostensibly democratic environment of post-war America. But, like the German *émigrés* Theodor Adorno and Hebert Marcuse, Arendt was also critical of the injustices and blind faith in progress that she discerned as underpinning Western humanism.

Frantz Fanon was more closely influenced by the rhetoric of French existentialism than Arendt (considering French is the official language of the Caribbean island of Martinique and Fanon studied medicine and psychiatry in France), but he worked through the implications of Sartre's thought to attack the power dynamics of European colonialism, particularly as they concerned racial oppression. Fanon's criticism of Eurocentrism is exemplified in his powerful Conclusion to *The Wretched of the Earth* (1961), in which he argues 'we must leave our dreams and abandon our own beliefs ... leave this Europe where they are never done talking of Man, yet murder men everywhere they find them'.[8] More than Sartre and Arendt, Fanon's concern was to redefine a space of agency for the dispossessed. His existentialism is much more militant than Sartre's and he argues, like Camus in *The Rebel* (1951), that in certain instances there are limits beyond which one should not be pushed and which even justify violence as a purifying force. Whereas Sartre claims that in an absurd universe there can be no real limits, Arendt and Fanon identify certain social and economic pressures that impinge on freedom and civil liberty. But they do not envisage an excessive nihilistic world without limits, nor do they reject humanist values *carte blanche*, seeking to affirm 'the human' as a resilient life force never entirely undermined by impersonal forces. In the words of the French novelist Alain Robbe-Grillet, all three thinkers reject the notion of 'our alleged "nature" and the vocabulary that perpetuates its myth' and refuse 'to accept the "pan-anthropic" content of traditional, and probably every other, humanism', but they do so to understand what humanism might mean when it has its back to the wall.[9]

Jean-Paul Sartre

Sartre's massive work *Being and Nothingness* is his fullest expression of the existentialist position he had been refining through World War II. Reflecting the uncertainty of European identity in the 1940s, Sartre developed a version of Heidegger's theory that there is nothing 'essential' in humans that explains their complexion and motivations, only at root a vacancy that exists prior to language and cannot be fully expressed by it. This theoretical starting point strips away humanist confidence in an autonomous and knowable self that matures through experience. Sartre believed the individual acts maturely by preparing to face the consequences of his or her actions, but he challenges the classical humanist notion of an essential self that underpins rational behaviour. This position appears to be a strain of moral philosophy, but in *Being and Nothingness* Sartre does not discuss identity explicitly in ethical terms (terms which he did not fully develop until *Notebooks for an Ethic*, 1947).[10] Rather he considers the most basic ontological dimensions of 'Being' once familiar social masks have been stripped away. In fact, there is little that helps us to understand Sartre's humanism in *Being and Nothingness* and, like Heidegger's *Being and Time*, the work can actually be interpreted as anti-humanist for its radical assault on the classical humanist conception of an indivisible self. It was Sartre's next statement on existentialism, his more accessible 1945 lecture *Existentialism and Humanism*, that enabled him to counter some of the general criticisms of his position and to explain existentialist thought in humanist terms.

Sartre begins *Existentialism and Humanism* by detailing four main criticisms of existentialism: first, that it is an 'invitation to people to dwell in quietism of despair' because it questions the validity of any course of action; second, that it dwells on 'all that is ignominious in the human situation' and neglects 'charm and beauty'; third, that it focuses on the individual at the expense of solidarity with others; and, fourth, that it avoids serious moral obligation because 'nothing remains but what is strictly voluntary'.[11] He takes his time to address these four criticisms, but starts by making the general claim that rather than being a 'gloomy' philosophy it actually renders 'human life possible'.[12] This emphasis on possibility develops Kierkegaard's notion of becoming and is part of the central thrust of Sartre's humanism: even though he encourages the individual to strip away habitual modes of action one is still left 'with a possibility of choice'.[13] In *Being and Nothingness* he had argued that Being has two primary aspects: Being 'in itself' (*en soi*) by which identity is constructed and Being 'for itself' (*pour soi*) in which human beings are always moving towards something, be it a desired object, goal or the future in general. In *Existentialism and Humanism* he distinguishes humans from moss, fungi, cauliflowers and most animals in that they are sentient creatures that 'propel' themselves 'towards a future'.[14] Because a choice is always a unique moment of self-becoming, the individual is responsible for the direction in which he or she is propelled and the consequences that follow from that choice. Rather than sheltering in a narcissistic life-world in which any action could be justified as 'good' for the self, Sartre argues that when one chooses responsibility one does so with 'an image of man such as he believes he ought to be'.[15] This argument suggests there is a close match between choosing what is valuable for the individual and choosing what is best for humankind. He substantiates this rather grand claim by giving two examples: the man that chooses to join a Christian rather than a Communist trade union commits himself to the idea that 'man's kingdom is not upon this earth' and the man that decides to marry and have children commits himself to the 'practice of monogamy' and to cherishing the sanctity of family life. In short, he believes that behind every individual choice is an ideal toward which everyone must strive: 'I am creating a certain image of man as I would have him be' and 'in fashioning myself I fashion man'.[16]

We will come to the criticisms of these claims presently, but it is worth dwelling on what Sartre conceives humanism to be in relation to his version of existentialism. He is anti-rationalist in arguing that it is impossible to prove indubitably whether a certain choice is 'good' rather than 'bad' (because there are no moral absolutes and some choices have adverse side-effects) or whether the urge to act is the result of good sense or irrational compulsion, but he suggests that all acts should be exemplary of the highest ideals. Sartre distinguishes between good faith in which the individual acts sincerely and with the good of all in mind and bad faith that is 'ashamed of itself and does not dare speak its name'. Bad faith obscures 'all its goals to free itself' from the 'anguish' that Sartre – following Kierkegaard and Heidegger – believes is one of the irreducible features of human existence.[17] He asserts that no true action can be made without a sense that the choice might prove undesirable (such as the military leader who sends his troops into battle), but his claim that when the individual acts he or she does so not just for him or herself but for everyone prevents, or should prevent, any action being purely self-serving. He challenges the charge that existentialism is a 'quietist' philosophy by claiming that whatever we do we cannot help but 'act', arguing that it is not a pessimistic theory because it stresses that an individual's destiny is his or her own.

Sartre is particularly interested in choices for which there are no clear solutions, when all possible routes are problematic and potentially disastrous. In *Existentialism and Humanism* Sartre chooses the example of a young man enlisting in the army in spite of his mother's concern for him, and he dramatises another scenario in his short story 'The Wall' (1939) in which the narrator refuses to tell a firing squad the location of the man they are hunting, not because his friend's life has more value than his own or because his friend is more socially useful, but because he simply 'refused to do it'.[18] Sartre's point is that whatever is decided in these scenarios – whether the individual values knowledge, love, fellowship, providence, or bravery – the commitment to act transcends the particular choice demanded by the situation. His emphasis on 'instinct' in these tricky cases reveals him to be more of a Romantic than an idealist, arguing that 'if values are uncertain, if they are still too abstract to determine the particular, concrete case under consideration, nothing remains but to trust to our instincts'.[19] His point is that one may act within a particular ethical or political framework, but freedom remains a defining feature of existence because the individual remains at liberty to act even in the most trying circumstances: thus, 'man cannot be free at times and a slave at other times: he is entirely and always free or he does not exist'.[20] This understanding is at the heart of Sartre's humanism, in which free choice transcends any situation in which one may find oneself (although Fanon would argue that this is unlikely to be the case for the slave or captive).

Sartre's task is to distinguish between two types of humanism. He mocks liberal humanism in *Nausea* as cherishing a naïve image of man, an image from which Roquentin tries to rescue himself. In this case 'man' is taken 'as the end-in-itself and as the supreme value', whereas in Sartre's revitalised humanism individuals are not fully formed and must commit themselves wholeheartedly to an ethic of self-becoming and to the realities of an uncertain future.[21] There are times in *Nausea* when Roquentin feels his identity stripped away entirely, such as when he wanders through the street and can 'no longer feel myself; I am won over by the purity surrounding me ... am I myself not a wave of icy air? With neither blood, nor lymph, nor flesh.'[22] At other times he experiences his self in transition from one uncertain state to another, neither of which can adequately be named. For Sartre, it is this notion of 'self-surpassing', rather than satisfaction at the wonderful accomplishments of humanist civilisation, that creates the condition for a more authentic strain of humanism.[23] He calls this 'existential humanism' since humans always seek beyond themselves (*pour soi*) and ends *Existentialism and Humanism* by claiming it has the aim 'of liberation or of some particular realization, that man can realise himself as truly human'.[24] While critics like Derrida may accuse him of simply sloganeering and admitting classical humanism through the back door, Sartre's existential humanism is self-critical because the individual will always be anxious that he or she may make wrong choices.[25] It is a critical humanism because it questions all established answers and historical analogies, forcing all individuals into being responsible by resolutely facing the consequences of their actions. It is also a critical humanism because it does not allow the thinker to hide in a world of abstract contemplation, but forces him or her into the maelstrom of existence with no clear path leading into a secure future and no Godhead to light the way. With this in mind, Sartre's translator Philip Mairet comments that 'detached deliberation' can only lead to the individual making 'minor decisions', whereas 'genuine critical dilemmas of the individual's life ... emerge through conflicts and tumults of the soul, anxieties, agonies, perilous adventures of faith into unknown territories'.[26]

While Sartre is persuasive in distinguishing between these two forms of humanism, there is actually something uncritical about his claim that every decision is an act of commitment to humankind: we might be lured into making choices by false consciousness or social manipulation, or might suffer from a medical condition that renders 'authentic' decision-making impossible. For this reason, in partial response to Sartre's lecture, Heidegger's 'Letter on Humanism' (1947) represents an attempt to distance his own work from the French thinker and, more generally, from humanist-based philosophy. Heidegger argues that it is not justifiable to locate human beings at the centre of the universe or as the basis for all action. His attack is on metaphysical humanism as the unassailable vantage point for all understanding, which also includes the priority of 'the individual' in Sartre's thought. Heidegger argues that for Sartre 'every humanism is either grounded in a metaphysics or is itself made to be the ground of one'.[27] On this view, Sartre is neither critical nor radical enough in rethinking the relationship between existentialism and humanism. In a characteristically abstruse manner Heidegger asks:

> Should we still keep the name 'humanism' for a 'humanism' that contradicts all previous humanism — although it in no way advocates the inhuman? ... Or should thinking, by means of open resistance to 'humanism', risk a shock that could for the first time cause perplexity concerning the *humanitas* of *homo humanus* and its basis?[28]

Perhaps Sartre is too accepting of humanism and does not see a problem in retaining the individual as the satellite for action, even though it is reconceived as a fledgling self moving towards an indistinct future. From Heidegger's perspective, Sartre's stress on subjective experience recycles the language of classical French philosophy and does nothing risky in reconceiving the problem of existence and its relation to death.

The crucial difference between Heidegger and Sartre is that the French philosopher begins with the concept of the human self, whereas Heidegger bases his philosophy on Being (*Sein*) which he describes as 'the most universal and the emptiest of concepts', eluding precise definition but without eliminating 'the question of its meaning'.[29] Heidegger discusses the way in which 'thrownness into Being' — a form of existential orphaning in which we are thrown into a bewildering environment — is a fundamental condition of sentient life, leading to the kind of anguish that cannot be overcome by reason or religious faith. We may try to make ourselves more secure by packaging notions of 'self', 'identity' and 'humanness' as knowable, but Heidegger would argue that the more security we ostensibly have the more insecure our existence becomes. Sartre would concur with this, but retains the notion of the individual fundamentally isolated from others and with responsibility primarily for itself 'as the incontestable author of an event or object',[30] whereas Heidegger stresses that Being is a relational term connected to a world of other Beings. For Heidegger, Being (*Sein*) should be approached as 'Being-in-the-world' (*Dasein*), implying an unbreakable connection with a shared environment. Where Sartre speaks in terms of 'my' responsibility and 'my' freedom and the pronoun 'I' suggests a separation from others, Heidegger's theory of 'Being' implicates those others 'from whom, for the most part, one does *not* distinguish oneself – those among whom one is too'.[31] In this way, Heidegger attacks the Cartesian subject for conceptually dividing the private self from those other shadowy entities that inhabit the world: the split rests on Descartes's association of the mind (or *cogito*) with the true self and the body with the contingent world in which the mind is suspended. Even though Sartre insists at times that 'we find ourselves in a world ... of "inter-subjectivity"', Heidegger charges him with putting too much emphasis on the individual.[32] While Sartre retains aspects of Descartes's model (he quotes the Cartesian mantra 'I think, therefore I am'[33]), Heidegger claims that *Dasein* is ontologically too basic to be split into mind and body, or subject and object. In contrast, he argues that the conjunctives 'with' ('Being-in-the-world-*with*-Others') and 'too' ('those among whom one is *too*') should be understood 'existentially' as relational terms that imply ready-made links between Beings. On this understanding, he differs from Sartre in his claim that the individual is never alone, but 'by reason of this *with-like* ... the world is always the one that I share with Others. The world of *Dasein* is a *with-world*.'[34]

Heidegger's criticisms appear sound, but according to Derrida he is not exempt from the charges he levels at Sartre. Indeed, many of Heidegger's differences from Sartre derive from the distinct national philosophical traditions to which they are heir. While Heidegger is as critical of German idealism as Sartre is of French rationalism, to Derrida's mind neither goes far enough with their critiques. True, they invent a new language that expresses the desire to reconceive selfhood in terms of 'good faith' or 'authentic existence'. Even though Heidegger goes further than Sartre in reinventing language, they both remain stuck in a discourse that speaks in terms of 'individual', 'self' or 'Being' that are themselves products of social, historical and linguistic convention. The implication of Derrida's extreme poststructuralist position – into which he has dipped periodically since the late 1960s – is that language necessarily binds the human being (or however else we may want to describe it) to a pre-existing network of signs into which we are born and by which we are acculturated. If this is the case, then it problematises the attempts by Sartre and Heidegger to distil authentic existence from the social codes that support it: for this reason Derrida calls 'the question of the truth of Being' the 'last sleeping shudder of the superior man'.[35] Although Derrida's critique of existentialist thought in 'The Ends of Man' has depth, there is also something to be retained in Sartre's and Heidegger's insistence that the void at the heart of Being cannot be expressed in language: that the 'ice-cold feeling' of homelessness will always evade any attempt to appropriate it or fix it in discourse. Moreover, Sartre's understanding that 'man is impossible' did not stop him trying to 'manifest this impossibility' to harness its creative and critical energies in the face of what he perceived to be a largely unquestioning society.[36]

Hannah Arendt

Hannah Arendt's writings on political, social and philosophical issues are even more diffuse than Sartre's and it is harder to pin down the humanist impulse in her work. For example, in *The Human Condition* (1958) Arendt declares that 'the problem of human nature ... seems unanswerable in both its individual psychological sense and its general philosophical sense' but she returned repeatedly to deal with the sustaining values of human life.[37] She reveals a strong existentialist current in her argument that 'it is highly unlikely that we, who can know, determine, and define the natural essences of all things surrounding us ... should ever be able to do the same for ourselves – this would be like jumping over our own shadows', but she had a troubled intellectual relationship with Sartre.[38] Arendt praised Heidegger's critique of Sartre's subjectivism in his 'Letter on Humanism', and on reading the translation of Sartre's *The Words* in 1964 she expressed her personal dislike for the French thinker, accusing him of 'highly complicated lying' and for fashioning 'a great show of sincerity' in his exaggerated claims to be politically engaged.[39] However, like Sartre, she also questions whether in fact we 'have a nature or essence', concluding that human life only emerges from inchoate existence through thinking and acting. And, like Sartre, she looks back to Kierkegaard (as well as to Marx and Nietzsche) for giving voice 'to the modern loss of faith, not only in God but in reason as well' and for giving an existentialist turn to modern thought 'against the alleged abstractions of philosophy and its concept of man as an *animal rationale*'.[40] But if we compare Arendt's description of 'jumping over our own shadows' to Sartre's conception of 'Nothingness' as the void of being, there is a subtle distinction between the two, in that Arendt believed there is more to learn and say about the shadowy human condition and the 'things' that surround us than Sartre acknowledges. This may be due to the strong Germanic current in her writing (she was taught by both Heidegger and Karl Jaspers), but this is offset by her wish to cut across fixed modes of inquiry that stemmed in part from her shifting national identity (she left her homeland for France in 1933 with the rise of National Socialism, then emigrated to America in 1941). Although she is often labelled a 'political philosopher' Arendt offers no systematic theory of politics or political action, but returned to the haunting existentialist – and humanist – questions: 'who are we' and 'what should we do'?

Arendt shared with Sartre the belief that the contemporary thinker is obliged to rebel against traditional metaphysics. She states in her collection of essays *Between Past and Future* (1961) that 'it began to dawn upon modern man that he had come to live in a world in which his mind and his tradition of thought were not even capable of asking adequate, meaningful questions, let alone of giving answers to its own perplexities'. If, on this basis, it is not the existentialist's task to resolve metaphysical problems, then engaged action seems 'to hold out the hope ... of making it possible to live with [problems] without becoming, as Sartre once put it, a *salaud*, a hypocrite'.[41] It is perhaps not surprising that existentialist thought arose in the second quarter of the twentieth century when ideology, class conflict and total war cleaved nations like never before in modern history. Arendt is more historically aware than Sartre. Writing most of her work in Cold War America, Arendt describes the contemporary situation as an 'odd in-between period ... an interval of time which is altogether determined by things that are no longer and by things that are not yet'.[42] This 'in-between' space is 'a gap in time' pressed in by revenants of the past and portents of the future; at the fulcrum of past and future stands the human being on whom the historical forces impinge and demand to be given shape.[43] The quietist would relax and let the 'clashing waves of past and future' wash over him or her; the pessimist would not act believing that action could not bring about a better state of affairs; and the nihilist would act randomly and without care of consequence.[44] Only the resolute individual is able to intervene in this clash of past and future, to create a third 'diagonal force' that would enable one to 'judge the forces fighting ... with an impartial eye' and yet be brave enough to actively intervene at the right moment.[45] The essays in *Between Past and Future*, ranging over topics of history, authority, freedom, education, culture and politics, are exemplary of Arendt's holistic existentialist position as she attempts both to think and 'to move in this gap' between past and future, combining 'criticism' and 'experiment' that she believes should not be 'sharply divided' from each other.[46]

Like Sartre, Arendt is concerned with exposing the masks 'which society assigns to its members as well as those which the individual fabricates for himself' in order to approach the 'naked' human condition once it has been stripped of its disguises.[47] Only when the individual becomes a 'challenger' and acts 'against tyranny and things worse than tyranny' will one be able to glimpse what Arendt calls the 'apparition of freedom'. This seems to adhere to Sartre's notion of good faith. But where Arendt differs crucially is in her stress on group identity over individual experience and by locating freedom in 'the public space' created between individuals. For example, in the essay 'What is Freedom?' she argues that freedom is wrongly conceived as an 'inward space into which men may escape from external coercion and *feel* free', a tendency which she argues may simply be seen as a sign of 'retreat from the world'.[48] Whether we speak in terms of the American emphasis on 'public happiness' or the French conception of 'public freedom', she argues that only in communal spaces can freedom as 'tangible reality' be glimpsed.[49] Too often this 'apparition of freedom' fails to solidify into something lasting, such as in Revolutionary France or Communist Soviet Union when oppressive conditions took root in the new soil that briefly promised freedom. Even though both these revolutions put emphasis on 'social' rather than 'individual' experience, in *The Human Condition* Arendt distinguishes between what she calls the creative 'public world' and the potentially repressive 'social world'. She claims the public world was prominent in Classical Greece, but in modern history has been eroded by social forces that reify human relations and enforce inhuman codes of behaviour. To her mind, whereas the factory-belt mentality of industrial modernity isolates and divides workers, the public culture of the Classical world nurtured creative interdependency in its citizens. This serves to emphasise the concrete good of the collective over the abstract subjectivity of the individual and those self-determining support groups such as the family. For example, in her first major work written in German *The Origins of Totalitarianism* (1951) she claims: 'the world found nothing sacred in the abstract nakedness of being human ... It seems that a man who is nothing but a man has lost the very qualities which make it possible for other people to treat him as a fellow-man.'[50] The implication is that when we forget our 'fellow-man' through thoughtlessness, introspection or malice then we lose sight of the true purpose of being human.

Arendt roots the contemporary understanding of humanism in the Roman concept of *humanitas* as the 'highest being we know of', a concept that she argues is absent in Greek culture with its emphasis on high education and the transcendent realm of ideas.[51] She relates this conception of humanism to notions of 'geocentrism' and 'anthropocentrism' as triumphant values before Darwinism and Marxism (together with the scepticism of Kierkegaard and Nietzsche) replaced them with conceptions of 'system' and 'process'. However, despite these theoretical assaults on *humanitas*, the fact that humanist values prevail even in the midst of the scientific and technical advances of modernity and postmodernity suggests that 'man' (to use Arendt's term) is much more 'than a special case of organic life'.[52] Anti-humanist modern science may claim it has freed itself 'completely from all such anthropocentric, that is, truly humanistic, concerns', but to Arendt's mind it does so by retreating into technical jargon that no longer speaks to the 'everyday language' of public culture.[53] On this issue Arendt's discussion foreshadows some of the debates surrounding technology and humanism (see Chapter 8), but the crux of her argument is that in pursuing abstract truth that 'lies *behind* natural phenomena', contemporary scientists (by which she means physicists associated with nuclear power and the space race) neglect the very 'pre-scientific' questions that motivate their project in the first place.[54] Science claims its 'pure' triumph over the relativity of human concerns by reconstructing 'the world we live in so radically' that it leaves 'the humanist' and 'the layman' floundering behind with their antiquated belief in 'commonsense'.[55] But Arendt goes some way to rescuing humanism by arguing that most scientists may transform the sphere of debate into technical language, but behind this they cannot help but be concerned with human issues. Those who are not, such as ideologically suspect eugenicists, turn their back on humanism in favour of a higher principle of authority, domination or fascistic will to power that does not simply lower 'the status of man' but utterly destroys its values.[56]

Arendt returned to the threat of totalitarianism throughout her work and the benign guises that often mask it, such as her famous exposure in *Eichmann in Jerusalem* (1963) of the 'banal' evil of the Nazi war criminal Adolf Eichmann and his inhuman participation in the Final Solution, not through cold calculation but through thoughtlessness. She sees that totalitarianism is likely to emerge in mass society at any point where humanitarian concerns have been eroded and the individual feels superfluous, when their space to be creative has been closed off by inhuman bureaucracy or self-interested politics. But rather than retreating from the political sphere to celebrate the inner life of the individual, she argues that politics is useful – in fact, essential – for preserving shared public space. To Arendt's mind the modern 'nuclear' age is characterised by a loss of a 'common world' that leaves humans either living 'in desperate lonely separation' or 'pressed together into a mass' with no room to breathe.[57] Although she places emphasis on the individual's ability to act out his or her own virtue as a mark of the health of culture, she is critical of the liberal emphasis on the existential richness of the individual's private life. Contesting the liberal notion that 'freedom begins where politics end' on the one hand, her vision of a pluralistic public culture and participatory democracy also counters the totalitarian ethic that imposes the will of the leader or the state on the people, and polices spaces in which creativity and dissent can thrive. She is clear that politics will continue to be used for corrupt ends, but argues that politics is all that we have for organising action and preserving the basic right of citizenship. Arendt echoes Sartre in her commitment to action, but takes two steps beyond him by stressing the importance of public participation and by arguing that emancipatory ideals are rarely realised in tangible ways. She nevertheless maintains that the political realm has the resources to compensate for existential anxiety and that political action can create conditions that make life bearable.

The existential dimension of Arendt's writing is most clearly discernible in *The Origins of Totalitarianism* and *The Human Condition*, but her 1950s essays collected in *Between Past and Future* are most useful for assessing her response to humanism. Like Sartre she emphasises the need to act, but is more hesitant about the positive outcome of ethical or political action and locates the urge to action outside the self, 'guided by a future aim' that emanates from a shared 'principle'.[58] What she does grant to the self is the ability to improvise in an uncertain environment, to perform an act with existential virtuosity (that she derives from Machiavelli's concept of *virtu*) in a creative 'theater where freedom could appear'.[59] This notion of improvising or starting over grants human beings the 'capacity to begin', but also politicises any individual act, unless it is to be a private or narcissistic act that would lack vitality and meaning. Although her theory of 'starting over' is very different from Heidegger's emphasis on death, this dimension reflects the existential idea more clearly apparent in Heidegger than in Sartre, that when we act we perform before another, who is not fully separated from the self (as in the philosophical distinction between subject and object), but a fellow being in the world.[60] This existential relatedness suggests a common humanity that cuts across distinctions of race, ethnicity, gender or creed as the basis of humanist interaction. This position is partly borne out by her own experience of anti-Semitism in Germany and helps to explain her belief that citizenship and ethnicity should be independent of each other. She argues in *The Origins of Totalitarianism*, for example, that anti-Semitism in Germany was 'an instrument for the liquidation not only of the Jews but of the body politic of the nation-state as well' and a desecration of the conditions of human existence.[61] Again, this claim resembles Sartre's argument that in cases of anti-Semitism the sphere of human relatedness is disrupted by the imposition of an arrogant and hubristic will: 'by treating the Jew as an inferior and pernicious being, I affirm at the same time that I belong to the elite [which] closely resembles that of an aristocracy determined by birth. There is nothing I have to do to merit my superiority, nor is there anything I can do to lose it. It is given once and for all.'[62] We will develop the existential humanist understanding of racial and ethnic difference in the next section on Frantz Fanon. Here it is worth noting that although there are major differences between Sartre and Arendt in terms of the role of public culture for providing the grounds for freedom, they both attempt to rescue the possibility of humanist action and interaction from the debilitating forces of technological modernity that coincide with, or even give rise to, totalitarianism.

Frantz Fanon

With the rise of postcolonial theory in the 1980s Frantz Fanon has become one of the most hotly debated of modern intellectuals. Although Sartre wrote a long introduction in praise of and in general sympathy with Fanon's treatise on the colonial situation in North Africa, *The Wretched of the Earth* (1961), when Fanon died that same year he was a marginal figure outside particular interest groups in France and Africa. As Nigel Gibson notes, Fanon's posthumous rise to prominence as a provocative thinker in Europe and North America coincided with the emergence of South African exiles in the late 1970s and the rise of African-American studies in universities.[63] While he might easily have been positioned elsewhere in this book, a discussion of Fanon's thought is germane to a consideration of existential humanism both in terms of Sartre's direct influence on him and Fanon's own attack on what he deemed to be the certainties and self-satisfactions of European humanism.[64] While it is possible to recruit elements of Fanon for anti-humanist or posthumanist causes in statements like 'when I search for Man ... I see only a succession of negations of man', his critical humanism is evident throughout his first book, *Black Skin, White Masks*, when he proclaims 'Mankind, I believe in you' and 'make of me always a man who questions!'[65] Among critics of Fanon, Edward Said, Nigel Gibson and Richard Onwuanibe all detect a strong humanist strain in his work, and Lewis Gordon claims that while Fanon 'rejects ontology' and a fixed notion of 'human nature', he 'does not reject the existential phenomenological impact of what he "sees". This is because he is fundamentally a radical, critical, revolutionary, existential humanist.'[66]

Where Sartre links philosophical and fictional inquiries and Arendt relies on the language of political theory (even though she is critical of it), the dominant discourses of Fanon's *Black Skin, White Masks* and *The Wretched of the Earth* are drawn from psychoanalysis and Marxism. He makes reference to both post-Freudian and neo-Marxist concepts, but attempts to bridge psycho-analytic and social-economic dimensions (with their respective emphasis on the individual and the collective) by sketching out the possibilities for attaining emancipation. Fanon is critical of both European existentialism and Western humanism – as Lewis Gordon claims, while Fanon 'wants to find Man ... he keeps bumping into White Man'[67] – but his work is imbued with an existential awareness of the forces that both hinder and enable individual and communal freedom to be enacted when the stakes are at their highest. Fanon's emphasis is upon demystifying popular misconceptions of the subaltern as 'disfigured' and not fully human, as well as giving voice to the traumas and desires of those oppressed by skin colour or colonialism.

At the beginning of *Black Skin, White Masks*, Fanon proclaims 'a new humanism' that challenges the racist and partisan foundations of European and American humanism (America being the 'monster' that Europe made, a country that racism 'haunts' and 'vitiates' like a 'dialectical gangrene').[68] All his writings can be seen as an attempt to move toward this new humanist position as the ultimate end, even though he, like Arendt, was aware that this may be forever just over the horizon. Although there is a clear emancipatory ethic in his work, Fanon's sight is rarely clouded by grand utopian dreams, but a sense that 'it would be good if certain things were said' that have hitherto been ignored or deliberately hidden. When it comes to the Enlightenment ideals expressed in the French Revolutionary slogan 'liberty, equality, fraternity' and the humanist rhetoric of the Declaration of Independence, Fanon is clear that these universalistic statements actually reinforce a partisan power base. On this issue, in his Preface to *The Wretched of the Earth*, Sartre stresses that authentic humanism has the ability to renew itself by turning on the pretensions of so-called universal humanism to speak for all individuals living under all conditions. While European humanism may speak with the language of universal rights, it is often a smoke screen to hide a 'racist humanism since the European has only been able to become a man through creating slaves and monsters'.[69] The claim to a common humanity by some has only come about by making others 'less-than-humans' by means of servitude, captivity and slavery. When slaves turn on the master they may still speak in terms of humanism and human rights but only, as Sartre says 'to reproach us [the white Europeans] with our inhumanity'.[70]

Rather than taking these slogans at face value, Fanon shares Sartre's willingness to face the 'vast black abyss' and 'zone of nonbeing' that lie at the heart of identity.[71] He is also interested in social inequalities that are often masked by political universalism in order that, as Richard Onwuanibe notes, he can 'really universalise' the humanist values of 'human dignity, freedom, love, care and justice'.[72] Where Fanon moves beyond Sartre is his focus on the racial marks and stigma of 'blackness', shifting away from an abstract philosophical treatise on the 'human condition' towards an affinity with Arendt's study of the relations between economics, sociology, politics and psychology that have stimulated the contemporary crisis in European human-ism and, to his mind, infected 'the worm-eaten roots of the [whole] structure'.[73] For Fanon, it is not only the responsibility of colonised peoples to control their destiny, but the pressing task of Europeans 'to wake up and shake themselves, use their brains, and stop playing the stupid game of the Sleeping Beauty'.[74]

Fanon's work can be seen to intensify Sartre's theory of rebellion and Arendt's interest in revolutionary theory, evident in Sartre's claim that 'from the point of view of a future society which will be born thanks to [the rebel's] efforts, his violence is a positive humanism ... Not a means of achieving humanism. Not even a necessary condition. But the humanism in itself, insofar as it asserts itself against reification.'[75] Like Sartre and Camus, Fanon is sensitive to the virtues of rebellion for radically disrupting intolerable conditions, even if one has to resort to violence. He is often dubbed an 'apostle of violence' and accused of sharing with the Black Panthers in late 1960s America a philosophy of armed militancy: 'the moment [the native] realises his humanity ... he begins to sharpen the weapons with which he will secure his victory'.[76] But, rather than tribal warfare, Fanon's emphasis is on violence as a purifying force that enables reintegration and reunification. He is critical of non-violent and gradualist approaches to colonial problems, seeing them as forms of inertia; arguing that the process of decolonialisation is necessarily a violent one with the ultimate goal to change 'the whole structure ... from the bottom up'.[77] For the individual, violence can be a form of self-empowerment in which the slave turns on the master – 'it frees the native from his inferiority complex and from his despair and inaction; it makes him fearless and restores his self-respect' – but such muscular violence can easily become an end in itself. Although this is the danger in Fanon's view of violence, his revolutionary theory differs crucially from Arendt's argument in *On Violence* (1969), written in the wake of counter-cultural protests and the Black Power movement, that violence paradoxically lacks the power to bring about new and lasting social relations.[78] But Arendt admits that Fanon's reputation for advocating violence is based largely on the opening chapter of *The Wretched of the Earth* and not on his more tempered statements, such as his claim that 'unmixed and total brutality ... invariably leads to the defeat of the movement within a few weeks'.[79]

Whereas Sartre discusses the responsibility of the individual and Arendt writes in terms of the potential creativity of the public sphere, Fanon focuses on the tensions between coloniser and colonised and between nation states, particularly as they affected the Antilles region of the West Indies and the Algerian war against the French in the 1950s (in which he actively participated as a member of the Algerian liberation front, the FLN). In *Black Skin, White Masks* he claims ironically that 'the Negro of the Antilles will be proportionately whiter – that is, he will come closer to being a real human being – in direct relation to his mastery of the French language'; the colonised people gain an inferiority complex 'by the death and burial of [their] local cultural originality' and their humanness can only be reclaimed (in a debased form) by adopting the values and the 'language of the civilizing nation'.[80] In the face of this psychic dilemma, the 'native' may try to whiten or objectify himself (and it is usually a 'he' for Fanon), but this would only be what Stuart Hall calls 'a profound misrecognition of one's own identity'; alternatively he can try to reinvent a primitive tribal past, but this may be only one or other version of primitivism as defined by the dominant culture (see Chapter 6 on pagan humanism); or he can take up arms against the oppressor to combat 'the violence which has ruled over the ordering of the colonial world'.[81] A number of critics have detected a Manichean logic in Fanon's thought: what he himself calls a 'world cut in two' between master and slave, between belonging and not-belonging, and between the settler's 'well-fed' and 'easygoing' town and the native's 'crouching village, a town on its knees, a town wallowing in the mire'.[82] There is certainly a set of binary oppositions in Fanon that reflect the opposition between self and world in Sartre, but Nigel Gibson claims that Fanon subsumes this motionless 'logic of equilibrium' into a dynamic and 'untidy' dialectic.[83] Gibson argues against Homi Bhabha's critique that Fanon often simplifies the ambivalence of colonial relations in favour of absolute closure that justifies his call to violence against the oppressor.[84] For Gibson, Fanon's 'dialectic of negativity' is not one in which the native simply substitutes the tyranny of the master with another equally tyrannical regime, but reveals 'the historical moment when the native begins to be released from the crushing objecthood of totalitarian colonial reality and disrupts the spatial ordering central to the colonial regime'.[85]

Fanon's 'new humanism' can be read critically as part of his over-confidence 'in the ability of the revolution to create a "new person"' or can be interpreted more positively as part of a self-determining theory of becoming in which the logic of colonisation is disrupted just as it is actively opposed.[86] Fanon was aware that militant nationalism could easily become 'an empty shell, a crude and fragile travesty' of a more meaningful revolution.[87] Because of this he wished to make African nationalists aware of the broader social and political needs that would transform their cause into a more inclusive pan-African oppositional humanism. He believed that such a revolutionary moment would come about through a combination of social organisation and the kind of creative spontaneity that reflects the existential improvisation that Arendt argues can meaningfully transform social relations. While Fanon's support of nationalist uprising as a means to purify human relations seems prescient with the violent nationalist upsurges in late twentieth-century Europe, Africa and the Middle East (but also ideologically suspect in the light of the rhetoric of 'ethnic cleansing' in the East European conflicts in the 1990s), the postcolonial critic Rajagopalan Radhakrishnan indicates that 'nationalism is not a monolithic phenomenon to be deemed entirely good or entirely bad ... the historical agency of nationalism has been sometimes hegemonic although often merely dominant, sometimes emancipatory although often repressive, and sometimes progressive although often traditional and reactionary.'[88] In other words, while Fanon's notion of nationalist consciousness may provide the energy to galvanise a movement that is both organised and spontaneous, if it rigidifies into 'the official ideology of nationalism' or becomes too narrow in its interests it will become a force of oppression and may lead to self-perpetuating terrorism. On these lines he argues that 'if nationalism ... is not enriched and deepened by a very rapid transformation into a consciousness of social and political needs, in other words into humanism, it leads up a blind alley'.[89] But, conversely, the adoption of Western humanist values by colonised and developing countries may simply mean the sacrifice of political self-determination to some higher and abstract notion of 'Man' that does not speak to specific historical and cultural issues: as Fanon asks at the end of *The Wretched of the Earth*, 'So, my brothers, how is it that we do not understand that we have better things to do than to follow that same Europe?'[90]

Richard Onwuanibe detects six features in Fanon's humanism: (i) the importance of dignity and recognition; (ii) the supreme value of freedom; (iii) values of justice, love and peace; (iv) the search for authentic universalism; (v) 'the emergence of a new man'; and (vi) its dialectical character.[91] Many of these features are also true of Sartre and Arendt, while all three agree on the equal importance of action and thought, and they are equally resolute in their existential and political commitment. Where Derrida's 1969 essay focuses on 'the ends of man', these three thinkers all focus on the possibility of starting over with a new beginning. In Fanon's case, Nigel Gibson claims his 'new humanism' is articulated with greatest clarity and with more attention to practical possibilities in *The Wretched of the Earth*, in which 'the dialectic of spontaneity and organisation' is central to its historical thrust.[92] While Fanon seems to complicate his humanism by advocating violence, it is born out of his concern that colonial stasis will triumph over social change and is in desperate need of being shaken out of its complacency. His energetic prose style mirrors the revolutionary vision in which 'the native's muscles are always tensed' and ready for combat.[93] But, despite his theoretical weakness when it comes to deal with gender issues and women's liberation, there are softer elements to his humanism that give his vision real nuance.[94] The masculine energy of Fanon's prose flows from the anger of the archetypal black existentialist anti-hero Bigger Thomas in Richard Wright's 1940 novel *Native Son* (from which Fanon learned about race relations in the USA), but his emphasis on personal and collective transformation expresses the same kind of spiritual striving described by the African-American writer June Jordan in the late 1960s: 'at this date when humankind enjoys wild facility to annihilate, no human study can sanely ignore the emergency requirements for efficient, yes, competent affirmation of the values of life, and that most precious burden of identity that depends, beggarly, on love.'[95] On this level, while Fanon's attention is often directed toward particular causes, he is always aware of the need to bridge local and international issues through fellow feeling. Similarly, although the case studies in *Black Skin, White Masks* reveal neuroses peculiar to the patients that Fanon treated as practising psychiatrist, they also expose universal fears about persecution and inferiority as debilitating conditions that can only be overcome by regaining self-respect and with the recognition and genuine support of others.

Primary Texts

Jean-Paul Sartre

Nausea [1938], trans. Lloyd Alexander (New York: New Directions, 1964).
Being and Nothingness [1943], trans. Hazel Barnes, 7th edn (New York: Citadel Press, 1971).
Existentialism and Humanism [1946], trans. Philip Mairet (London: Methuen, 1973).
Notebooks for an Ethic [1947], trans. David Pelhauer (Chicago: University of Chicago Press, 1992).
The Communists and Peace [1952], trans. Martha H. Fletcher (New York: G. Braziller, 1968).

Hannah Arendt

The Origins of Totalitarianism [1951] (San Diego, CA: Harcourt Brace, 1966).
The Human Condition [1958], 2nd edn (Chicago: University of Chicago Press, 1998).
Between Past and Future: Eight Exercises in Political Thought [1961] (New York: Penguin, 1993).
Eichmann in Jerusalem: A Report on the Banality of Evil [1963] (New York: Penguin, 1977).
On Violence [1969] (New York: Harcourt Brace, 1972).

Frantz Fanon

Black Skin, White Masks [1952], trans. Charles Lam Markmann (London: Pluto Press, 1986).
The Wretched of the Earth [1961], trans. Constance Farrington (Harmondsworth: Penguin, 1974).
Toward the African Revolution: Political Essays [1963], trans. Haakon Chevalier (Harmondsworth: Penguin, 1967).

CHAPTER 3

Dialogic Humanism
(Freud – Irigaray – Levinas)

The cultural form of the dialogue as a conversation between two people goes back as least as far as Plato's philosophical exchanges between Socrates and the young men he hopes to instruct into reasoned logic. For Plato, the participants in philosophical dialogues are always unevenly matched: Socrates is a figure of wisdom, experience and cerebral agility, whereas his companion often finds it difficult to apply a particular train of thought to tangential or apparently unrelated issues. The notion of the conversation suggests both an engagement with a subject of discussion (love in *The Symposium*, the ideal city in *The Republic*) and an intellectual 'turn' (*conversare*) in which a line of inquiry brings about a new idea or sparks off associations in a different area. Plato's writings suggest that, even though Socrates retains his wisdom in solitude, he needs another participant to work on and against in order to pursue his thoughts and perform his civic duty. Whereas Socratic dialogues are external, the internal dialogue (or *psychomachia*) recurs in Western culture, from medieval morality plays, through the various versions of the Faust legend, to modernist writing of psychic fragmentation. Although the internal dialogue may be more complex and the knowledge differential between opposing elements is rarely as stable as in the Socratic dialogue, the theory of a dramatic exchange between two participants has remained largely the same. The danger is that, in literary and theoretical discourse, the internal dialogue (whether projected, imagined or personified) will not result in a 'true' conversation between two people, but confirm a single perspective (or *doxa*) by subordinating the second voice to the authority of the first. However, while conversations often involve more than two people, in a pure philosophical form (as in the Hegelian dialectic) the interplay between two forces usually creates the condition for a third element to emerge. Although historically it has taken on different inflections, the theory that only through such exchange can humans affirm their identity (as individual beings and conversing subjects) is central to the strains of dialogic humanism discussed in this chapter and develops our discussion of dialogue in the Introduction.

There are three broad twentieth-century traditions that privilege the dialogue as central to understanding the dynamic relation between individuals:

psychoanalysis, phenomenology and a particular form of civic thought. While the next chapter considers civic humanism and Chapter 6 discusses Mikhail Bakhtin's theory of dialogism, this chapter features three prominent intellectuals – the Austrian psychoanalyst Sigmund Freud (1856–1939), the French feminist Luce Irigaray (1932–) and the Jewish philosopher Emmanuel Levinas (1905–95) – as representatives of psychoanalytic, ethical and phenomenological thought. Although these thinkers are all European, the transatlantic movement of psychoanalysis to America in the 1930s (through *émigrés* such as Erik Erikson and Herbert Marcuse), together with the interest in phenomenology among American-based academics like Paul de Man and the dissemination of European ideas in American universities over the last fifty years, makes the following discussion pertinent for thinking through forms of American cultural conflict which hinder dialogic exchange, such as the urban melting pot and institutional racism.

All three thinkers situate the dialogue at the heart of their theory of human exchange. In Freudian psychoanalysis the dialogue occurs between the analyst, who must remain detached and impartial, but also engaged and alert, and the patient (or analysand), who in the course of therapy switches between the poles of subordination and empowerment until a healthy middle ground is established. Freud began writing in the 1890s with the aim to formulate psychoanalysis as a purely natural science, but his meta-psychological writings from the 1910s display his growing belief that a more dynamic and non-specific model would be needed on which to base his theories. The notion that successful analysis will enable the individual to reestablish his or her sovereignty (and independence from debilitating forces) lies at the heart of psychoanalysis understood as a humanist practice, but this theory is complicated in Freud's consideration of the individual's inability to 'see' his or her unconscious and dependence on others. In contrast, although she was trained as an analyst, Irigaray's dislike of the rigidity of Freudian analytic exchange and her sceptical attitude towards the goals of therapy led her to develop a form of poetic philosophy in which she considers the interchange between individuals not held in an institutional bond. For Irigaray, humanist dialogue (once it has been stripped of the imperial pretensions to convert or dominate the Other) should not just be intellectual, but physical, emotional and spiritual as well. Her reconception of the human subject as an 'identity envelope' suggests a more fluid sense of intimate interchange than the rational model that Freud sought. Lastly, Levinas' emphasis on dialogue represents a refinement of the phenomenology of the German philosopher Edmund Husserl, as he tried to extract the irreducible essences of human thought from the phenomena of everyday life. Levinas considers the possibility that these essences do not exist in a pure form but are always mediated through language and culture. Moreover, he argues that phenomenological inquiry should not be solitary and introspective, but always practised in relation to another being in an act of beholding, with the participants recognising their differences and together working through issues of Otherness.

The theory of Otherness connects all three thinkers into a distinctly twentieth-century tradition that, since the 1970s, has inflected poststructuralist, feminist and postcolonialist thought. One of the problems we have already encountered with theoretical discourse is that it tends towards abstraction, with the danger that the human subject under inquiry is ungrounded and the inquirer becomes more of an observer than a participant in a humanist enterprise. To counter this tendency, recent Other-related discourses attempt to position the inquiring self in relation to the topic of inquiry by including both figures in the theoretical frame in order to highlight gender, racial or cultural difference. Not only does this methodology help to expose power differentials that always exist between individuals, but it positions the exchange in terms of the institutional, historical and ideological forces that bear upon human relationships. While the humanist ideal may be to reach a point where the open exchange of ideas between individuals radiates out into the wider social and political spheres (following the Romantic idea that reform of the self is the only way to facilitate lasting social change), Freud, Irigaray and Levinas all indicate the barriers that prevent that ideal being attained. Interestingly, each thinker privileges a particular mode of dialogic exchange: Freud emphasises mind-to-mind interaction; Irigaray focuses on body-to-body relationships; while Levinas concentrates on the face-to-face encounter. These emphases characterise Freud as a cool scientific figure whose conversation with his patients is distanced and professional, while Irigaray is a passionate and affective thinker who stresses the corporeal and libidinal bond of sexual relationships, and Levinas is an earnest theorist whose encounter with another individual concentrates on the face as the defining, but most vulnerable, aspect of human identity.

Despite these basic differences, whether they are focusing on the mind, body or face, all three are not just interested in how the Other speaks or thinks, but also in the physical and physiological apparatus of communication (vocal tone, touch, gesture or smile), suggesting that it is impossible to behold the Other without attending to the context in which the dialogue takes place. They would also all concur on different levels with Paul Ricoeur's claim (discussed in the Introduction) that human identity is never transparent, but possesses 'an opaque subjectivity'. Ricoeur argues that a philosophical and cultural 'detour' is inevitable when approaching the question of 'the human' because there is no easy way to determine identity or any simple model for interpersonal communication. As such, the Other will always demand close attention, but the danger is that he or she will become diminished or even violated in the process of interpretation. This hermeneutics of Otherness is a strong connecting theme throughout their work. But, although Freud, Irigaray and Levinas all detect a textual quality to subjectivity that both demands and frustrates interpretation, none of them would claim the Other is completely unknowable, even in situations when one is faced with what Levinas calls 'the radical Other'.

As with the other triads in this book, a comparative study of the three thinkers raises problems in their methodologies that do not so much disable the humanist aspects of their thought, but help to define dialogic humanism as a trend that emerges only through exchange between different and sometimes competing discourses. Particularly in relation to Freudian psychoanalysis, a number of critics (including Irigaray) have challenged what they perceive to be the constraining exchanges at the heart of analysis. However, even though Freud has his detractors, in most instances his methodological concepts are reworked rather than jettisoned for being intellectually defunct. Instead of reifying Freudian concepts, these ideas are freely mobilised by Irigaray and Levinas to enhance debates about intimacy and cultural exchange that take them far beyond their original usage. However, Irigaray and Levinas do not solve these problems and one might argue that Freudian science is actually more grounded than the, at times, free-floating imaginative and ethical discourses of these two. As such, this chapter will play the thinkers off each other, instead of constructing a simple progression of Other-oriented thought. A detailed study of three thinkers (rather than a single pairing) suggests a more fluid model of exchange than the rigid philosophical definition of a conversation between two thinkers, suggesting that dialogic humanism should be prepared to respond equally to polyphony, critique and dissent.

Sigmund Freud

Throughout his work between the early 1890s and the late 1930s the Austrian psychoanalyst Sigmund Freud rarely wrote explicitly in terms of 'the human', preferring 'patient', 'neurotic', or a medical name to designate the subject of his study. This tendency can be explained partly by the detached scientific approach Freud tried to refine and partly through the desire early in his career to describe the workings of the human mind using the language of natural science. In his 'Project for a Scientific Psychology', written in a few weeks in 1895, abandoned and unpublished until 1950, he outlined his model of mind 'in terms of increase, diminution, displacement and discharge of energy ... conceived as flowing through and accumulating within a differentiated network of neurones'.[1] On this model mental life derives from 'specifiable material particles' and behaviour can be explained in terms of the 'flight from pain' and avoiding 'unpleasure', while consciousness seems to be a 'bolted on' aspect of humans defined fundamentally as biological and neurological creatures.[2] Even in his later writing when he diluted his scientific language and developed a more flexible psychoanalytic vocabulary, he often wrote in terms of 'human material' (for example, in *Introductory Lectures on Psychoanalysis*, 1916), suggesting that psychoanalysis can excavate biological and psychic 'riddles in the life of human communities' for which 'exact science' fails to account.[3] His sparing use of the word 'human' is understandable in its lack of specificity to an object of study and because the German *menschlich* or *Menschen* can refer variously to a human being, a man, a person, or the general state of humanity. However, despite his reluctance to write in humanist terms, Freud's search for a hybrid language of psychoanalysis, somewhere between natural science, social science and the arts, can be interpreted as an expression of his vocation to understand the 'riddle' of the human.

One problem with his early scientific work is that it seeks to explain the workings of neurological mechanisms in the abstract, with little attention to the external stimuli that create a particular reaction in individuals. The interpretative dimension of psychoanalysis which grew in importance in his work, from Freud and Josef Breuer's *Studies in Hysteria* (1890) and Freud's *The Interpretation of Dreams* (1900) through to his important *Papers on Metapsychology* (1915), suggests that he was increasingly interested in the interchange between the inquirer and the subject of inquiry. Freud often adopted the role of the impartial scientist standing above his field of analysis with the belief that progress can be made with his patients and, as Adam Phillips argues, he assumed that his patients were scientifically minded as regards the acquisition of knowledge.[4] However, Freud acknowledged that there is always something baffling about the unconscious and realised that patients will inevitably transfer their anxieties onto the analyst in the course of therapy (and so need to work through psychic transference in which the analyst becomes a surrogate parent figure). For these reasons, he developed a more inclusive and interactive psychoanalytic model that gradually replaced the static conception of his early work. Ricoeur and Phillips argue that there are two sides to Freud – the scientist and the interpreter – which are always in tension, implying that not only is there an external dialogue between analyst and patient, but an internal dialogue between the different discourses Freud adopted to describe psychic phenomena, in his efforts to extend the scope of nineteenth-century medical psychiatry.

Tony Davies describes Freud as an '*Aufklärung*, a humanistic rationalist of the old school, dispelling error and superstition and throwing the murkiest corners of the psyche open to the sunlight of scientific reason'.[5] Davies goes on to argue that this search for certainty is undermined by Freud's theory that the individual is enslaved to irrational forces that cannot be controlled, while Kate

Soper discusses this tension in terms of anti-humanist forces that 'besiege' the agency of the human subject.[6] Both humanist and anti-humanist elements are certainly present in Freud's work, but these elements do not necessarily undermine each other considering the complex field of data he wished to analyse. As Judith Ryan suggests in *The Vanishing Subject* (1991), Freud 'was able to allow for a divided self while at the same time showing the way for its reintegration', while his 'reorganization of the self' in analysis 'was in no sense a return to more commonplace or more robust conceptions of selfhood'.[7] It is perfectly reasonable to argue (as the younger analysts Otto Rank and Ludwig Binswanger claimed) that Freud undervalued the interpretative implications of psychoanalysis and subordinated the 'willingness to listen with openness' to the scientific desire to 'expose and abolish idols which are merely the projections of the human will'.[8] But it is perhaps fairer to see the two tendencies constantly jostling for dominance in his writings. Freud describes his project as an attempt to 'understand something of the riddles of the world'; but, with the realisation that the world and self are intertwined, in his mature work he outlines a modern humanism (without writing explicitly in humanist terms) that acknowledges and explores the fissures in human identity.[9]

Freud's essay *The Question of Lay Analysis* (1926) proves useful for summarising these mature ideas and for distancing his theory of psychic life, first, from the Enlightenment humanist conception of the rational individual as a unified and self-defining entity and, second, from the understanding that psychoanalysis should be seen as the handmaiden of medicine. On the scientific level he remained convinced that 'strong and persistent' feelings must 'be based on something real, which it may perhaps be possible to discover' while, on the interpretative (or hermeneutic) level, he focused attention on the 'powerful instrument' of language that patients use to describe their own experiences.[10] The form of *The Question of Lay Analysis* is interesting in itself for propelling Freud's ideas towards a dialogic model of interaction. He invents an imaginary figure, 'the Impartial Person', who asks a series of commonsense questions based on the observation of analysis: an outsider-figure who, Freud is quick to point out, would be an undesirable presence during analysis if it is to be truly therapeutic. The Impartial Person questions the differences between medicine, psychiatry and psychoanalysis, wonders how far the patient is ignorant of the reality of his or her condition, and queries the relationship between religious confession and analysis. Freud does not just invent the Impartial Person as a straw target, but as a figure who is interested in, but perplexed by, the goals of psychoanalysis. He responds to the 'impartial' questions with patience and humility, rather than the certainty of a scientist seeking objective accounts of human behaviour. Indeed, Freud claimed that his science 'is not a revelation' because it 'still lacks the attributes of definiteness, immutability and infallibility' that characterised the aims of nineteenth-century scientific research; he developed a theory based on a series of metaphors, because no single analogy could do justice to the complexity of human psychology.[11]

The primary intention of *The Question of Lay Analysis* was to make analysis understandable to a general audience and to refute the charges of 'quackery' levelled at Freud.[12] His awareness of the interchange between individuals is demonstrated both in terms of the content and dialogic form of his essay and is central to his aim to interpret mental life. Even though his work is haunted by a search for a 'deep' truth that goes beyond factual evidence and lies beneath the veneer of reality, his understanding that this search is always under way also marks his writings with a sensitivity to the multiple layers of interpretation in which the analyst must engage. Freud's notion of a dynamic psychology should be understood both in terms of the careful interpretation of the conflicting data gleaned from the patient in analysis and in terms of the interplay between the forces (some psychic, some biological, some social) that contribute to the complexity of mental life. He challenges the criticism that interpretation is little more than analytic guesswork, by stressing the rigorous analysis (and self-analysis) the trainee must undergo before he or she can gain an 'unprejudiced reception of the analytic material'.[13] Freud is quick to refute the charge that psychoanalysis does not have a stable methodology, but he fails to substantiate how interpretative agreement can be reached given the 'private' dialogue of analysis. Ricoeur argues that Freud actually underplays the personal factor of analysis and his ideas rest too heavily on finding the 'right interpretation' or psychoanalytic truth that would explain an individual's mental life.[14] Nevertheless, Freud's emphasis on the analyst's 'sharpness of hearing' (acquired through natural ability and training) positions him closer to the literary critic or the musicologist who can interpret complex symbols or sounds, than it does to the empirical scientist. Moreover, the moral dimension of psychoanalysis means the analyst has responsibility for the patient's welfare by choosing the right moments to intervene, particularly on the topic of sexuality which he insists should be treated with tact and care.

One of the major charges from anti-humanist quarters in the 1970s was that the humanist understanding of rational behaviour as meaningful activity is both uncritical and shortsighted. From a structuralist viewpoint, the forces of class, ideology, history, language and biology combine to overwhelm the self-determinism of the individual, who is forced to respond passively to this combination of pressures. On one level, Freud's psychoanalytic theories concur with this challenge to humanist thought. By positioning the conscious subject in passive relationship to unconscious desires and psychic urges, Freud counters the commonsense belief that humans can and do act rationally.

However, on another level, Freud demonstrates the way in which individuals develop agency in their coming-to-terms with, and even mastery over, potentially painful or debilitating experiences. John Carroll comments on Freud's humanist, and to his mind, 'naive' optimism, as he carries forward the Enlightenment torch in foreseeing a future for the individual 'in which reason had reshaped the instincts'.[15] But Freud's thought is not just concerned with the individual's quest for rational knowledge, nor is he wildly optimistic as he believes there are always impediments to self-knowledge. Indeed, he argued that human agency does not derive from an over-reliance on reason, but the existence of 'a strong tendency towards the pleasure principle' that opposes other 'forces or circumstances' and seeks to direct activity towards a 'yield of pleasure'.[16]

One example of this theory is in *Beyond the Pleasure Principle* (1920) in which Freud describes the *fort-da* game that a young boy plays on his own; he throws away a wooden reel and other objects 'so that hunting for his toys and picking them up was often quite a business'.[17] Freud observed that this game of 'disappearance and return' was accompanied by expressions of 'interest and satisfaction' in the boy when the object is retrieved, and he interprets the simple game as the child acting out a family drama in which the mother disappears temporarily to leave the child alone. The child compensates for this pain by 'staging the disappearance and return of the objects within his reach', compensating for the pain of loss with the pleasure of relocation.[18] This 'instinct for mastery' turns the child from a passive subject, helpless in the face of parental behaviour, into an active agent who expands his repertoire of control over this instinctual loss by turning it into an experience of pleasure. Rather than retreating into a lonely and isolated world, the child's relationship with the 'lost' object represents a displaced dialogic relationship with, in this case, the mother. On Freud's view, a healthy relationship between child and object prepares him or her for meaningful and mature relationships with others. As the American thinker Walter Lippmann argued in his *A Preface to Morals* (1929), this theory incorporates the humanist belief that maturity consists of understanding that 'the universe is not composed' of the child's wishes, of realising 'how much is beyond' the child's immediate gratification, and of appreciating that others 'have their preferences and their wishes' which are often different to the child's own.[19] It also links up to Martha Nussbaum's claim (discussed in Chapter 1) that primary feelings are related to an individual's need for things outside the self that cannot be controlled.

This overcoming of anxiety and the creation of a 'new environment' (as Lippmann calls it) through game-playing suggests that for Freud agency is possible, but it does not ward against the game becoming compulsive or neurotic in its repetition (with the object becoming an end in itself), or preventing narcissism and megalomania from developing in which the manageable play-world impedes the formation of real relationships.[20] What the example does suggest is that even in a realm of 'things', the instinctual impulse is to develop psychic attachments; not to renunciate the reality principle but to override it with a gain of pleasure. One obvious complication with this model for older children and adults is that in a social world of individuals striving for personal pleasure over collective enjoyment, self-interest is likely to neutralise the possibility of generosity or establishing a sharing environment. Alternatively, those relationships that are formed can be explained purely in terms of the 'need' to form psychic attachments within a small family unit. As the following section on Irigaray discusses, another problem with this kind of example (also evident in Levinas' description of the ethical encounter, as discussed below) is that it is an existential abstraction: it describes the child, the mother and the analyst, without reference to siblings or a wider communal network which may complicate, or even reinforce, Freud's interpretation. His tendency to write in universalist terms is a facet of his desire to arrive at a general theory of psychic life, but reveals weaknesses when he deals with individual cases (as feminist criticisms of his published case studies show). Nevertheless, his discussion of the *fort-da* game illuminates the humanist scope of Freud's project to analyse personal relationships by focusing on the interchange between unconscious forces and the individual's conscious (if not entirely self-aware) coming-to-terms with situations.

Luce Irigaray

Luce Irigaray's early work from the 1970s (and for which she is best known) reassesses Freud's psychoanalytic insights from the perspective of psycho-linguistics, particularly the manner in which individuals represent themselves and how identities are constituted through language. These ideas emerge from Jacques Lacan's linguistic reworking of Freud's natural-scientific perspective, in which Lacan indicates that psychological symptoms and the markers of individuality ('I', 'me', 'you', 'us') are embedded firmly in language. When we use the word 'I' to designate what is 'mine', we are not only using a linguistic phrase (the indexical marker 'I'), but suggesting a relation between what is mine (or attributes 'I' associate with 'myself') and what is 'not-mine' (what is 'yours' or what is related to the external world). Each of these linguistic signs designates a relationship even if they are not fully articulated. While, as this section discusses, there are strong humanist elements to Irigaray's thought, she dispels what poststructuralists see as the illusion that the self is an autonomous agent by focusing on those moments when sexual desire manifests itself in daily life, suggesting an excessive dynamic flow between elements that cannot be contained by the boundaries of the self. As such, Irigaray challenges the classical humanist view of the self conceived as an individual unit (which survives to some extent in Freud's thought) with a theory of plural selves that are always implicated by, and entangled with, one another. This idea is crucial for understanding her emphasis on dialogic exchange and her continued engagement with psychoanalysis; as Margaret Whitford has argued, although Irigaray has turned her attention from Freud in her later work, 'the psycho-analytic model of dialogue – a *here* and *now* in which two interlocuters meet, and in which the question of desire or transference is central – continues to reverberate throughout her entire oeuvre'.[21]

Irigaray's work in the 1970s dealt centrally with psychoanalysis, but from an early stage she distanced herself from Freud's and Lacan's preoccupation with the ego and the phallus by emphasising the complexities of gender identity and the ways in which dynamic relationships form between indivi-duals. She is often associated with Kristeva and Cixous as feminist thinkers interested in exploring the possibility of *écriture féminine* as a mode of expression distinct from the power ideologies of patriarchal discourse (see Chapters 1 and 5). In *This Sex Which is Not One* (1977), Irigaray is eager to expose what she describes as 'the sexual indifference that underlies the truth of any science', which she sees to be as true of Freudian psychoanalysis as of other discourses that make knowledge claims.[22] Her earlier book *Speculum of the Other Woman* (1974) had created a rift between Irigaray and the psycho-analytic establishment, particularly the way she used psychoanalytic ideas to destabilise Freud's meta-psychological principles, to expose how little he attended to the identity of girls (for example, in the *fort-da* game), and to attack the bias in Lacan's thought for conceiving of female identity as a 'lack'.[23] In her passionate assault on the masculine emphasis of Freudian and Lacanian theory, 'The Poverty of Psychoanalysis' (1985), Irigaray focuses on the effects that psychoanalytic discourse has on women and other epistemologies that ignore sexual difference: 'Do women remain divided and assigned to their lot so that men can remain one?'[24] She is particularly concerned by the way this phallic bias disguises itself in the name of neutral or universal theory and her feminist dialogue with psychoanalysis is an attempt to check this impulse. However, although many aspects of Irigaray's work have feminist aims, in terms of her exploration of the relations between individuals it is also possible to consider her as a humanist thinker for whom the concept of dialogic exchange is theoreti-cally prior to her feminist concern to demarcate distinct sexual characteristics.

One of the major reasons that Irigaray took issue with psychoanalysis in the 1970s is that her perspective on selfhood is more inclusive than Freud's scientific viewpoint. Indeed, Freud was resistant to approaching psycho-analysis as a *Weltanschauung* (a worldview or 'philosophy of life'), which he believed would artificially provide a 'unified solution of all the problems of existence'.[25] While his concern was that such a totalising philosophy would undermine the scientific basis of his ideas, he often failed to examine the theoretical implications of his work or to consider what Irigaray calls 'the development of consciousness and History' as they impact on personal identity.[26] The fusion of psychoanalytic and Marxist ideas in the mid-twentieth century in the work of transatlantic intellectuals, such as Herbert Marcuse, countered Freud's narrow view of the self and set the groundwork for Irigaray's radical theory of sexual difference. Marcuse's *Eros and Civilization* (1956) questions the inevitability of Freud's conception of social order as a structure that repudiates desire and encourages conformity, suggesting it is only 'a specific historical organization of human existence' that may change (or be changed) in the future towards 'a non-repressive civilization based on a fundamentally different experience of being … and fundamentally different existential relations'.[27] Irigaray's theoretical interrogation of Freud follows similar lines to Marcuse in terms of a critical assessment of the social implications of psychoanalysis. But, whereas Marcuse places emphasis on alienated labour, Irigaray considers the ways in which gender differences have become rigidified in the 'masculine' economy that underpins the current social order (what Lacan called 'the Law of the Father'). Marcuse and Irigaray both offer radical critiques of Freudian thought by sketching different modes of human relations to those based on normative and (to their mind) repressive sexuality, but neither are as pessimistic as the Austrian analyst on the issue of overcoming psychic problems. While, for the most part, Freud assesses the state of the individual in the present by looking backwards to the root cause of neurosis in early childhood, Marcuse and Irigaray look to the future for overcoming social injustice through the transforming power of love.

For Irigaray, the relationship between analyst and analysand is never as stable as Freud outlines, mainly because she believes the demarcation of differences between self and world and between individuals is never clear cut. However, while Irigaray discusses 'desire' as the dynamic force that propels the self between experiences as a way of countering Freud's scientific perspective on mental life, her theory of gender identity is not that simple. For example, in her reading of the *fort-da* game she criticises Freud's oversight concerning the different ways boys and girls enter into language and become socialised; in *Sexes and Genealogies* (1987) she argues that rather than attempting to master their environment by controlling objects, girls try 'to give birth to themselves. They only stoop to mastering the other … when they are unable to engender their own axis.'[28] She proposes that women feel 'with' themselves and others rather than acting 'on' their environment as a substitute for intimacy; in the case of the *fort-da* game, 'woman always speaks *with* the mother, man speaks in her absence ... This *with* has to try to become a *with self*.'[29] On this view, it may seem that the biology of the sexes determines the 'penile thrust or its manual equivalent' in boys, whereas girls 'enter into language without taking anything inside themselves'.

While Irigaray emphasises the relation between self, body and language much more carefully than Freud, it raises the essentialist question about how far gender characteristics are determined by biological differences. Some critics see Irigaray as promoting an undeconstructed idea of 'Woman', but Margaret Whitford and Naomi Schor have argued that she deploys a 'strategic essentialism' (rather than an 'essential essentialism') for discussing an alternative experiential realm that evades the controlling phallocentric and logocentric discourses which she detects in Freud and Lacan. As Schor argues, Irigaray's emphasis on 'a sexually marked language, a *parler-femme*' is merely part of her project to debunk 'the universal subject' and to problematise the view that the self can be adequately expressed in language.[30] Although the self is always positioned in language, the 'I' or the 'you' that designates the self is an inadequate marker that cannot wholly express identity. In fact, following Lacan's theory of the mirror stage, Irigaray sees that these markers only create the illusion of a unitary self (imaged in the mirror) that is, in fact, fragmentary. On this view, in the *fort-da* game the child actually throws a fragment of himself or herself away, suggesting that the self is always incomplete without the missing Other. For Irigaray, only in the dialogic relation between terms (both within the self and between selves) can a more fluid notion of identity emerge which dispels the illusion of unitary essence and evades the strict demarcation of gender differences.

In her collection *An Ethics of Sexual Difference* (1984), Irigaray develops this 'in-between' position for considering the relationship between binary oppositions. For example, desire and morality are often positioned as polar opposites in terms of the individual's relationship to others, with the former being associated with indulgence, selfishness and sin (Freud's pleasure principle), and the latter with restraint, control and moderation (the reality principle). Irigaray argues that these groupings often serve to gender moral theory, public affairs and philosophy as male pursuits, while 'women are left the so-called minor arts: cooking, knitting, embroidery, and sewing; and, in exceptional cases, poetry, painting, and music'.[31] Not only does Irigaray attack this historical sanctioning of gender roles and the 'artificial scission' between private and public life as either desirable or necessary,[32] but she also rejects the idea of sexual specificity by suggesting that gender binaries and the 'space-time' of the 'living subject' should both be reconceived in terms of 'containers, or envelopes of identity' rather than fixed entities.[33] She believes that such a reconception will transform the way in which individuals and social units relate and so create a new kind of humanism; as she says, 'this change in perspective is, precisely, a matter of ethics'.[34] In later work like *Je, Tu, Nous* (1990) and *Democracy Begins Between Two* (1994) Irigaray has concentrated on social relationships, public identities and issues of citizenship, but she often returns to consider the desire for, and sexual attraction between, intimate partners that 'makes possible speech, promises, alliances': a 'half-open' existence that develops the conception of the self as both receptive to, and coextensive with, its environment.[35]

Irigaray argues that ethics can emerge from rethinking sexual difference as mutually complementary (rather than combative) and by questioning 'masculine' and 'feminine' as essentialising terms. The either-or logic that places divisions and limits on concepts and social spaces alike, suggests an atomised world of distance and opposition in which dialogues are problematic, rather than establishing an environment that nurtures reciprocity. Irigaray suggests that 'the maternal–feminine' can intervene in a traditionally male world of 'right' behaviour (in which impulse is resisted in favour of good sense), to reveal a realm of libidinal intimacy that belongs neither to male nor female, but exists in the plenum of overlapping identity-envelopes. Such a realm has its obvious dangers when one individual subjects another to his or her power, with 'the one who offers or allows desire' usually 'engulfing the other'. But, Irigaray implies, rather than accepting a binary model of empowerment and submission, the existence of a third term in 'relation to the divine, to death, to the social, [or] to the cosmic' can limit narcissism and self-aggrandisement at the expense of the Other and open a space for mutual interaction: the 'rubbings between two infinitely near neighbors that creates a dynamics'.[36] She hopes to replace the dialectic model of master–slave with a model based on what she calls the 'first passion': a sense of wonder or joy in the face of the Other, beholding 'what it sees always as if for the first time, never taking hold of the other as its object. It does not try to seize, possess, or reduce this object, but leaves it subjective, still free.'[37] Rather than founding her humanism on the repudiation of desire, this theory (influenced by the Romantic belief that moral reform must stem from within) implies that morality emerges from the dialogic space between individuals, with the intertwining of selves becoming excessive: 'an alchemical site' that cannot be contained.[38]

On Irigaray's model, morality is coextensive with the discovery of the self in the Other as an angelic 'messenger of ethics', revealing a primitive human desire to reach out to others. This sensibility is better associated with the primal sense of touch as a coming and going between selves, than with the higher sense of sight that divides the visual field into subject and object.[39] In her essay 'An Ethics of Sexual Difference', she contrasts these angelic ethics of intimacy with the neutral ethics of classical philosophy and the nineteenth-century natural sciences, in which the human subject is understood to be universal and ungendered. While Irigaray illustrates her ideas with distinctly feminised images – the meeting of vaginal lips and the touch of the placental membrane – she admits that the only way such an ethics could be mobilised is through interaction and giving over the self to the Other: 'it can be accomplished only through the combined efforts of the two halves of the world: the masculine and feminine'.[40] Her theory raises moral questions about monogamy and fidelity, but she is less concerned with normative ethics, than in reconceiving a meta-ethical sphere based on sexual difference that influences moral behaviour. Throughout her work, Irigaray displays this humanist desire to establish an ethics of difference through union (rather than the erasure of difference in unity): 'a "we are" or "we become", "we live here" together'.[41] It is this humanist 'philosophy of life', to recall Freud's phrase, that stimulates Irigaray's vision of a 'future civilisation' facilitated by the 'transformation of relations between the two genders'.[42] While this future is dialogic at root (she insists that the revolution will occur 'first and foremost in the couple'), she stresses its unpredictability and defends herself against the charges that this is a utopian vision: 'I am … a political militant for the impossible, which is not to say a utopian. Rather, I want what is yet to be as the only possibility of a future.'[43]

Emmanuel Levinas

As a thinker whose work spans the whole of the twentieth century, Emmanuel Levinas was influential among French intellectual circles in the 1940s, but did not rise to prominence in the English-speaking world until late in his career, aided by the translation of Jacques Derrida's influential essay 'Violence and Metaphysics' (published 1964; translated 1978) which positioned Levinas as one of the most distinctive of major modern theorists. A Jewish thinker from Lithuania, educated in Strasbourg, spending much of World War II in a prisoner of war camp as a French soldier, and later working as a scholar in Israel and France, Levinas epitomised the versatile intellectual, his work creating dialogues between different linguistic and cultural traditions (Jewish, Russian, German and French) and between theological, philosophical and social discourses. He did, in fact, contribute to the two most influential philosophical trends of the first half of the century – phenomenology and existentialism – but is now best known for his work on the ethics of Otherness. Levinas links his personal experience of captivity to the much broader unease with humanist ideals after the Holocaust in his critique of classical humanism. However, rather than falling in line with the anti-humanist cries of French intellectuals in the 1960s and abandoning humanism as a metaphysical hangover of the Enlightenment project (cries which Levinas dismisses as the accumulation of 'apocalyptic ideas and slogans of intellectual high society ... imposed with the tyranny of the latest fashion'), he tried to preserve what he calls the 'humanism of the other man' as a defining factor of his philosophy.[44] As this section will make clear, while it is easier to position Levinas' ideas concerning Otherness within a conventional philosophical framework than in relation to psychoanalysis or feminism, it is interesting to consider his contribution to the development of a dialogic humanism, both on his own terms as an ethical philosopher and in relation to Freud and Irigaray.

Levinas' humanism derives directly from the priority of ethics in his work, while his place as one of the most influential of late-twentieth-century theorists stems from his books *Humanisme de l'autre homme* (1972) and *Otherwise than Being, or, Beyond Essence* (1974), in which he moved beyond the traditional humanist/anti-humanist debate over essentialist categories. Here, Levinas responded to Heidegger's 'Letter on Humanism' and the anti-humanist critique of the classically conceived human subject (see the previous chapter for discussion). Levinas believed that the anti-humanist attack on metaphysics not only challenges the pretensions of theorists seeking absolute grounds for defining 'the human', but also jettisons 'the idea of person, goal and origin of itself, in which the ego is still a thing because it is still a being'.[45] Rather than adopting the poststructuralist dismantling of the human, Levinas based his humanism on the theory that the self is 'hostage' to and has 'a responsibility' for the Other. He argues that we cannot decline this double challenge if we are to become 'ourselves' in the fullest sense of the word by overcoming psychic rifts in the self and cultural, ideological and political schisms in the world. Although Levinas was not a theologian, throughout his work he discussed this kind of human relatedness as if it were a religion (what Derrida calls 'the religiosity of the religious'[46]) in an attempt to identify the holiness of being. His finely nuanced theory implies that although the individual is a passive 'hostage' to the Other, one also has an active 'responsibility' to give oneself over to the Other to increase the possibility of overcoming alienation and persecution on personal and social levels. As Levinas says in *Otherwise than Being*: 'the influences, complexes and dissimulations that cover over the human do not alter this holiness, but sanction the struggle for exploited man.'[47] While need, perversity, caprice or even misplaced pathos may undermine the best efforts of individuals to meet the Other half-way, this attempt to rescue the holiness of the human from selfishness and complacency is central to understanding Levinas' work as a prime example of dialogic humanism.

All of Levinas' writings are inflected by this primary responsibility to others, indicating that relationships between individuals and cultures holding different values lie at the heart of his dialogic humanism. This theory of the ethical dialogue based on the encounter of the self with the Other derives from Levinas' development of the theological work of the religious existentialist Martin Buber. As Jewish thinkers, Levinas and Buber share the optimistic view that although interpersonal intimacy is rarely achieved, the possibility of dialogic understanding should be a continual motivation. On this topic, in his most famous book *I and Thou* (1923) Buber foreshadows the work of the French structuralists by claiming that 'primary words are not isolated words, but combined words' (such as 'I–Thou' and 'I–It') which hold the 'I' in relation to another, and by which the signification of 'I' is determined.[48] Levinas concurs with Buber in maintaining that others can be met, but only by elevating the Other to a 'Thou' instead of obliterating the Other through narcissism (an 'I–I' relationship) or by debasing it to an 'It'. Only the 'I–Thou' relation is authentic, for it 'can only be spoken with the whole being', whereas the 'I–It' implies an instrumental relation where the Other becomes an object to be used or appropriated.[49] In his numerous essays on Buber, Levinas concurs with this theory of relational humanism, even agreeing that the true meeting of self and Other can transcend and exalt the banality of daily life. For example, in his 1968 essay 'Martin Buber's Thought and Contemporary Judaism', Levinas writes:

> [T]he contact of the divine with the exalted instants is, for Buber, meeting, dialogue, opening to others but at the same time to self. The instant is not transcended in the impersonal, but in the interpersonal. Persons who speak to one another confirm one another, unique and irreplaceable.[50]

Levinas respects Buber's belief that this special meeting is an awakening of self to Other and cannot be reduced 'to any relation with the *determinable* and the objective' (on this view, even in language Otherness is misrepresented or even violated), but he is critical of the spiritual exclusiveness of Buber's meeting (Levinas prefers the term 'encounter') which seems far removed from the social and cultural spheres.[51] Levinas questions how 'the voice' of God enters into the moment to seal the pact between self and Other and wonders how Buber's 'purely formal meeting' relates to the immanent world of Others if it is conceived as being always outside of time and social relationships.[52] To address these existential ideas it is important to consider another strong current in Levinas' thought – his response to phenomenology – which helps to explain his emphasis on the face-to-face encounter in his later work.

In his early essay 'The Phenomenological Theory of Being' (1930), Levinas develops the phenomenological ideas of Edmund Husserl by suggesting that philosophy cannot be based solely on the empirical knowledge the mind gleans from external phenomena. Levinas' reading of Husserl moves away from epistemology and empiricism to a 'theory of being' which privileges

consciousness and existence over anything we can extract from our environment or we can know about ourselves.[53] Reacting against Husserl's introspective method of inquiry, in which past and future are 'suspended' for a still
moment of clear reflection, Levinas shifts his attention from abstract thought
to the immanent realm of existence. He describes consciousness as the 'absolute
sphere of life' that cannot be surpassed and goes on to divide this 'sphere' into
regions in which the self exists in different forms. Developing these ideas in a
much later essay, 'Ethics as First Philosophy' (1984), Levinas returns to
Husserl by suggesting that all knowledge is predicated on 'man's concrete
existence in the world he inhabits, in which he moves and works and possesses'.[54] Rather than leading a contemplative life in which the self exists in and
for itself, appropriating 'things' to shore up personal boundaries or making a
home out of another's misery, Levinas suggests the face of the Other always
jolts the individual out of a self-affirming existence. He argues that the Other
cannot be known or understood in its entirety, but challenges the personal
boundaries of the self and calls into doubt moral certainties. Not only does the
Other force the self to confront mortality and finitude (the possibility that the
self may not exist or will not exist permanently), but it also impels the
individual to face the Other. Instead of ignoring cultural forms and mediations
(as Husserl and Buber tended to) or allowing differences of nationality, class,
race or gender to discourage the self from responding to particular individuals,
Levinas argues (like Fanon) that the Other forces us, often against reason and
will, to confront these marks of difference.

   In this way, Levinas goes much further than Freud in dealing with the
nuances of personal contact. Rather than the inquiring self (or analyst, for
Freud) trying to understand the Other (the analysand) through impartial
procedures, Levinas' self is destabilised and humbled in the presence of the
Other. Indeed, Levinas believed his work to be free from the language and
pretensions of psychoanalysis, which, as Simon Critchley makes clear, he
viewed as 'simply part and parcel of the anti-humanism of the human sciences'.[55]
Levinas was also sceptical about Freud's theory of the unconscious as a
repository of repressed desires, preferring to understand identity in terms of
subjectivity (the relation between 'me' and 'you') and sensibility (an ethical
feeling of love for the Other). However, although Levinas is generally dis-
missive of Freud, at times there seem to be strong parallels between the two
thinkers, particularly on ideas of trauma, the primal fear of darkness and night
terrors. Critchley even argues that without this conception of a 'traumatized
self' there could be no ethics for Levinas, because fellow feeling and compassion arise when the self confronts its own incapabilities and weaknesses.[56]
Again, the face is important in the encounter with the Other: what is the most
human of all – the face – is also the most inhuman: behind the eyes lurk images

of death and the inexpressible void of Being. This void can be read as a version of the unconscious, but needs to be understood within the context of intimate care and not formulated through scientific procedures. Levinas develops the existentialist idea that social masks often conceal the truth of Being (while stressing relatedness over solitary existence); for him 'the proximity of the other is the face's meaning ... in a way which goes beyond those plastic forms which forever try to cover the face like a mask'.[57] He believes these social masks can never wholly conceal the Other, because 'always the face shows through the forms' and 'calls for me' in a moment of 'extreme exposure, defencelessness, vulnerability'.[58]

Levinas addresses many issues pertinent to Otherness (including violence, mastery, evil, trauma, prayer, justice and shelter), but one aspect of the personal encounter he does not fully address is that of sexual difference, when gender boundaries become part of the fabric of dialogic humanism. The theoretical differences between Irigaray and Levinas are interesting on this topic, particularly as they stress two different forms of relationship: for Irigaray, a bodily encounter in which two beings curl around and even enter into each other and, for Levinas, an intimate, loving, but respectful, face-to-face encounter. Irigaray emphasises the loss of boundaries between individuals as ushering in a physical and moral reliance on another being, whereas Levinas sees the negotiation of those boundaries as a cornerstone of ethical relatedness. Indeed, in her essay 'Questions of Emmanuel Levinas' (1991), Irigaray is critical of Levinas for not attending carefully to the primal sense of touch: as she says, 'to caress, for Levinas, consists, therefore, not in approaching the other in its most vital dimension, the touch, but in the reduction of that vital dimension of the other's body to the elaboration of a future for himself'.[59] She argues that the Levinasian encounter is not risky enough: if differences prove insurmountable then the individual will try to secure a future for him or herself by retreating from the Other. In short, whereas Irigaray's humanism is full of primal energy – 'a fluid universe where the perception of being two persons ... becomes indistinct, and above all, acceding to ... an energy produced together' – where relationships are risky and liable to go awry, Levinas' 'open' encounter occurs on an elevated plane, level with 'the height of the face' and corresponding to what Derrida calls an 'expression most-high'.[60]

It is unfortunate that Levinas had not the opportunity to respond to Irigaray's critique of his work (he died in 1995). However, although there are marked differences in their visions of dialogic humanism, both thinkers are optimistic that relatedness can occur, both privilege the transcendence of everyday life, and both focus on events which occur between individuals: Irigaray writes of the caress as 'an awakening to intersubjectivity, to a touching between us which is neither passive nor active' and Levinas stresses that I am

actively responsible for, but also a passive hostage to, the Other.[61] The
conversation for both thinkers is sometimes in the form of words (as it was
largely for Freud), but also in terms of gesture, touch and spiritual communion: what Irigaray calls an 'in-stasy in us and between us, and not an ecstasy
outside us'.[62] However, although Irigaray and Levinas overcome some of the
dialogic problems in Freud's scientific approach and indicate how Levinas'
'humanism of the other man' (and woman, for Irigaray) still has currency in
contemporary thought, because dialogues always occur in a cultural context, it
is important to consider the space (as well as the substance) of dialogue. All
three thinkers struggle in rooting their dialogic humanism in the material
world: the institutional restrictions that impact on analysis are rarely addressed
in Freud's work; Irigaray's intimate relationships seem to occur in private or
domestic spaces; and, despite Levinas' critique of the exclusivity of Buber's
spiritual meetings, his encounters with the Other have the ethereal quality of
undisturbed tranquillity. This inattention to material and geographical detail
contrasts with social and postcolonial thinkers, such as Edward Said and Paul
Gilroy, whose attention to actual space (whether Palestine or the Atlantic
passage) lends their work a cultural specificity which the thinkers discussed
here sometimes lack.[63] This space of human dialogic and cultural exchange will
be dealt with in the next chapter on civic humanism.

Primary Texts

Sigmund Freud

'Project for a Scientific Psychology' [1895], in *The Standard Edition of the Complete
  Psychological Works of Sigmund Freud*, ed. and trans. James Strachey, Volume 1
  (London: Hogarth, 1966).
The Interpretation of Dreams [1900], ed. Angela Richards, trans. James Strachey (London:
  Penguin, 1991).
Introductory Lectures on Psychoanalysis [1916], in *The Standard Edition of the Complete
  Psychological Works of Sigmund Freud*, ed. and trans. James Strachey, Volume 15
  (London: Hogarth, 1966).
On Metapsychology, ed. Angela Richards, trans. James Strachey (London: Penguin, 1991),
  particularly *Papers on Metapsychology* (1915), *Beyond the Pleasure Principle* (1920) and
  'A Note on the "Mystic Writing Pad"' (1924).
Historical and Expository Works on Psychoanalysis, ed. Albert Dickson, trans. James
  Strachey (London: Penguin, 1991), particularly *The Question of Lay Analysis* (1926).

Luce Irigaray

An Ethics of Sexual Difference [1984], trans. Carolyn Burke and Gillian C. Gill (London:
  Athlone, 1993).
Je, Tu, Nous: Toward a Culture of Difference [1990], trans. Alison Martin (New York:
  Routledge, 1993).

The Irigaray Reader, ed. Margaret Whitford (Oxford: Blackwell, 1991), particularly 'The Poverty of Psychoanalysis' (1985) and 'Questions of Emmanuel Levinas' (1991).

To Be Two [1994], trans. Monique M. Rhodes and Marco F. Cocito-Monoc (London: Athlone, 2000).

I Love To You: Sketch of a Possible Felicity in History, trans. Alison Martin (New York: Routledge, 1996).

Emmanuel Levinas

Humanisme de l'autre homme (Montpellier: Fata Morgana, 1972).

Otherwise than Being, or, Beyond Essence [1974], trans. A. Lingis (The Hague: Martinus Nijhoff, 1981).

Outside the Subject [1987], trans. Michael B. Smith (London: Athlone, 1993).

The Levinas Reader, ed. Seán Hand (Oxford: Blackwell, 1989), particularly 'The Phenomenological Theory of Being' (1930), 'Martin Buber and the Theory of Knowledge' (1958) and 'Ethics as First Philosophy' (1984).

Entre Nous: On Thinking-of-the-Other, trans. Michael B. Smith and Barbara Harshav (London: Athlone, 1998).

CHAPTER 4

Civic Humanism
(Wollstonecraft – Habermas – Hall)

At the heart of civic humanism is the belief that human beings are naturally citizens by virtue of their innate sociability, and that consequently the highest form of activity in which we can engage is the pursuit of the common good. Aristotle has gone in and out of fashion several times during his afterlife, but the Aristotle of *The Politics* and *The Nicomachean Ethics* gives particularly clear expression to one of the recurring principles of civic humanist thought: that citizenship is both natural and virtuous. 'It is our affections for others', writes Aristotle in *The Politics*, 'that causes us to choose to live together' and it is the city state or *polis* that for Aristotle 'belongs to the class of objects which exist by nature' as a means, initially, 'of securing life itself' and subsequently of securing 'the good life'.[1] For Aristotle, we are citizens first and individuals second, for the state is held to be 'prior to the individual'.[2] Serving the state is thus not a duty in the sense of an external imposition foisted upon reluctant individuals, for citizenship on this model is the true expression and fulfilment of what it means to be human.

There are several further features of Aristotle's civic humanism which are relevant to the ensuing discussion, because of the way that they anticipate some of the later variations upon, and problems within, civic humanist thought. First is Aristotle's notion that the *polis* is in a process of organic evolution towards its final form. Here Aristotle anticipates subsequent Romantic ideas of organic form, but with the difference that Aristotle is more interested in bringing such concepts to bear on 'outer' phenomena, such as the *polis*, than on phenomena whose private character demarcates a separation between the citizen and the individual.[3] Like a sapling which achieves its *telos* in becoming a tree, the *polis* grows towards a state where it will eventually realise its true purpose. However, unlike a tree, whose mature form is apparent, the final shape and purpose of the *polis* are subject to debate, and to enter into such debate is what partly defines the roles of the citizen and political theorist. The second, closely related feature of Aristotle's thought is that citizenship is not therefore an exact science. In *The Nicomachean Ethics*, Aristotle distinguishes between several kinds of knowledge, holding prudence or practical wisdom to be the form of knowledge most appropriate to citizenship. Because, writes Aristotle, 'it is impossible to deliberate about things that are *necessarily* so, prudence cannot be science'.[4] The common good cannot be as easily quantified as an object of exact science, although this does not prevent Aristotle from claiming that the good state is naturally hierarchical and should exclude women and slaves from citizen status on the basis that the predetermined *telos* of these groups is to provide middle- and upper-class male citizens with the means of survival (a variation of this argument was used for pro-slavery propaganda in nineteenth-century America). Nevertheless, Aristotle's insistence that political science is inexact opens up a space for deliberation about the common good, the nature of citizenship, and the purpose of the state. The *polis* may be a predetermined and naturalised category, but human beings – or some of them at least – should discover for themselves what this means. As we shall see in this chapter, this model of civic humanism also comes under pressure from other ways of thinking about the human.[5]

The high points of European civic humanism arguably occurred during the Renaissance and Enlightenment. As Chapter 1 argued, the Renaissance itself gave rise to a variety of humanisms, but, as we also suggested, an influential aspect of Renaissance humanism was its reorientation of education towards the active life of the citizen.[6] *A Defence of Poetry* (1595), by the sixteenth-century English poet and courtier Philip Sidney, is one of numerous texts that debate the merits of the active as opposed to contemplative life. For Sidney, 'well-knowing' is only of value if it leads to 'well-doing', the 'end of all earthly learning being virtuous action'.[7] Mediating between the overly abstract discipline of moral philosophy on the one hand and the overly concrete discipline of history on the other, poetry, according to Sidney, is a highly effective form of rhetoric because it teaches by example using emotion as part of its appeal. Sidney's notion of the social and educational value of poetry identifies a key aspect of what might be called a civic humanist understanding of literature, which also links up to functionalist theories of emotion discussed in Chapter 1. Erasmus' *Praise of Folly*, briefly referred to in the Introduction, is another text that is representative of a public-spirited Renaissance outlook, intent on recasting Christianity in the light of classical values as a species of civic humanism capable of operating as a practical force of good in the world and remedying the logic-chopping and reclusive nature of late medieval scholasticism. However diverse and problematic Renaissance humanism is, what distinguishes it, according to Martin Davies, was that it 'stood apart from the traditional centres of book production in the religious houses and universities' and that behind the 'varied and not always successful enterprises' of humanists 'lay a simple and for centuries very powerful idea: the humanist conviction that good letters lead, under God's guidance, to good men'.[8] Renaissance humanists were thus partly responsible for establishing a virtual public sphere in the form of a republic of letters, existing outside traditional enclaves and devoted, in Aristotelian fashion, to the pursuit of the common good.

It would of course be reductive to rely on Renaissance humanist caricatures of the medieval period as homogeneously reclusive, just as it would be equally reductive to characterise the Renaissance itself as uniformly insistent upon the active life of the citizen. Other traditions with their own already existing or emerging anthropologies are present in the Renaissance: for example, relevant to the following discussion, are the Augustinian tradition of looking inwards to find God and the fledgling Romantic humanist sense of inwardness. These emphases upon inwardness contributed towards the 'denaturing' of citizenship by dismantling the Greco-Roman classical idea that, to quote Charles Taylor, 'the order of things embodies an ontic logos whereby ideas and valuations are ... seen as located in the world, and not just in subjects'.[9] The interesting difference suggested here by Taylor is the distinction between seeing external phenomena, such as nature, the world and other people, as inherently valuable, and attributing value instead to individuals who make choices about value. In the first case, it is the object of value in and for itself that is important, whereas in the second, significance is conferred (as with Sartrean existentialism) upon the valuing subject, upon the fact of choice and who chooses, rather than what is chosen. An updated version of the difference that Taylor has in mind here would be the difference between someone who contributes to a charity out of a sense of concern for the hardship suffered by the people involved, and some-one who contributes to charity because a celebrity has attributed importance to the issue. The cult of personality which dictates that who says what is more important than what is said is a commodified version of subject-centred humanisms that internalise the external. However, the individualism of an inward-inclining Romantic humanism and the concern for the common good of an outward-looking civic humanism have not always been strangers to one another. As such, this chapter will be partly devoted to showing how individualism and civic humanism both couple and uncouple.

The three writers discussed here are the proto-feminist and Enlightenment thinker Mary Wollstonecraft (1759–97), the neo-Enlightenment thinker Jürgen Habermas (1929–), and the post-Enlightenment practitioner and theorist of cultural studies Stuart Hall (1932–). An outward-looking civic consciousness informs the work of each of these writers, but there are significant cultural and conceptual differences between them. Whereas Wollstonecraft and Habermas can be seen as sharing in common certain Aristotelian and Enlightenment ideas about the collective good and grounding this idea of commonality upon (an albeit contested) anthropology, Hall will be considered here as a post-Enlightenment figure whose civic humanism is pragmatic rather than grounded upon a systematic theory of human nature.

Mary Wollstonecraft

In his essay 'An Answer to the Question: "What is Enlightenment?"' (1784), Immanuel Kant aims to provide for the Enlightenment a kind of mission statement. The 'motto of enlightenment', writes Kant, is: 'Have courage to use your *own* understanding.'[10] Kant opposes the '*public use*' of one's reason' which he says 'must always be free' and 'alone can bring about enlightenment among men' with the '*private use*' of reason, by which he means the use of reason which is thrust upon an individual in a 'particular *civil* post or office with which he is entrusted'.[11] Private reason, here, means thought that has an investment in maintaining a social institution or business interest. It is thought that is tied into a particular job description, like the reasons an estate agent might give for buying a particular house. Public reason, on the other hand, is more capacious, universal, and 'disengaged', to recall the term Charles Taylor uses to describe some of the effects of rationality.[12] There are also echoes of the Renaissance humanist construction of a virtual public sphere in Kant's description of public reason as 'that use which anyone may make of it *as a man of learning* addressing the entire *reading public*'.[13] In addition, a principle of dialogue is implied in the evocation of a reading public composed of independent thinkers whose views are not automatically taken to be true, but have to be tried and tested by other independent thinkers.

Independent reason is thus the basis, not just for a complacent objectivity, but for a critical, questioning form of citizenship that is given expression in the work of the late eighteenth-century English social thinker Mary Wollstonecraft. Wollstonecraft challenged those naturalised social constructions of gender which allocate men to the realm of reason and citizenship and women to the realm of feeling or 'sensibility'. In *A Vindication of the Rights of Woman* (1792), she asks why women should not be 'educated in such a manner as to be able to think and act for themselves'.[14] She also questioned reason itself, or at least that improper male employment of reason 'to justify prejudices' which maintain sexual inequalities. 'The mind must be strong', writes Wollstonecraft, 'that resolutely forms its own principles; for a kind of intellectual cowardice prevails which makes men shrink from the task' of rooting out such prejudices.[15] Resolute independent thinking is thus what Wollstonecraft calls for and herself practises in her appeal to women – and men – to liberate themselves from the prison house of ascribed social identities.

The value Wollstonecraft places on autonomous reason is clearly an expression of individualism. As such, it is potentially in conflict with civic humanism, for to assert the primacy of the self-reliant, autonomously reasoning individual could be seen as reversing the Aristotelian principle of the *polis* being 'prior to the individual'. Wollstonecraft is undoubtedly an individualistic thinker who inherits – as well as anticipates – several different strains of individualism. As an Enlightenment intellectual, she values independence of thought. As a Christian, drawn towards the religious dissent that was very much alive in the late eighteenth century (and often commensurable with Enlightenment independence), she favours personal conviction and experience of God over those 'Romish customs' and 'irksome ceremonies' which are thought to obstruct our 'free-will offering to Him'.[16] As a precursor of Romanticism, she has an ambivalent attitude towards that cluster of terms, including sensibility, sentiment, genius, feeling and imagination, which were used to define a more thoroughgoing subjectivist epistemology. And as a contributor to liberal theories of natural right which underpinned American and French revolutionary thought, she privileges the freedom and rights of the individual.

If these individualisms identify a humanism that by asserting the natural priority of the individual appears to part company with its civic counterpart, then this tendency towards divergence is tempered in Wollstonecraft's writing by an equal emphasis upon universalism, the common good and participation in 'critical citizenship'. Reason, for example, is not so thoroughly individualised as to prevent Wollstonecraft from affirming the value of 'truth' which should ideally be 'common to all' and asserting that if reason is 'an emanation of divinity', then 'the nature of reason must be the same in all':

> Reason is ... the simple power of improvement; or, more properly speaking, of discerning truth. Every individual is in this respect a world in itself. More or less may be conspicuous in one being than another; but the nature of reason must be the same in all, if it be an emanation of divinity, the tie that connects the creature with the Creator; for, can that soul be stamped with the heavenly image, that is not perfected by the exercise of its own reason?[17]

This might be read as an expression of a hubristic subjectivism, in that it appears to sanctify individual reason by identifying it with the divine and the universal. The appeal to authorities outside the self such as God could be seen as a ruse designed to lend legitimacy to the autonomous thinker. Nietzsche, who arguably takes Romanticism to its extreme, will read virtually everything according to a subjectivist epistemology, by insisting that the will to (objective) knowledge is 'really' about the will to (subjective) power. Alternatively, Wollstonecraft may be seen as genuinely attempting to locate truth and authority both inside and outside the individual: looking 'inwards' also involves looking 'upwards' towards a higher being and authority who is also the guarantor of the values which already exist in the world. Those values might need to be rediscovered, but they are in the world rather than purely in the minds of subjects who create meaning and value *ex nihilo*.

The classical idea that, to recall Charles Taylor, 'the order of things embodies an ontic logos whereby ideas and valuations are ... seen as located in the world, and not just in subjects' is thus still applicable to Wollstonecraft, for the classical mimetic perspective whereby the mind is thought to mirror what already objectively exists is in keeping with a critical civic humanism that focuses upon 'issues' rather than 'personalities'. The primary focus of attention in *A Vindication of the Rights of Woman* falls upon the issue of the injustice of denying women the right to education and reason. This view does not depend on Wollstonecraft herself for its validity. Of course, the issue of injustice arises out of particular experiences of gender inequalities, but these particulars naturally find a place in the larger and pre-given ethical scheme of things. Wollstonecraft's individualism is thus the means to critical civic humanist ends, rather than an end in itself. Independence is important, not just for its own sake, but because by challenging prejudice it is the means of restoring women's God-given social rights. Wollstonecraft's writing thus moves 'inwards', 'upwards' and 'outwards' simultaneously.[18] To remain at the level of the individual is to prove incapable of generating general principles from solitary examples. As Wollstonecraft herself writes: 'The power of generalizing ideas, of drawing comprehensive conclusions from individual observations, is the only acquirement, for an immortal being, that really deserves the name of knowledge.'[19]

So far the discussion has said little about the role of feeling in Wollstonecraft's work and the impact that it has upon her civic humanism. It would be tempting, in the light of Wollstonecraft's own work together with that of other civic humanist thinkers, to reach the conclusion that citizenship is an altogether rather cold and unfeeling affair, to do with the head rather than the heart. True, thinkers like Aristotle and Sidney embrace functionalist attitudes towards the emotions as part of their civic humanism. True, also, Aristotle refers in *The Politics* to the 'affections' that we have 'for others' as the basis of citizenship, although this is a fleeting reference in a text devoted to the classifying, dividing and sub-dividing procedures endemic to rational enquiry. In general, reason has been associated with the public and emotion with the private sphere, and civic humanism identified as a critical rather than affective activity. Wollstonecraft herself has often been seen as an arch-rationalist who is deeply suspicious of the 'empire of feeling' to which women are stereotypically consigned.[20] It is not difficult to find passages, particularly in *A Vindication of the Rights of Women* that support this view:

> [W]omen, in general, as well as the rich of both sexes, have acquired all the follies and vices of civilization, and missed the fruit. It is not necessary for me always to premise, that I speak of the condition of the whole sex, leaving

exceptions out of the question. Their senses are inflamed, and their under-
standings neglected, consequently they become the prey of their senses,
delicately termed sensibility, and are blown about by every momentary gust of
feeling ... Ever restless and anxious, their over exercised sensibility not only
renders them uncomfortable themselves, but troublesome, to use a soft phrase,
to others. All their thoughts turn on things calculated to excite emotion; and
feeling, when they should reason.[21]

'Sensibility' is disparagingly referred to here as a term which signifies the
intense preoccupation with affective life in the late eighteenth century, particularly by Romantic thinkers. Sensibility and its (sometimes) near analogues,
sentiment, pity, passion, sympathy, fancy, imagination and the sublime, weave
their way through a variety of eighteenth-century and early nineteenth-century
texts, from Rousseau's *Discourse on Inequality* (1755) and his widely read sentimental novel *Julie, ou La Nouvelle Héloïse* (1791) to Jane Austen's *Sense and
Sensibility* (1811). Such texts, including Wollstonecraft's *A Vindication of the
Rights of Woman* and her two novels of sensibility, *Mary, A Fiction* (1788) and
The Wrongs of Woman (1798), contributed towards the creation of a rich, often
finely discriminating, but also intensely contested, vocabulary of feeling. The
key question surrounding sensibility, and particularly 'the woman of sensibility'
referred to in the Preface to *The Wrongs of Woman*, is the question of where
sensibility belongs in relation to the discourses of individualism, civic humanism,
enlightenment and reason.[22]

In the above passage, 'over exercised' sensibility is equated with the turbu-
lence of unregulated emotions, which prevent women from becoming autonomous, reasoning citizens. Emotion here is reason's 'other' and not amenable to
rational analysis. Elsewhere, Wollstonecraft defines love, against friendship,
as a passion 'in which chance and sensation take the place of reason and choice'
and which 'draws the mind out of its accustomed state'.[23] But the conclusion
which might be reached on the basis of these passages, that Wollstonecraft the
rationalist citizen is the enemy of passion and feeling, is false. 'Passions',
continues Wollstonecraft, 'are spurs to action, and open the mind; but they
sink into mere appetites, become a personal and momentary gratification,
when the object is gained, and the satisfied mind rests in enjoyment.'[24] If
passion, as 'mere' appetite and the source of temporary personal gratification,
is the enemy of reason, then passion, insofar as it opens the mind to new
possibilities, can also be the helpmate of reason. The latter sense harmonises
with Wollstonecraft's sometimes rhapsodic association of 'genius' with the
'quick perception of truth, which is so intuitive that it baffles research, and
makes us at a loss to determine whether it is reminiscence or ratiocination, lost
sight of in its celerity, that opens the dark cloud'.[25] Understood in this way, the

effects of sensibility do undermine the autonomy of reasoning individuals, but to their advantage in that they move autonomous reason beyond the circumscribed realm of the already thought and known.

As emotion is for the Romantic humanists discussed in Chapter 1, so sensibility for Wollstonecraft can be productive or unproductive, purposeful or purposeless. It can be indolent, hedonistic and temporarily gratifying or it can contribute towards the 'serious duties of life' by accompanying reason in the pursuit of individual and collective enlightenment.[26] If there is a sense of strain present in Wollstonecraft's attempt to elevate one version of sensibility over the other, then that is arguably because the aesthetic of capricious personal feeling is in danger of eclipsing that other version of sensibility which lends itself to the civic humanist and Enlightenment pursuit of the common good. Sensibility needs a helping hand if the 'right' and 'proper' version of it is to feel as natural to the human heart as its 'improper' counterpart. If caprice is identified with childishness, then it will seem, especially in the light of Rousseau's equation of childhood with nature, as though capriciousness is a naturally narcissistic state which has to be vigilantly policed by adult duty and responsibility.[27]

The helping hand needed by true sensibility to offset what Wollstonecraft herself refers to as the 'natural selfishness of sensibility' and to 'renature' the civic realm from the point of view of the emotions, comes in the shape of those dialogic verities discussed in the last chapter: compassion, care and fellow feeling.[28] These virtues take their cue from the capacity for feeling which women are already encouraged to cultivate, but working with rather than against reason, they further humanise and positively feminise citizenship. Women with 'heated' imaginations and 'fastidious' feelings are 'often amiable', writes Wollstonecraft, and 'their hearts are really more sensible to general benevolence, more alive to the sentiments that civilize life, than the square-elbowed family drudge; but wanting a due proportion of reflection … they only inspire love'.[29] Thus the Enlightenment thinker, whose free and independent use of reason contributes towards the creation of a critical citizenship, attempts to bring the woman of feeling with her into the masculinised public realm to balance critique with care, reason with emotion, sense with sensibility. These attempted marriages may not completely assuage the feeling that public virtue and private gratification are in danger of going their separate ways, but Wollstonecraft's enduring legacy is to ask difficult questions about how and where passion and feeling fit in with civic humanist aspirations when they are simultaneously contributing towards the intensification of private life.

Jürgen Habermas

As a neo-Enlightenment thinker who revises rather than jettisons Enlightenment categories, writing two centuries later the German social philosopher
Jürgen Habermas shares in common with Wollstonecraft a preoccupation with
the value of non-solipsistic reason in the pursuit of the collective good.
However, given Habermas' self-characterisation as a post-metaphysical thinker,
who has also lived through the apparent failure of the Enlightenment to deliver
a better world, there are also profound historical and intellectual differences
between them. Wollstonecraft is in the end a metaphysical thinker in that she
believes that reason is a transcendent, God-given faculty, which connects the
autonomous thinker's mind with the value immanent in the world. Her way of
overcoming the loneliness of the solitary mind is to affirm that reason is
common to all and that it leads to a recognition of already present truths. For
the post-metaphysical Habermas, this convergence of mind and world might
well constitute an example of what he refers to in *The Theory of Communicative
Action* (1981) as pre-modern, mythical thought. Drawing on the work of
Claude Lévi-Strauss, Habermas characterises pre-modern societies by their
conflation of the individual with his or her social role (from this point of view,
Aristotle's insistence that the *polis* is prior to the individual is an example of
mythical thought), and by their simultaneous conflation of culture with nature.
'From this reciprocal assimilation of nature to culture and conversely culture to
nature, there results' writes Habermas,

> on the one hand, a nature that is outfitted with anthropomorphic features,
> drawn into the communicative network of social subjects, and in this sense
> humanized, and on the other hand, a culture that is to a certain extent
> naturalized and reified and absorbed into the objective nexus of operations of
> anonymous powers.[30]

Modern or proto-modern theories of immanent meaning, theories which blur
the distinction between the 'internal relations among meanings' and the
'external relations among things', would thus fall under the category of
mythical thinking.[31] Humanisms which seek to ground their interpretations of
human nature on what it is 'really' like, could themselves be construed as
examples of mythical thinking which attempt to mend the rifts within modernity between mind and world, knower and known, culture and nature, value and
fact. As we discussed in Chapter 1, organicist concepts of the human appealed
to by Romantic thinkers, such as Keats, would fall under this category.

Habermas himself, however, does not seek to close these gaps, or at least not
without the reasoned deliberation which characterises one aspect of modernity.
Whereas mythical thought assimilates the individual to the social and the social

to the natural, thereby making of consensus a naturalised 'given', modernity according to Habermas separates out the spheres of the objective, the social and the subjective. These three spheres correspond respectively to the domains of science (understood by Habermas as the 'the totality of facts' about reality, where facts correspond to truths), morality (defined as 'the totality of all interpersonal relations that are recognized by members' of the social world 'as legitimate') and art (characterised by Habermas in terms of a Romantic aesthetic of individual expression which 'delimits from the objective and social worlds a domain for each member of *what is not common*').[32] In the ideal world of communication that is also the basis for an ideal form of citizenship, all three spheres are subject to critical debate and reflection. Thus individuals not automatically assimilated to naturalised social roles can question conventions; conversely, individuality can be delimited – as well as potentially expanded – through dialogic encounter with others; 'scientific' claims can be treated as 'validity claims – and thus exposed to criticism and open to revision'; and worldviews can be 'identified *as* worldviews' and understood as 'interpretative systems that are attached to cultural traditions'.[33] While these spheres of the subjective, objective and social can each go their separate ways, with the result that, for example, 'art that has become autonomous pushes toward an ever purer expression of the basic aesthetic experiences of a subjectivity that is decentered and removed from the spatiotemporal structures of everyday life', the ideal communciative space imagined by Habermas is one in which science, morality and art are in critical dialogue with one another. 'Thus nonobjectivist approaches to research within the human sciences' writes Habermas, 'bring viewpoints of moral and aesthetic critique to bear – without threatening the primacy of questions of truth.' Likewise, 'in realist art and *l'art engagé*, moments of the cognitive and of the moral-practical come into play again in art itself'.[34]

Given the rigour and complexity of Habermas' thinking, together with his wide-ranging engagements with the classics of sociological, philosophical, anthropological and linguistic enquiry (Marx, Weber, Durkheim, Adorno, Horkheimer, Kant, Husserl, Lévi-Strauss, Austin and Piaget), one might be forgiven for suggesting that the ideally critical dialogue which might take place both within and between art, science and morality can only be undertaken within the thick, specialised tomes of Habermas' *The Theory of Communicative Action*. There is, however, a populist strain in Habermas' thought, which is evident in the way he locates critical citizenship within ordinary, everyday human consciousness. In particular, it is Habermas' conception of the 'life-world' which places a participatory citizenship within the reach of all communicating human subjects and which overcomes the tendency for the three spheres of art, science and morality to fall 'under the control of specialists', as he writes in 'Modernity – An Incomplete Project' (1980).[35]

Habermas uses the term 'life-world' (*Lebenswelt*) to designate the unspoken values, beliefs and assumptions which all human communities draw upon in order to understand and communicate with one another. The concept of the life-world also comes closest in Habermas' writing to the way mythical thought is seen by him as functioning, for both share in common the tendency of their worldviews to become so naturalised that they are not visible *as* world-views. What happens to life-worlds in modern societies, however, is that they become denatured. As a result, reason begins to play a hugely significant role in modernity, since once values and consensus are no longer givens, they have to be rationally argued for: in other words, reasons have to be given for the beliefs that a community holds where formerly no such rationalisation was necessary. 'A lifeworld', writes Habermas, 'can be regarded as rationalized to the extent that it permits interactions that are not guided by normatively *ascribed* agreement but – directly or indirectly – by communicatively *achieved* understanding.'[36] If the important difference between pre-modern and modern life-worlds is 'reason', then their equally important shared characteristic is the 'inherent telos of human speech' of 'reaching understanding' with one another.[37] The rationalised life-world only makes explicit what was implicit in the unrationalised life-world, that human communication is really about human solidarity. Speech for Habermas is thus what sensibility, at least in one of its versions, is for Wollstonecraft: the glue that at least potentially binds us together.

However, what prevents members of a rationalised life-world from real-ising their potential as communicating, deliberating, reflexive citizens in search of a non-coercive consensus is the colonisation of the life-world by the negative forms of rationality embedded in capitalist and administrative systems. Capitalist rationality privileges 'egocentric calculations of success' over authentic communication.[38] Meanwhile, state administration and the capitalist economy itself constitute 'increasingly complex, formally organized domains of action' which hinder the life-world from exercising its different form of rationality.[39] In the absence of a shared mythical worldview, two conflicting models for achieving consensus therefore present themselves: an organic as well as populist model rooted in the natural features of ordinary, everyday communication versus an inorganic, externally imposed, administered con-sensus, evident in late capitalist cultures in an increasingly pervasive audit culture littered with performance indicators.

Habermas' neo-Enlightenment confidence in the progressive nature of reason – a confidence which underpins his version of civic humanism – needs further discussion, since reason has come under increasing attack from different quar-ters during the twentieth and early twenty-first centuries.[40] Habermas is himself aware of, and critically responsive to, these counter-Enlightenment perspectives. To the tendency of Weber, and later Adorno and Horkheimer, to condemn Enlightenment reason for its instrumentality, Habermas in *The Theory of Communicative Action* responds by differentiating communicative rationality from its instrumentalising counterpart. In *The Philosophical Discourse of Modernity* (1985), he tackles those various different 'others' of reason upon which anti-Enlightenment thinkers have based their critiques of the perceived hubris of an 'enlightened' reasoning subject aspiring to universally valid knowledge. To the counter-Enlightenment claims that reason excludes various limit experiences, such as eroticism (Bataille), mysticism (Heidegger through to Derrida), madness (Foucault), Dionysian ecstasy (Nietzsche), or that it ignores its own historicity and discursivity (Foucault again) or will to power (Nietzsche and Foucault), Habermas responds by again arguing that there is more to reason than the subject-centred version of it invoked by these thinkers:

> [B]oth cognitive-instrumental mastery of an objectivated nature (and society) and narcissistically overinflated autonomy (in the sense of purposively rational self-assertion) are derivative moments that have been rendered independent from the communicative structures of the lifeworld, that is, from the intersubjectivity of relationships of mutual understanding and relationships of reciprocal recognition.[41]

It is a moot point as to when this derivation began. Habermas himself often cites Kant as the perpetrator of a subject-centred rationality, but Kant himself, like Wollstonecraft, does not totally subjectivise reason. Also debatable is the extent to which quasi-Romantic appeals to liminal experiences destabilise the rational subject only to release him or her into a richer kind of subjectivity. Passion, to recall Wollstonecraft, may disturb the composure of the autonomous thinker, but only to deepen the sense of an inner life inaccessible to reason.

These backward glances to Kant's and Wollstonecraft's own qualifications of autonomous reason bear out Habermas' argument that the 'New Critique of Reason' denies continuity with the counter-Enlightenment tendencies that were already present in the Enlightenment itself (but which were given fuller expression in Romantic thought).[42] This kind of perspective also closes the gap between Habermas and his postmodern adversaries, for both can be seen as standing in the tradition of the Enlightenment's own self-critique. Although Habermas sets himself apart from his critics, there is some common ground. True, Habermas explicitly embraces Enlightenment concepts of universality to which subjective (or in his case, intersubjective) reason aspires, whereas postmodern thinkers, such as Foucault, tend to see universality as the hubristic elevation of subjective reason to the status of universal truth. However, Habermas' concept of universality is really quite humble. 'Stability and absence of ambiguity', writes Habermas, 'are rather the exception in the communicative practice of everyday life.' As a result, 'commonality' can only ever be 'occasional'.[43] Communication amongst citizens in pursuit of a non-reified common good is thus a precarious, open-ended affair, which is premised upon the heterogeneity of life-worlds and their diverse rationalisations.

Habermas is not a total pluralist, however, for he holds that some arguments and rationalisations are better than others. His criteria for 'better than' are those of the 'pure' rationalist, the sociologist and the civic humanist. The logician in Habermas claims that some arguments are more internally coherent than others (such that a certain postcolonial, feminist or patriarchal proposition might be regarded as more coherent than another). With his social scientist's hat on, Habermas maintains – against a relativist thinker like Richard Rorty (see Chapter 7) – that some propositions about social reality have more purchase than others. Finally, as a thinker who can be located within the tradition of civic humanism, Habermas maintains the view that some arguments are better than others on the basis of their vision of the good and just life. Intersubjectivity and non-coercion are the key terms within Habermas' civic humanist court of appeal.

Stuart Hall

In *Culture, Media, Language* (1980), co-edited by the black British cultural critic and theorist Stuart Hall for the pioneering Centre for Contemporary Cultural Studies at Birmingham University, there is a section at the end of the volume entitled 'Selective Guide to Further Reading and Contacts'.[44] The contacts include the Federation of Worker Writers, a London-based feminist theatre group, the academic journal *Literature and History*, and various independent bookshops, including Sisterwrite and Compendium in London and Grassroots in Manchester.[45] That a primarily academic textbook should also supply a brief guide to what is happening 'on the ground' in terms of left-wing and feminist, cultural and political activity speaks to Hall's pragmatic attempt to bring intellectual work into close relationship with practical politics and everyday life. In this respect, Hall is the postmodern equivalent of the kind of citizen-poet admired by Philip Sidney, for whom 'well-knowing' is insufficient without 'well-doing'. Citizenship is not the densely theorised phenomenon that it is for Habermas. Neither is Hall's work explicitly grounded in an anthropology based on reason and intersubjectivity (Habermas), or reason and sensibility (Wollstonecraft). Such large underpinning ideas as God, justice, reason and human nature are not normally part of Hall's vocabulary, for these concepts are features of grand narratives whose explanatory force always has to be put to the test, for Hall, of changing economic, cultural and political circumstances. The 'object of [my] work' says Hall 'is to always reproduce the concrete in thought – not to generate another good theory, but to give a better theorized account of concrete historical reality'.[46] Hall's suspicion of totalising theories and universalist claims to truth thus makes it possible to characterise him as a post-Enlightenment thinker. What is interesting about the example of Hall is that while the engagement in all of his work with the politics of culture and representation speaks to a persistently deep commitment to citizenship, the simultaneous post-Enlightenment emphasis in his work on difference and plurality raises the question of whether the collective goals of citizenship are still possible, or even desirable.

In their jointly authored essay 'Citizens and Citizenship' (1989), Hall and David Held suggest that 'difference' is 'the joker in the citizenship pack'.[47] Where citizenship has according to Hall and Held 'tended to absorb "differences" into one common universal status – the citizen', postmodernity begs recognition of differences of various kinds: from ethnic and cultural diversity; to the diversification of the language of citizen rights so as to include 'the animal species', 'Nature itself' and 'vulnerable minorities, like children'; to 'the differentiated ways in which people now participate in social life';[48] to the 'breakdown of a sense of community and interdependence' engendered by the unbridled economic self-interest of the Thatcherite (and post-Thatcherite) era in Britain, to which close parallels can be made to Ronald Reagan's and George Bush Sr's Republican administrations in 1980s America.[49] There is also the problem, Hall and Held write, 'of what political entity the citizen is a citizen *of*', given that 'the nation state itself – the entity to which the language of political citizenship refers – is eroded and challenged', both from within (by 'regional and local "nationalisms"') and from without (by 'the processes of economic, political, military and ecological interdependence'). They refer, for example, to the problem posed by the chemical disaster which took place in an American-owned factory in Bhopal, Central India in the 1980s: 'how to give effects to the "rights" of the citizens of Bhopal against chemical pollution caused by a multinational company registered in New York and operating world-wide'.[50] Finally, if there can be any finality given the proliferation of differences, the 'long and rich history' of citizenship itself means that there is 'no "*essence*" to citizenship, but instead 'three leading notions': namely, 'membership', 'rights and duties in reciprocity' and 'real participation in practice'. Each notion gives rise to its own set of problems (discussed by Hall and Held), as well as existing in a potential state of tension with the other concepts.[51]

One solution to these complexities might be to opt for the contemplative as opposed to active life, or for a reclusive form of individualism. These are not real options, however, for the civic humanist. Hall may at times suggest that postmodern culture is just too fragmented for citizenship to have any purchase – 'we don't have alternative means', he writes, 'by which adults can benefit from the ways in which people have released themselves from the bonds of traditionalist forms of living and thinking, and still exert responsibilities for others in a free and open way' – but he retains an optimism which translates fragmentation into a sense of dialogic possibility.[52] For Hall, alive to the poststructuralist insight that language is slippery but wanting to use this on behalf of a civic humanist ethic of active social engagement, all concepts and practices, from citizenship to liberal individualism to the National Health Service, are sites of struggle, which need to be actively contested to avoid handing them over to right-wing ideologues.[53]

Hall's time as acting and actual Director of the Birmingham Centre from 1964 to 1979 itself has a close bearing upon the issue of whether an active and shared sense of citizenship can or cannot combine with a 'post-traditional' commitment to plurality. This period witnessed a boom in theory and since cultural studies was an emerging 'discipline' without firm disciplinary boundaries, it engaged in a succession of critical dialogues with both established and emerging theoretical paradigms, from functionalist sociology to the new Marxisms and feminisms, structuralism, poststructuralism, discourse theory, postcolonialism and postmodernism. Hall resisted the idea of being a 'keeper of the conscience of cultural studies, hoping to police you back into line with what [cultural studies] was if only you knew'.[54] At the same time, writes Hall, cultural studies 'can't be just any old thing, which chooses to march under a particular banner'. For Hall, what distinguishes cultural studies without prescriptively fixing it, is its political commitment 'to make a difference in the world'. 'I don't believe knowledge is closed', he writes, 'but I do believe that politics is impossible without what I have called "the arbitrary closure".'[55] For Hall, discussion has at some point to end, so that ideas can materialise into practice and actively participate in the struggle over meaning. Cultural studies thus is and can be a broad church, but its critical identity would be lost if it withdrew from an active and questioning citizenship.

The figure who has continually inspired Hall because he provides a model of the engaged intellectual is the Italian political thinker Antonio Gramsci. For Hall, Gramsci is the antidote to the tendency of intellectual knowledge to become ever more refined and internally divided. 'We have attempted', writes Hall,

> to *work towards* a greater unity, without expecting to conjure it out of thin air or the 'will to knowledge'. Our aim, in this respect, could be defined as the struggle to form a more 'organic' kind of intellectual. Gramsci spoke of the distinction between those 'traditional' intellectuals who set themselves the task of developing and sophisticating the existing paradigms of knowledge and those who, in their critical role, aim to become more 'organic' to new and emergent tendencies in society ... He also designated two tasks for those aiming to become 'organic' intellectuals: to challenge modern ideologies 'in their most refined form', and to enter into the task of popular education.[56]

The liberationist spirit of 1968 is expressed here and elsewhere in Hall's writing in the desire to mobilise 'organic' intellectuals into alliances with popular constituencies that may together articulate a unified counter-culture. However, the lesson of both 1968 and the subsequent emergence, in the 1980s, of the New Right, is the Gramscian lesson that any given hegemony 'once achieved, must be constantly and ceaselessly renewed, reenacted'.[57] This constant renewal is necessary because the 'plurality of discourses', out of which a hegemony, such as Hall's bugbear Thatcherism, is constructed, is always liable to fragment or become contradictory. 'Hegemony', writes Hall, 'points to a way of conceptualizing the emergence of Thatcherism in terms of the struggle to gain ascendancy over a whole social formation, to achieve positions of leadership in a number of different sites at once, to achieve the commanding position on a broad strategic front.'[58] The concept of hegemony is thus close to the precarious and open-ended consensus towards which Habermas' rationalised life-world works. And it is the in-built tendency of any hegemonic formation towards fragmentation which is its saving grace, as therein lies the possibility for transformation and renewal.

Unity and plurality are thus both struggled for by Hall, and always together, so that plurality is either contained within a fragile synthesis or can dismantle a prescriptive synthesis in order to work towards a better one. If, in his analysis of Thatcherism, Hall seems reluctantly impressed by the New Right's successful conversion of plurality into synthesis, then elsewhere Hall expresses concern about the downside of a unity which subsumes difference beneath sameness. In 'Cultural Studies and its Theoretical Legacies' (1992), Hall writes that he wants to 'absolve himself' of the 'black person's burden' which requires that 'I'm expected to speak for the entire black race on all questions theoretical, critical, etc., and sometimes for British politics, as well as for cultural studies'.[59] Instead of identifying himself as a representative spokesperson, who in the manner of an Enlightenment writer like Wollstonecraft uses the particular to illuminate a general social or human experience, the post-Enlightenment Hall is wary of speaking on behalf of others who thereby become silently absorbed into a collective humanist 'we'. Hall continues in this anti-totalising vein in his work on race and ethnicity. In 'New Ethnicities' (1989), for example, he argues that the 'displacement of the "centred" discourses of the West entails putting into question its universalist character and transcendent claims to speak for everyone, while being itself everywhere and nowhere'.[60] And in 'What is this "Black" in Black Popular Culture?' (1992), Hall once again emphasises the need to attend to various kinds of difference:

> [I]t is to the diversity, not the homogeneity, of black experiences that we must
> now give our undivided creative attention. This is not simply to appreciate the

historical and experiential differences within and between communities, regions, country and city, across national cultures, between diasporas, but also to recognize the other kinds of difference that place, position, and locate black people. The point is not simply that, since our racial differences do not constitute all of us, we are always different, negotiating different kinds of differences – of gender, of sexuality, of class. It is also that these antagonisms refuse to be neatly aligned; they are not simply reducible to one another; they refuse to coalesce around a single axis of differentiation.[61]

One of the end-points of the emphasis upon difference would be to suggest that life experiences are so different from each other that they are radically incommensurable. The point of autobiography, from this point of view, would be to solidify a Romantic sense of irreducible particularity. When Hall writes or speaks autobiographically, he does so in this particularising vein. However, the 'we' of citizenship is never totally lost sight of, for the autobiographical 'I' used by Hall is always in critical dialogue with, rather than in total flight from, a collective 'we'. Such dialogue is evident in 'The Formation of a Diasporic Intellectual' (1992), in which Hall talks about his difficult relationship with left-wing politics in the late 1950s and 1960s:

> I always had problems in that period, about the pronoun 'we'. I didn't know quite who I meant, when I said 'We should do X.' I have a funny relationship to the British working-class movement … I'm in it, but not culturally of it. I was one of the people, as editor of *Universities and Left Review*, mainly negotiating that space, but I didn't feel the continuity that people who were born in it did … I did have a diasporic 'take' on my position in the New Left.[62]

The diasporic non-assimilation of the 'I' to the 'we' of collective politics does not mean that Hall gives up on the collective, but that he is alive to the genuine difficulties of building 'forms of solidarity and identification which make common struggle and resistance possible but without suppressing the real heterogeneity of interests and identities'.[63]

Moreover, the concept of difference may be individualised (to the point where autobiography seems inevitable), but a sense of individuality is once again not an end in itself, but a means of serving the higher civic humanist end of cultural politics. The issue, raised by Hall in his work on race and ethnicity, of who or what gets to represent 'black' culture, of whose black voices are thereby empowered or disempowered, forms part of the repertoire of questions dealing with power and marginality which cultural politics addresses. It is possible, therefore, to speak of a broadly civic humanist use of auto/ biography, either to illustrate, as in the case of Wollstonecraft, a general social or human condition, or, as in the case of Hall, to question representativeness itself and to redraw the relationship of the particular to the general.

The concept of the diaspora itself points to the always unfinished dialogue between 'we' and 'I', belonging and not belonging, identification and estrangement, which takes place between and within cultures. Hall describes the diasporic experience of postcoloniality – and a version of postmodernism – as the experience of 'being inside and outside', of knowing places 'intimately', but of never wholly belonging to those places.[64] The feeling of not belonging anywhere is in a sense compensated for through Hall's invocation of a tradition of cultural diaspora, stretching back to the onset in the fifteenth century of the '"Euro-imperial" adventure'. Since that time, suggests Hall, 'in the "contact zones" of the world, culture has developed in a "diasporic" way'.[65] Conceived of as a key constituent of modernity, the condition of diaspora is comparable with the denaturing of communities and cultures that both Wollstonecraft and Habermas deem necessary for an enlightened, critical citizenship. For Hall, as for Wollstonecraft and Habermas, the citizen is an outsider who at the same time continues to search for the ideal community which is expressive of both difference and solidarity.

Hall's moving autobiographical account, 'The Formation of a Diasporic Intellectual', gives considerable emotional and experiential depth to the concept of the diaspora. This depth accords perfectly with the view of politics that the term cultural politics implies. If, from a Habermasian perspective, the instrumental practice of modern politics exalts one aspect only of the human, then cultural politics restores to politics a depth and fullness which are in tune with the civic humanist identification of politics with humanity itself. Cultural politics is in this sense akin to Habermas' richly imagined life-world and Wollstonecraft's equally rich concept of the role of the thinking and feeling citizen. All three thinkers expand citizenship and politics in such a way as to invite the recognition that politics is no more and no less than the art of living together and that this difficult art draws on a range of human needs and capabilities.

The received history of cultural studies, told by Hall himself, has it that cultural studies inaugurated a radical break with the formerly elitist model of 'Culture with a capital "C"', thereby shifting the 'whole ground of debate from a literary-moral to an anthropological definition of culture'.[66] The literary-moral definition of culture is summarised in Raymond Williams' *Keywords* (1976) in his characterisation of the nineteenth-century use of the term 'to attack what was seen as the "mechanical" character of the new civilization then emerging: both for its abstract rationalism and for the "inhumanity" of current industrial development'.[67] In its insistence upon 'cultures' and not 'Culture', cultural studies is supposed to have broken with an aesthetic tradition epitomised by Leavis' notion that high culture salvages endangered human values.[68] However, recent historians and theorists of culture such as Francis

Mulhern and Ian Hunter have revised this account by identifying continuities between the concepts of culture invoked by both cultural studies and the 'literary–moral' tradition.[69] Hall's persistent attempt to avoid vulgar Marxist reductions of culture to economics is one example of such a continuity, for in both the elitist and popular traditions, the word culture comes to define a domain which is regarded as being outside of, and often in opposition to, the economic. The corollary of this is that 'culture', whether high, popular, subcultural or subaltern, signifies a form of life that is not reducible to the alienating and commodified social relations of capitalism. Indeed, cultural politics, as Francis Mulhern suggests, may offer such an expansive and nuanced concept of culture that it loses sight of a more practical politics. 'No politics', writes Mulhern, 'in so far as it respects its constitutive function, which is to determine the order of social relations as a whole, can adequately replicate the contours and textures of the cultural formation in which it seeks to have effect.'[70] The phrase 'contours and textures' that Mulhern uses to describe 'the cultural formation' suggests a richness which recalls the Romantic sense of complexity and depth discussed in Chapter 1, but where Romantic humanists tend to locate these inside the individual, civic humanists tend to locate them outside, in the diversified cultures and communities we inhabit. The resulting concept of non-quantifiable culture thereby takes over the function attributed by baggy humanists like Leavis to literature and high art. While cultural politics continues to focus its attention on the rich, irreducible field of 'identities, interests and values' that constitutes culture, practical politics may indeed get ignored.[71] However, Hall's insistence that politics, of a practical kind, is impossible without 'arbitrary closure', together with his persistent emphasis on live everyday issues, such as the fate of the National Health Service in Britain, discussed in 'Learning from Thatcherism' (1988), indicate his own effort to combine awareness of complexity with active social engagement.

In the case of all three thinkers discussed in this chapter, civic humanism is richly and complexly conceived: Wollstonecraft's combined emphasis on reason and sensibility, Habermas' three spheres of art, morality and science and Hall's insistence upon diversity, construct citizenship as an art that draws upon a range of human skills and experiences which extend some way beyond 'politics' as we have come to know it. The problem of translating such a richly conceived civic humanism into concrete practice is never far away, for without this practical dimension, the simultaneous emphasis of civic humanism on participatory citizenship is thwarted.[72]

Primary Texts

Mary Wollstonecraft

A Vindication of the Rights of Woman [1792], 2nd edn, ed. Carol Poston (New York: Norton, 1988).
Mary, A Fiction [1788] and The Wrongs of Woman: or, Maria. A Fragment [1798], in Mary and The Wrongs of Woman, ed. James Kinsley and Gary Kelly (Oxford: Oxford University Press, 1980).

Jürgen Habermas

'Modernity – An Incomplete Project' [1980], in Modernism/Postmodernism, ed. Peter Brooker (London: Longman, 1992).
The Theory of Communicative Action, Volume 1 [1981], trans. Thomas McCarthy (Cambridge: Polity, 1984).
The Theory of Communicative Action, Volume 2 [1981], trans. Thomas McCarthy (Cambridge: Polity, 1987).
The Philosophical Discourse of Modernity [1985], trans. Frederick Lawrence (Cambridge: Polity, 1987).

Stuart Hall

'Cultural Studies and the Centre: Some Problematics and Problems', in Culture, Media, Language: Working Papers in Cultural Studies, ed. Stuart Hall et al. (London: Hutchinson, 1980).
The Hard Road to Renewal: Thatcherism and the Crisis of the Left (London: Verso, 1988), particularly 'Learning from Thatcherism' (1988).
'The Toad in the Garden: Thatcherism among the Theorists', in Marxism and the Interpretation of Culture, ed. Cary Nelson and Lawrence Grossberg (Basingstoke: Macmillan, 1988).
(with David Held) 'Citizens and Citizenship', in New Times: The Changing Face of Politics in the 1990s, ed. Stuart Hall and Martin Jacques (London: Lawrence & Wishart, 1989).
'Cultural Studies and its Theoretical Legacies', in Cultural Studies, ed. Lawrence Grossberg et al. (New York: Routledge, 1992).
Stuart Hall: Critical Dialogues in Cultural Studies, ed. David Morley and Kuan-Hsing Chen (London: Routledge, 1996), particularly 'New Ethnicities' (1989), 'The Formation of a Diasporic Intellectual' (1992) and 'What is this "Black" in Black Popular Culture?' (1992).

CHAPTER 5

Spiritual Humanism
(Benjamin – King – Kristeva)

Spiritual humanism may appear to be a contradiction in terms, for humanism has often been defined against religion. According to this perspective, only when God is perceived to be irrelevant or dead can the human come into its own and define itself on its own terms, even though those terms have varied considerably between thinkers. Friedrich Nietzsche, whose work will be discussed in the next chapter, exemplifies this attitude towards religion in *Human, All Too Human* (1878), for he sees the death of God as the condition for an impulsive human creativity to have its day.[1] In a similar vein, Mikhail Bakhtin's paganism, also discussed in the next chapter, is based in part upon the notion of a secularised and self-determining human world liberated from the confines of theology.[2] God, from the perspective of such a secular humanism, is the limit that human beings have to overcome in order to determine their own fate and identity.[3]

Spiritual humanism nevertheless often presents itself as a humanism of a superior kind to its secular counterpart, by pointing to the latter's deficiencies. From a spiritual point of view, secular humanism is too materialistic and soulless, its 'gods' often being the false gods of money, power, sexuality, technology or rationalism. 'What shall it profit a man', asks Martin Luther King, Jr (1929–68), one of the key thinkers discussed in this chapter, 'if he gain the whole world of externals – aeroplanes, electric lights, automobiles, and colour television – and lose the internal – his own soul?'[4] The Renaissance and eighteenth-century Enlightenment saw a shift, according to King, from a 'God-centred universe' to a 'new man-centred religion', the effect of which was that 'the laboratory began to replace the church, and the scientist became a substitute for the prophet'.[5] While King does not totally decry reason, science and technology, he criticises them for their spiritual short-sightedness and for the inflated view of 'man' to which they give rise.

But what is the spiritual? For King, as we shall see, there is a fairly clear answer to this question, since for him 'God is love'.[6] Spirituality according to King is based upon both the recognition of that love and its re-enactment in human relationships. If we lose our capacity for love, we lose our soul. The German theorist Walter Benjamin (1892–1940), another thinker featuring in this chapter, suggests that 'like every generation that preceded us, we have been endowed with a *weak* Messianic power'.[7] This can be taken to mean that our sense of God, as a tangible force in human life, is necessarily weak because of our condition as fallen human beings. It is also weak because of the demise in secularised cultures of organised religion; people whose outlook is secular may still use a theological register and speak, for instance, of an institution or person as 'soulless' or of the 'mental hell' they have experienced or of children as 'angelic', but these phrases are merely the colloquial and leftover traces of theology. King's spirituality, however, is at the opposite end of the spectrum to the weakened sense of theology exemplified in Benjamin's reading of Franz Kafka's 'cloudy' modernist parables that seem to have lost their doctrinal grounding.[8] King's strong messianism is instead unambiguously and conventionally scriptural, the holy scripture being the place where God is understood by King to reveal himself. There are thus two related features of 'strong messianism': one is that God is immanent; the other is a belief in the timeless relevance of a holy writ. King's belief is of course just one version amongst countless other versions, past and present, of a strong messianism, which pits itself against the forces of secularisation. Many different things have been done and said in the name of the holy word or God/prophet felt to be present in the world, from the Islamic fundamentalist fatwah issued against Salman Rushdie in the late 1980s, to the inherited conviction of George Bush Jr at the turn of the millennium that America is blessed and has certain divine rights. King has been chosen to represent the strong sense of the messianic because his is a mainly benevolent, humane example and has a strong political subtext. He has also been selected because while he reverses the displacement of a 'God-centred' by a 'man-centred' religion, a human-centred sense of spirituality is optimistically felt by King to be achievable through love.

Although King's ideals went against some of the theological orthodoxies of his time that placed greater emphasis upon human sinfulness and distance from God, they are still couched in conventionally religious terms. The conventional aspect of 'strong messianism' means that it may be somewhat blind to forms of spirituality that are not obviously or systematically theological. For example, in *The Trumpet of Conscience* (1967), King is partly sympathetic to the spiritual ideals of the 1960s counter-culture, but at the same time suggests that 'the hippies will not last long as a mass group' because 'there is no solution' in the 'flight from reality' and the separatism which according to King characterise the hippie movement.[9] One of the implications of the weak messianic power referred to by Benjamin is that religion does not totally disappear from modern secularised life, but that it mutates, as with the hippie movement, into different forms. For Benjamin, as for many nineteenth- and twentieth-century advocates of high art and Romantic aestheticism such as Adorno, the aesthetic realm is one such form of surrogate theology. The use of the theological term 'canon', as in 'literary canon', to designate a body of revered quasi-sacred texts, points to the surrogate religious role that high art has often been assigned in fulfilling spiritual needs and human aspirations. But Benjamin, as we shall see, does not identify great works of art as the only dwelling place for a weakened theology, for ordinary, everyday capitalist life is also seen by Benjamin as the site of a certain theology.

The third thinker whose work will be discussed in this chapter is the French practitioner and theorist of psychoanalysis, Julia Kristeva (1941–). Kristeva's work can also be considered as a form of weak theology, in that rather than theology 'proper' it is psychoanalysis that is perceived by Kristeva to have a redemptive healing power. Kristevan psychoanalysis also acts as a surrogate religion because it appeals to a form of mysticism. Kristeva's style of psycho-analysis is influenced by poststructuralism and particularly by the idea that concepts – all concepts – are never completely intelligible or 'present'. We may like to think that the concepts we live by – such as self, love, freedom, truth, God, justice, human, experience – are transparent, but such transparency is a metaphysical illusion. The concept of God may be mostly transparent for King, but his emphasis on God as love is one among a plethora of concepts that have waxed and waned during the course of Christian history. Every strong version of messianism will by definition lay claim to the truth about the nature and purpose of God as revealed in the scriptures, but the scriptures (or at least some of them) have been continually reinterpreted and retranslated, often with the radical effect of making one generation's heresy the next generation's ortho-doxy. Total knowledge of God, from this point of view, is a rationalist fallacy.

Kristeva's poststructuralist psychoanalysis is one way in which postmodern culture and theory have turned against the perceived confidence of modern science and reason to penetrate all aspects of reality and have helped to rehabi-litate quasi-religious concepts of Romantic mystery. In 'The Sublime and the Avant-Garde (1988), Jean-François Lyotard examines modernist and post-modernist variations on the Romantic aesthetic of the sublime (discussed further in the Conclusion), while in *The Postmodern Condition* (1979), he enthusiastically embraces what he calls the 'unpresentable': 'let us be witnesses to the unpresentable', he writes, in an attempt to move us beyond the illusion of a reality which is fully penetrable by reason.[10] King's spirituality also stands partly against modern science and reason, but whereas his God is nevertheless rational and knowable, the God of postmodern theology, as represented in this chapter by Kristeva, is an elusive 'Other'. One important strand of theological thought, namely negative theology, holds that God cannot be named or fully understood in human terms.[11] It is this negative or weak theology which informs Kristeva's notion, not just of the spiritual *per se*, but of other concepts such as the body, motherhood and femininity which are themselves 'spiritual-ised' by being treated by Kristeva as partly unnameable. Thus weak messian-ism is manifested in Kristeva's work both in her negative theology (where God is an absent presence), and in her theologising of phenomena existing on the margins of official religious discourse.

This last point is vital, because it raises the key question of whether weak theology constitutes a 'watering down' of conventional religion or a produc-tive challenge to it, a challenge which furthermore revitalises spirituality by finding religion in unexpected or neglected places. In an article on religion in Heidegger's thought, John Peacocke suggests that 'thinking, in the sense of meditative thinking, retains the character of openness, piety and receptiveness only so long as it does not intend an object of belief'. 'Sadly,' he concludes, 'Heidegger abandons his "openness to the mystery" for the neurotic striving to find God.'[12] There are echoes of certain forms of Buddhism here, in the notion that only when the mind empties itself of a possessive intention towards an object can true spirituality occur. Weak theology, from this point of view, paradoxically turns out to be more authentic than its conventional counterpart, because it does not seek to possess God, and because its openness towards religion allows the spiritual to emerge in disregarded or unnoticed places. Weak theology can therefore be said to enable different stories to be told about spirituality. Weak theology also enables us to identify the otherwise hidden mutations of a religious sensibility which have persisted into modernity and postmodernity. Of postmodern culture, Carl Raschke has written:

> [T]he theological thinker privy to the aesthetics and the poetics of the post-modern can begin to envision 'sacrality' not simply as a complex of stock theological emblems or representations, but as a veritable marquee flashing with the evanescent tokens and hints of religious sentimentality in the twentieth century.[13]

For Raschke, so-called 'new religiosity' in postmodern culture 'is nothing new at all. It is simply old-time esotericism, and in many instances archaic super-stitions or dangerous obsessions, repackaged for present-day consumer tastes.' Raschke's invocation of consumerism is not intended as a slur on what he goes on to refer to as 'the *commodification of the arcane and obscure*', but then neither does he display a totally enthusiastic and uncritical acceptance of postmodern consumer religion, such as TV evangelism.[14] The neither/nor attitude points us in the direction of the key questions with which this chapter will be concerned: should those multifarious forms of spirituality engendered by a weakened sense of the messianic be celebrated for their diversity and for their challenge to conventional religion? Or do we need the more conventional anchor that King's spirituality offers? Are some forms of spirituality more 'authentic' than others? Which of them best might serve the interests of a revitalised and critical humanism?

Walter Benjamin

Much of Benjamin's writing, from the mid-1910s to his death in 1940, takes the form of modernist fragments and, as such, does not form a unity. Disunity and fragmented perception are themselves explicitly and persistently thematised by Benjamin, as part of his characterisation of the shock-effect of modern and especially urban life. Where theology, in the scriptural mode, promises to give a meaning and a ground to human life, Benjamin's modernism lends itself more to sporadic glimpses of the divine within the human. The sources of revelation, both profane and sacred, are also many and varied. As Benjamin himself writes in an essay on 'Surrealism' (1929), 'the reader, the thinker, the loiterer, the *flâneur*, are types of illuminati just as much as the opium eater, the dreamer, the ecstatic. And more profane. Not to mention that most terrible drug – ourselves – which we take in solitude.'[15] While the emphasis on profane illumination resulted at times in an attempt by Benjamin to purge his vocabulary of all traces of the theological, religion is nevertheless a persistent, though variably inflected, strain in his thought.[16] Sacred revelation is not the preserve of a single canonical text or tradition: Judaism, Marxism, the proletariat, works of art, books in general, traditional storytelling, the phantasmagoric nature of modern life, are all differently attributed with revelatory, redemptive or 'auratic' power. If this list, like the list of illuminati given by Benjamin, suggests a dissipation of the spiritual, such that it can attach itself to virtually anything, then it simultaneously points in the direction of its renewal. An analogy with Protestantism may be helpful here, for just as Protestantism disturbed the monopoly by official mediators on the word of God, so Benjamin may be seen as de-authorising authorised religion. A Parisian arcade can be the site of an 'auratic' experience just as much as a conventional scripture can be. But the question with which Benjamin is concerned is which kinds of religious or quasi-religious experience are more or less 'quasi', more or less 'authentic' than others.

Modernist fragmentation of the spiritual is at once invoked and parried in Benjamin's 'Theses on the Philosophy of History' (written in 1940). Here Benjamin valorises a 'conception of the present as the "time of the now" which is shot through with chips of Messianic time'.[17] The phrase 'chips of ... time' belongs to a modernist vocabulary of shards and fragmentary moments. This modernist concept of time as disjointed and unpredictable replaces an Enlightenment conception of time as linear, progressive movement.[18] The Messiah may appear at any time and may in fact be already present. Within the Judaic theological tradition to which Benjamin appeals in 'Theses', 'every second of time is the strait gate through which the Messiah might enter': *might enter*, but there is no definite knowing 'when'.[19] Such a modernist conception of time lends itself to a concept of the spiritual as sporadically 'immanent': here today, gone tomorrow.

However, the unknowability of the 'when' of the Messiah or the promised land of Judaism, is offset by the greater certainty about the 'how' the Messiah will make his or her presence felt in human history. In the 'Theses', Benjamin explicitly theologises Marxism. The combination of historical materialism and theology is granted considerable revelatory power by Benjamin with respect to human understanding, ethics and happiness. In terms of understanding, 'only a redeemed mankind', writes Benjamin, 'receives the fullness of its past – which is to say, only for a redeemed mankind has its past become citable in all its moments. Each moment it has lived becomes a *citation à l'ordre du jour* and that day is Judgement Day.'[20] At the day of reckoning, the modernist 'chips of messianic time', which give only momentary insight into the truth of human history, will be transformed into total understanding. Benjamin's future-oriented vision of redeemed perception is based upon the Marxist model of true as opposed to false consciousness. Humanity's fall into false consciousness is manifest in the silence to which the losers of history are condemned by history's ruling-class winners. History viewed from above – from the perspective, that is, of those who have benefited from it – might look like progress and civilisation, but as Benjamin famously puts it in the 'Theses on the Philosophy of History', 'there is no document of civilization which is not at the same time a document of barbarism'.[21] The barbarism of human exploitation is in other words the repressed underside of civilisation. What Benjamin in an essay of 1931 on the Austrian writer Karl Kraus calls 'materialist humanism', undermines the emphasis of 'classical humanism' on civilisation and progress.[22] The impossibility of thinking one thing (civilisation) without the other (barbarism) is an example of the dialectical approach which informs Benjamin's Marxism, as well as other more unambiguously secular Marxist thinkers like Bertolt Brecht. Any account of historical time that ignores this dialectic and speaks only of progress will be guilty of perpetuating a one-sided view: 'the concept of the historical progress of mankind', writes Benjamin, 'cannot be sundered from its progression through a homogeneous, empty time.'[23] In contrast, the messianic and Marxist conception of history involves destroying the false 'continuum of history' in the name of the 'oppressed past'.[24]

In terms of ethics, also, Benjamin's theologised Marxism is the source of revelation. Only when the empty, homogenous time of so-called progress is interrupted, does an ethically 'redemptive' view of the past become possible. Those who have already suffered at the hands of civilisation can be redeemed by a present and future no longer forgetful of them and determined to build on their behalf and in their memory a world free from exploitation. Human fulfilment is also at stake, for while 'the fight for the crude and material things' carries on between classes, human beings cannot fulfil themselves through the 'refined and spiritual things' that life also offers.[25] The theologised Marxism of the 'Theses' is thus granted the power to salvage cognitive, ethical and spiritual truths. This power is nevertheless described by Benjamin as a '*weak* Messianic power', a power that is only available in modernist 'chips' and has to be struggled for against the tide of fallen perception and false consciousness.[26]

In the 'Theses' a version of Marxism and a version of Judaism are the combined sources of the spiritual. Elsewhere, Benjamin turns to other sources. In 'On Some Motifs in Baudelaire' (1939), for example, he develops a theological conception of art. This is in sharp contrast with the anti-theological conception of art proposed in an earlier essay, 'The Work of Art in the Age of Mechanical Reproduction' (1936).[27] In 'On Some Motifs', Benjamin quotes the French poet Charles Baudelaire's claim that art is the place 'on which man has bestowed an imprint of his soul'.[28] Developing the contrasts which Baudelaire draws between photography and art, Benjamin writes that the 'aura' of art is based upon its capacity to return 'our gaze':

> What was inevitably felt to be inhuman, one might say deadly, in daguerreotypy was the (prolonged) looking into the camera, since the camera records our likeness without returning our gaze. Where this expectation is met (which, in the case of thought processes, can apply equally to the look of the eye of the mind and to a glance pure and simple), there is an experience of the aura to the fullest extent.[29]

Auratic art is conceived by Benjamin in both humanist and theological terms. Art is holy and sacred because it speaks to us and 'reflects back at us that of which our eyes will never have their fill'.[30] In contrast with the cold inhuman stare of early photography, auratic art exchanges with us an intimate look.

Photography is one of several, interrelated phenomena which are used in 'On Some Motifs' to characterise modernity. These (mainly) Baudelairean phenomena or motifs include the 'shock experience' of urban life; the 'web of … numberless interconnecting relationships' which exist in 'giant cities'; the aimless wandering of the urban *flâneur*; the 'atrophy of experience' engendered by the replacement of 'narration by information' and 'of information by sensation'; the construction of human beings as 'automatons'; and the fragmentation of time, modern time being likened to 'time in hell' which is 'the province of those who are not allowed to complete anything'.[31] Against these images of anonymity, ephemerality and dehumanisation, Benjamin pits the restorative, revelatory and humanistic power of auratic art, which is nevertheless in decline due to the modern forces of disintegration.

Benjamin does not spell out the nature of art's revelatory power. He does not say what image of the human it invites us to recognise. The implication is that art answers to a need for integration, ground and intimacy, but too much spelling out would bring art too close and would ruin its aura. Towards the end of 'On Some Motifs in Baudelaire', Benjamin writes of Baudelaire's insistence on the 'magic of distance'.[32] Thus if one theological conception of the work of art is based upon the idea of an intimate communion in which we recognise our needs, then the 'magic of distance' represents another more mystical conception, which breaks up the magic circle of complete communion and encourages a sense of wonder. The aura of distance, as opposed to the aura of communion, exceeds the human and thereby renders the spiritual within the human less definable. It is the partial ineffability of the spiritual that also allows it to keep appearing in Benjamin's work in different guises and with the attendant danger that it becomes too dissipated, too elusive. Against this perspective, however, we might say that Benjamin productively multiplies the sources of 'redemption' beyond the authorised channels of conventional religion and high art. This expansion of the spiritual occurs in 'On Some Motifs', when Benjamin, via Baudelaire, likens the blankly staring eyes of the urban crowd to 'eyes of which one is inclined to say that they have lost their ability to look'.[33] The inference, here, is that it is not just in auratic works of art that the human gaze is lovingly returned, for the stranger in the modern urban crowd who does reciprocate the look of another stranger would also be a source of spiritual illumination.

In another piece on Baudelaire, 'Modernism' (written in 1938), Benjamin quotes Baudelaire's definition of a new kind of poet as 'ragpicker':

> Here we have a man who has to gather the day's refuse in the capital city. Everything that the big city threw away, everything it lost, everything it despised, everything it crushed underfoot, he catalogues and collects. He collates the annals of intemperance, the *caphernaüm* (stockpile) of waste.[34]

The image of the ragpicker illuminates Benjamin's own practice as a gleaner of seemingly insignificant or minuscule phenomena, such as the invention of matches.[35] The poet-as-ragpicker is also comparable with the practice of Surrealist poets like André Breton and Paul Éluard, for the Surrealist wrenches objects out of their customary contexts and reassembles them within a new, revelatory constellation.[36] Benjamin's interest in the figures of the ragpicker and the Surrealist is closely connected to his ongoing concern with the theological theme of redemption, in other words, with salvaging the concealed significance of phenomena from the 'throw-away' mentality of consumer capitalism. This involves Benjamin in a search for redemptive meaning in places and in objects where such meaning might not normally be found.

The nature of the redemptive light that Benjamin casts on the 'refuse' of modern life is often profane rather than sacred.[37] Indeed, it is against capitalism's own quasi-theological characteristics that Benjamin poses his profane, demystificatory analyses. As Rainer Rochlitz has suggested, Benjamin diagnoses modern life in two different ways.[38] On the one hand, there is the analysis offered in 'The Work of Art in the Age of Mechanical Reproduction' and 'On Some Motifs in Baudelaire', where Benjamin shows how the cold impersonal stare of technology and modern life has led to the decline of aura. Rochlitz points out that this diagnosis corresponds with Max Weber's influential disenchantment thesis, also drawn on by Taylor and Habermas (see Chapters 1 and 4), which proposed that religion in modernity has been displaced by science and rationalisation.[39] On the other hand, capitalism is characterised by Benjamin in terms of its production of pre-scientific and pre-rational 'phantasmagoria', of which the commodity is a primary example. Writing of the nineteenth-century vogue for 'national exhibitions of industry', he suggests that the 'world exhibitions' which succeeded them 'were places of pilgrimage to the fetish Commodity'. He continues by invoking Marx's reference to the '"theological capers" of the commodity'.[40] From the profane, ascetic perspective of a Marxism bent on exposing the illusions of capitalism, commodities are phantasmagoric because they conceal the actual, profit-driven conditions of human labour under which they are produced (see the discussion of Marx in Chapter 1). The profane conditions of the commodity's production are thereby 'transcended', to use a religious term, in the illusory independence of the commodity. The past and present tendency of advertisers to anthropomorphicise commodities might itself be seen, along Benjaminian lines, as appropriating from religion and high art their auratic ability to return our gaze. Benjamin's profane response to the phantasmagoric nature of capitalism is to demystify it. Thus just as barbarism is exposed in 'Theses on the Philosophy of History' as the concealed underside of progress and civilisation, so the hidden life of the commodity is hinted at as part of Benjamin's redemption of human suffering from forgetfulness and false consciousness.

It would be misleading, however, to characterise this aura-breaking aspect of Benjamin's writing only in terms of a profane redemption, which impels us to wake up from the 'dream-world' of capitalism. Because capitalism, from the perspective of Weber's disenchantment thesis, is itself destructive of its own aura, there is something to be salvaged – namely a potentially more authentic form of spirituality – from what Benjamin refers to as the 'ruins of the bourgeoisie'.[41] As a tireless ragpicker with a theological cast of mind, Benjamin invests with redemptive significance what has been, or is about to be, discarded or emptied of meaning. Hannah Arendt describes Benjamin's often employed method of quotation as 'the modern equivalent of ritual invocations, and the spirits that now arise invariably are those spiritual essences from a past that have suffered the Shakespearean "sea-change" from living eyes to pearls, from living bones to corals'.[42] Given the demise, partly welcomed by Benjamin, of authorised religious and communal traditions, the sources of the spiritual are both threatened and dispersed. It is the self-appointed task of Benjamin partly to preserve those failing traditions, but also to look for redemption in unlikely or forgotten places.

Martin Luther King, Jr

Of all the thinkers discussed in this book, it is probably the African-American civil rights activist Martin Luther King, Jr who offers the clearest message about the meaning and purpose of human life. 'What is the *summum bonum* of life?' asks King in a sermon preached in Montgomery, Alabama in 1956. 'I think I have discovered the highest good,' he continues: 'It is love. This principle stands at the center of the cosmos.' This principle for King is the central message of the Christian gospel: 'As John says, "God is love." He who loves is a participant in the being of God. He who hates does not know God.'[43] Throughout his writings, speeches and sermons on civil rights, racism, segregation, the philosophy of non-violence, Vietnam, communism and capitalism, he argues for the founding principle that love completes us, that love is what God intended us for, that love fulfils our innermost needs and desires, and that love is therefore the answer to the problems of the world. For King, love is unambiguously the source of human well-being and the principal message of his primary text, the Bible. Where the sources of profane and spiritual redemption in Benjamin's writing are many and varied, and where the magic of intimate communion jostles with the magic of distance in Benjamin's conceptualisation of aura, King's writings and speeches find their primary inspiration in the Bible and in love.

Racial discrimination, and the hatred and fear that underpin it, are specific social and moral evils for King, which he saw as part of the history of Euro-American colonisation and enslavement. But racial discrimination is also implicated by King in a universal, theologised history of the struggle between good and evil, love and hate, freedom and subjugation, homecoming and exile. These are familiar Biblical themes, whose present relevance to black and Asian populations is established through King's use of typology: thus the freedom fighter Moses prefigures Mahatma Gandhi;[44] the opening of the Red Sea prefigures the emancipation of the 'oppressed masses in Asia and Africa' as well as the entry of the American black population into the promised land of equal citizenship;[45] the 'extremist for justice', Amos, prefigures Jesus who prefigures Paul who prefigures Martin Luther who prefigures Abraham

Lincoln who prefigures Martin Luther King himself.[46] The one sacred text, the one Book of Life, thus makes sense of the whole of human history, through the perceived recurrence of archetypal experiences.

Where the universalising mode of typology employed by King threatens at times to reduce concrete human beings to mere ciphers within a preordained scriptural history, human participation is safeguarded through King's persistent emphasis upon human compassion as a mirror of divine compassion. In this way the history prefigured in the scriptures does not operate behind people's backs, as it were, but within people's hearts. 'At the heart of reality', says King, 'is a Heart.'[47] This grounding of human reality upon the bedrock of love is pitted against the decentring and degrading of human beings that racial segregation entails. In his famous 'Letter from Birmingham City Jail' of 1963, in which he replies to eight prominent white churchmen and critics of his work, King writes that 'segregation' is an 'existential expression of man's tragic separation, an expression of his awful estrangement'.[48] Here, as in previous writings, King is selectively drawing upon the existentialist notion of a precarious and meaningless world in which human existence outstrips any attempt to define an unchanging human essence.[49] Where certain existentialists, like Sartre, tend to treat essences as permanently irrecoverable and the human condition as a condition of permanent exile (see Chapter 2), King's scriptural humanism confidently names the 'home' to which we might return. Home is the God of love, the God who enables us to overcome the tragic separation of race from race, and of human beings from themselves:

> When we are staggered by the chilly winds of adversity and battered by the raging storms of disappointment and when through our folly and sin we stray into some destructive far country and are frustrated because of a strange feeling of homesickness, we need to know that there is Someone who loves us, cares for us, understands us, and will give us another chance.[50]

The notion that God is love – and that God as love is within us – serves to humanise God, at the same time as it beckons us home to our fully human selves.

Scripture is also humanised by the implication that black Americans are themselves now key players in the universal history of good versus evil, not only in their struggle against the God-forsaken evils of oppression, but in the non-violent and therefore compassionate means of achieving liberation. 'Nonviolent resistance', writes King in 'Nonviolence and Racial Justice' (1957), 'does not seek to defeat or humiliate the opponent, but to win his friendship and understanding.'[51] In contrast to Frantz Fanon's combative philosophy, King's emphasis on non-violence towards the oppressor is based upon loving 'the person who does the evil deed while hating the deed that the person does'.[52] Non-violence, he writes in 'The Current Crisis in Race Relations' (1958) thus breaks 'the chain of hate by projecting the ethics of love into the center of our lives' and contributes towards 'the creation of the beloved community', a redeemed community based on 'reconciliation'.[53] Black American non-violent protesters are thus cast in the role of enlightened spiritual mentors for white America and for humanity in general. 'If there is a victory', writes King, 'it will be a victory, not merely for fifty thousand Negroes, but a victory for justice and the forces of life.'[54] As we discussed in relation to Fanon in Chapter 2, where white Americans and Europeans have in the past associated 'white' with enlightened humanity and 'black' with the less than fully human, King inverts this binary. It is not simply an inversion, however, for the implication is that no previous humanism can have a claim to authentic universality if it fails to take account of the sacredness of all human life. Non-violent protest demonstrates the black person's respect for the white man as a sacred human being, even if the latter fails to return the compliment.[55]

King had his critics, both during and after his lifetime. Malcolm X characterised him as 'just a twentieth century Uncle Tom', who was subsidised by the white man 'to teach the Negroes to be defenseless'.[56] From the perspective of the advocates of the Black Power and black consciousness movements, such as Malcolm X and Harold Cruse, King's pursuit of integrationist policies, which were based on the universality of love and also in partial harmony with the ideals of the white American constitution, were at the expense of black cultural and political autonomy.[57] King's pacifism was itself seen as playing into the hands of white America by entreating upon black Americans a passivity that reinforced the racial stereotype of the humble slave who knows his or her place. The charges that King was not black enough can be offset by the attempts of some subsequent critics to reclaim King on behalf of one or another version of African-American cultural identity. Thus Keith Miller argues for the continuity between King and the tradition of black slave songs and sermons based upon the typology of deliverance;[58] John Patton argues that the creation in primarily oral contexts of 'empathy and identification' is 'characteristic of much of King's public discourse and reflected a central feature of the tradition of black preaching' – Patton also suggests as a source for King's 'I Have a Dream' speech of August 1963, the call-and-response pattern of traditional West Indian calypso music;[59] Robert Harrison and Linda Harrison likewise stress the importance of the oral call-and-response tradition, but trace it back to the 'African oral tradition known as *nommo*'.[60] There are some common strands here, participation and 'the emotionality of conventional black religion', as Richard King puts it, being two of them.[61] According to these perspectives, Martin Luther King *was* black, in the sense that he drew on aspects of a distinctively African-American pulpit and slave song culture which itself drew on older African traditions. However, in every attempt to invoke a black (or female or working-class) tradition as the site of alternative value to white (or male or bourgeois) traditions, there is the danger of the falsely homogenising stereotype. Moreover, King's own concern, as a humanist and integrationist, is not to insert himself self-consciously within a distinctive cultural tradition, but to emphasise what human beings might share in common. The tradition of African-American spirituality can teach racist and materialist America the way, but the end is not the assertion of cultural tradition *per se*, but the universality, based on love, which is present in the tradition.

King himself engages with some of the criticisms, past and present, of the Christian view of love. Against Nietzsche's view that Christian love saps the vitality of 'pagan' instincts by elevating the morality of compassion above the natural will to power, King writes, in *Where Do We Go From Here: Chaos or Community?* (1967):

> One of the greatest problems of history is that the concepts of love and power are usually contrasted as polar opposites … It was this misinterpretation that caused Nietzsche, the philosopher of the 'will to power,' to reject the Christian concept of love … What is needed is a realization that power without love is reckless and abusive and that love without power is sentimental and anemic. Power at its best is love implementing the demands of justice. Justice at its best is love correcting everything that stands against love.[62]

King attempted to overcome the polarisation of love and power, by persistently empowering love and the non-violence which demonstrated the principle of love-in-action in the civil rights protests. King empowered love and non-violence in various ways: by citing the success of Gandhi in India; by making of love a world-transforming principle and associating it with humanity's homecoming; by opposing inner to outer strength – the non-violent method, says King in 'An Experiment in Love' (1958) 'is passive physically but strongly active spiritually';[63] by elevating the moral status of the non-violent campaigner; by emphasising the way that love and non-violence liberate the self from the age-old cycle of retaliatory violence; and by showing that love is by no means a soft option since it is hard to love someone from whom one receives 'hostility and persecution'.[64] This last principle expresses one of the characteristics which King identified with *agape* love. Drawing on Greek ideas, King distinguishes between three types of love: *agape*, *eros* and *philia*. Of these three, *agape* is the most difficult because according to King, it is 'unmotivated, groundless, and creative. It is not set in motion by any quality or function in the object.'[65] The person who expresses hate is easier to hate rather than love, but that person, according to King, is in need of love. 'Since the white man's personality', says King, '[is] greatly distorted by segregation, and his soul is greatly scarred, he needs the love of the Negro. The Negro must love the white man, because the white man needs his love to remove his tensions, insecurities, and fears.'[66] This is controversial: why should the African-American attend to the white American's needs, given the latter's failure to reciprocate such care? Why add to the African-American's own troubles by placing this moral burden of responsibility upon him or her? The counter-perspective is that King empowers the love shown by the oppressed towards his or her oppressor, by turning the oppressor into the victim and the oppressed into the potential healer of all victimisation.

Agape also enabled King to differentiate between the person and the institution, self and society. Non-violent resistance, according to King, 'is directed against the forces of evil rather than against persons who happen to be doing the evil. It is evil that the nonviolent register seeks to defeat, not the persons victimised by evil.'[67] The emphasis upon the institutional aspect of racism goes some way towards accommodating the more pessimistic insistence, voiced by such leading American Protestant theologians as Reinhold Niebuhr, upon collective human sinfulness. King refers in an interview from the mid-1960s to Niebuhr's contention, in *Moral Man and Immoral Society* (1932), that 'individuals may see the moral light and voluntarily abandon their unjust posture, but groups tend to be more immoral, and more intransigent, than individuals'.[68] One of the implications of this argument for King was that, like Levinas' intimate spirituality (see Chapter 3), love might work on an interpersonal face-to-face level, but not on an institutional level. Christianised *agape* offers a partial solution to this problem, for it has a depersonalising effect by focusing attention upon the sin and not the sinner, upon the collective forces that shape the individual. At the same time, Christianised *agape*, by distinguishing the person from the social, maintains the notion of a self that might be released from his or her entrapment within the false values of this world into the higher and more authentically human reality of love. The transformed self might then make a difference to those intransigent institutions which use human beings as their mouthpieces. 'The hardhearted individual', writes King in *Strength to Love* (1963), 'never sees people as people, but rather as mere objects or as impersonal cogs in an ever-turning wheel.'[69] To totally identify sinner with sin would be to reduce the person to a mere cog in the machine of institutionalised injustice. Thus *agape*, by separating sin from sinner, focuses on the institutionalised sin that 'speaks through' the individual, at the same time as it maintains a notion of the person freed from false values.[70]

This dialectic of freedom and entrapment is applicable to King himself. Refusal of the unjust and violent ways of this world expresses his nonconformity. King at times self-consciously places himself in a tradition of Christian nonconformists who 'refused to shape their witness according to the mundane patterns of the world'.[71] But nonconformity to the ways of this world involves conformity to the higher reality of God. In his earlier *Stride Toward Freedom* (1958), which tells the story of the Montgomery Bus Boycott of 1955, King writes of his anxiety before giving a particular sermon. Having been catapulted into the public eye, he wonders how he should present himself. He finally tells himself: 'Keep Martin Luther King in the background and God in the foreground and everything will be all right. Remember you are a channel of the gospel and not the source.'[72] Although King was a potent leader and agitator, he emphasises that he himself is a mere mouthpiece for both the spirit of a people and for the gospel. However, the serving as a mouthpiece for the gospel does not draw us away from our selves, but closer to them. This is the central message of King's scripturally grounded spiritual humanism.

Julia Kristeva

'Do you have a soul?' asks Julia Kristeva at the beginning of her *New Maladies of the Soul* (1993). 'This question', she continues, 'which may be philosophical, theological, or simply misguided in nature, has a particular relevance for our time. In the wake of psychiatric medicines, aerobics, and media zapping, does the soul still exist?'[73] Having explicitly invoked the obvious bearing that theology has on this question, Kristeva proceeds to offer a partly theological diagnosis of modern life as a 'fallen', soulless realm of misplaced values: 'we have neither the time nor the space needed', she writes, 'to create a soul for ourselves'; 'modern man' she continues, is a 'narcissist' who 'becomes swept away by insignificant and valueless objects that offer a perverse pleasure, but no satisfaction'.[74] However, if Kristeva's theological register tells us that we have lost touch with the deeper realities associated with the soul, then the remedy to this malady is not necessarily provided by theology. There are, she writes, '*different* models of the soul', different ways, in other words, of rediscovering human depth.[75] Unlike Martin Luther King, Kristeva is thus no scripturalist, she is not a 'believer', as she says in *In the Beginning was Love* (1985).[76] Her principal way of reintroducing the soul into a soulless world is not through theology, but psychoanalysis. For 'soul' we should therefore read 'psychic life', for it is psychic life, in all its complexity, that is impoverished by modern values: 'today's men and women – who are stress-ridden and eager to achieve, to spend money, have fun, and die – dispense with the representation of their experience that we call psychic life.'[77] Kristeva's version of psychoanalysis nevertheless borrows from theology certain religious themes. Psychoanalysis is, in this respect, a surrogate theology or, to recall Walter Benjamin, a '*weak*' form of 'messianic power', in that it attempts to be redemptive, but without recourse to theology proper. Psychoanalysis for Kristeva is an attempt to resurrect psychic life, to redeem 'subjectivity' from 'its amputated state'.[78]

But if psychoanalysis is a form of surrogate theology, then theology, and specifically Christian theology, is a form of surrogate psychoanalysis.[79] The beginnings of the history of interiority – of a deep and complex psychic life – are difficult to pinpoint, but for Kristeva in *New Maladies of the Soul*, the Bible and particularly the New Testament stand near the beginning of this history. What the New Testament does for Kristeva is to, as it were, 'heat up' language, to give language a revitalised affective and expressive dimension. Words are not merely words, therefore, but part of an intense psychodrama. In John's Gospel, 'John's interpretation of signs', writes Kristeva, 'starts off as a sensualism, if not as a replenishment of affects (what the Evangelist essentially says is "you are hungry and thirsty.") ... John insists that the *sense of sight* alone does not represent the intensity of your experience with these signs.'[80] Kristeva is echoing the way many believers, like King, may often feel that a scripture such as the Bible is speaking intimately to them about who they are. And the New Testament for Kristeva is especially intimate. However, what it reveals is not only love but also, following Freud, a complex Oedipal drama.

In her work, Kristeva offers challenging accounts of the Oedipal drama, but the essence of the Oedipal scenario at work in Western religious discourse is described in her book *In the Beginning was Love*. It is worth quoting at length, because it contains within it some vital Kristevan themes:

> [I]n reading about famous mystical experiences, I felt that faith could be described, perhaps rather simplistically, as what can only be called a primary identification with a loving and protective agency. Overcoming the notion of irremediable separation, Western man, using 'semiotic' rather than 'symbolic' means, reestablishes continuity or fusion with an Other that is no longer substantial and maternal but symbolic and paternal. Saint Augustine goes so far as to compare the Christian's faith in God with the infant's relation to its mother's breast. 'What am I even at the best but an infant sucking the milk Thou givest, and feeding upon Thee, the food that perisheth not?' What we have here is fusion with a breast that is ... succoring, nourishing, loving, and protective, but transposed from the mother's body to an invisible agency located in another world. This is quite a wrench from the dependency of early childhood, and it must be said that it is a compromise solution, since the benefits of the new relationship of dependency are of an imaginary order, in the realm of signs.[81]

As in some versions of religion, so, also, in Kristevan psychoanalysis, exile and separation are key human experiences: in religious terms, our fallen, sinful state separates us from God; in psychoanalytic terms, we are exiled from our first love object, the mother or mother figure. In the above passage, Kristeva in fact views God as a surrogate mother-figure, mystical fusion with whom repairs some of the damage done by the original separation from the mother.

But there is an important additional surrogate referred to in this passage that Kristeva inherits from Jacques Lacan: namely language. Where the first dependency on the mother was concrete and physical, subsequent attempts to re-enact the fusion we once experienced take place in language, in signs. Language itself is a kind of banishment, therefore, in that it exiles us from the body into the realm of abstract and disembodied signs. However, the abstract nature of language can be overcome by what Kristeva refers to as 'semiotic' language, for semiotic language puts us back in touch with our psychic life, and in particular with the all-important (for psychoanalysts) pre-history of our psychic life. It reminds us of the trauma of exile, of our human needs, and of the origins of what we call 'identity' in a complex and unresolved series of identifications (with the mother, with the father, with surrogate mothers, with language itself). The Bible, for Kristeva in *New Maladies of the Soul*, is therefore a semiotic text, because it probes into '*the ambivalent desire for the other*, for the mother as the first other, *which is at the base, that is, on the other side of that which makes me into a speaking being* (a separating, dividing, joining being)'. 'The Bible', she continues, 'is a text that thrusts its words into my losses.'[82] The Bible is thus granted the revelatory power to reveal the human soul or, in psychoanalytic terms, psychic life to us.

Sometimes Kristeva unambiguously names the origin of our loss in a similar manner to King. In each case it is love: God as love for King; desire of and for the mother in the case of Kristeva. However, it is also important for Kristeva that home is the place to which one cannot return. The maternal origin lies '*on the other side of that which makes me into a speaking subject*'. Whereas the divine origin, for King, can be rescued in the *agape* love that we show for each other, the maternal origin, for Kristeva, cannot be fully articulated since the imagined fusion with the mother occurred before language. Moreover, the pre-linguistic state of infancy is not characterised by Kristeva solely in terms of a sheltering mother figure, for early infancy is a more volatile and unruly affair. Babies, in other words, know no boundaries, not only in the sense that they do not differentiate between persons (hence the idea of the infant existing in a state of fusion with the mother), but also in the sense that their bodies are unco-ordinated (or what Lyotard would call a positive inflection of 'the inhuman'; see the Conclusion). In her earlier book *Revolution in Poetic Language* (1974), Kristeva suggests that the bodily drives of the infant are as 'full of movement' as they are 'regulated'.[83] Semiotic language will be unregulated, therefore, and disturb the composure of adult identity that has repressed its origins in the excitable state of the infantile body.

In her materialist and worldly emphasis on the body, Kristeva departs from those varieties of orthodox religion which see the body as a curse to be trans-cended. In this respect, Kristeva could have been discussed in the following chapter as a pagan humanist, who questions the conventionally high humanist discourses of mind and spirit and articulates instead a species of humanism grounded in the body. Indeed, Kristeva is at times so materialist that any kind of spiritual humanism seems a comforting illusion. In *Black Sun: Depression and Melancholia* (1987), her discussion of the painting *The Body of the Dead Christ in the Tomb*, by the sixteenth-century artist Hans Holbein, emphasises the way that the laws of nature seem to have consumed Christ's divinity, for the picture according to Kristeva 'seems to give expression to the idea of a dark, insolent, and senseless eternal power, to which everything is sub-ordinated'.[84] Here, the physical body and its decay are realities which give the lie to divinity. However, Kristeva never entirely relinquishes a mystical conception of the body. Although her tendency to identify femininity with motherhood has been criticised for its essentialism, Kristeva's rapturous mysticism means that the maternal body defeats precise definition.[85] As the inspiration for imaginary as much as for real identifications we can play creatively with different metaphors of maternity, knowing that the reality on which those metaphors are based is elusive. In her experimental essay 'Stabat Mater' (1983), Kristeva combines physical and supra-physical, semiotic and symbolic registers, the effect of which is to render the experience of mother-hood simultaneously concrete and metaphorical.[86] 'Stabat Mater' also spirit-ualises motherhood by recreating, through its historical account of the cult of the Virgin Mary, a theology of the mother which challenges male-centred religion. Kristeva is paradoxically at her most mystical and materialist when she invokes such terms as *chora*, body, mother or woman, because they are simultaneously within and beyond what we can know and represent. If physical decay is an undeniable fact of human existence, then the 'pre-linguistic' origin and 'post-linguistic' destination of the body wrest a realm of freedom and imagination from this realm of necessity. In *The Feminine and the Sacred* (1998), written in epistolary form with Catherine Clément, Kristeva asks: 'What if what we call "the sacred" were the celebration of a mystery, the mystery of the emergence of meaning?'[87] She goes on in a subsequent letter to differentiate between 'belief and religion' on the one hand and 'the sacred' on the other.[88] Religion and belief are consoling and empowering, whereas the sacred is associated with borderlines, thresholds and incompleteness.

By thinking about the sacred in this open way Kristeva, like Benjamin, creates the spiritual as a movable feast, whose limits cannot be firmly set. This weak messianism is, also, for Kristeva a humble messianism that is bound up with the question of gender. Women are said by Kristeva to be 'more apt to agree "humbly" to play a "minimal role" in the vast universe'.[89] Consequently '"they" do not really aspire to give meaning'.[90] If this appears to support another gender stereotype of feminine passivity and humility, then these qualities can also be a potential source of resistance to what Kristeva refers to as 'the Spectacle in which the religion of the Word culminates'.[91] By 'religion of the Word', Kristeva means the faith placed in the ability of language to name everything, while the term 'Spectacle' recalls her diagnosis (at the beginning of *New Maladies of the Soul*) of mass-mediated, late capitalist society as a society in which superficial and addictive images replace the depth of psychic life: 'You are overwhelmed with images. They carry you away, they replace you, you are dreaming. The rapture of the hallucination originates in the absence of boundaries between pleasure and reality, between truth and falsehood. The spectacle is life as a dream.'[92] This also recalls Benjamin's account of the phantasmagoric nature of capitalism, but in Kristeva's case the antidote to a society that attempts to reduce reality to the image is the cultivation of a sense of the irreducible.

It would be misleading, however, to over-emphasise Kristeva's mysticism, for it is the provocative border between meaning and the suspension of meaning which interests her. Elsewhere in *The Feminine and the Sacred*, she writes of the advantages as well as disadvantages of secrecy. Drawing attention to the way that 'the sacred and secrecy have journeyed side by side throughout history', Kristeva suggests that a complacent secrecy would be just as harmful as a theology or psychoanalysis committed to 'display' in that it would render the soul or psychic life too opaque, too invisible.[93] Given, also, the long-standing association of men with 'presence' and selfhood and women with 'absence' and selflessness, feminine mysticism might only reinforce another gender stereotype.[94] The 'rehabilitation of secrecy' recommended by Kristeva in *The Feminine and the Sacred* thus suggests a form of spirituality that exists on the threshold between mystery and conspicuous display.[95] The spiritual in the human remains concealed, but not so concealed that it cannot be brought to light in the non-orthodox ways suggested by Kristeva's feminised religion.[96]

Kristeva's emphasis on physical decay and Benjamin's on human barbarism point to an irredeemably fallen human world, where human spirituality is questioned from the perspective of certain inescapable facts about human existence. In stressing the material limits of the human, both can be seen as foundationalist thinkers, although in a mainly pessimistic sense, in that their notion of limits is tinged with postlapsarian sadness. The emphasis of both thinkers on limits also persists in the more spiritual aspects of their writing, through their insistence on those aspects of material and non-material reality that as mortal beings we cannot fully know. However, one effect of this emphasis on limits is to simultaneously evoke a sense of hidden realities that can sometimes be accessed and rescue us from our finite and fallen existence. Moreover, such is the nature of Benjamin's and Kristeva's weakened theology that the spiritual is located in unexpected places within the otherwise finite world of human beings. King, too, is a foundationalist thinker, but more optimistically so, since his sense of the gulf separating individuals from their higher, spiritual selves is not so great. King's theology is also less mystical than the other two thinkers, for the spiritual can be confidently named as love.

Primary Texts

Walter Benjamin

Charles Baudelaire: A Lyric poet in the Era of High Capitalism, trans. Harry Zohn (London: NLB, 1973).

Illuminations, trans. Harry Zohn, ed. Hannah Arendt (London: Fontana, 1973), particularly 'Franz Kafka' (1934), 'The Work of Art in the Age of Mechanical Reproduction' (1936), 'On Some Motifs in Baudelaire' (1939) and 'Theses on the Philosophy of History' (1940).

One Way Street and Other Writings, trans. Edmund Jephcott and Kingsley Shorter (London: Verso, 1985), particularly 'Surrealism' (1929) and 'Karl Kraus' (1931).

Martin Luther King, Jr

A Testament of Hope: The Essential Writings of Martin Luther King, Jr, ed. James Washington (San Francisco, CA: Harper & Row, 1986), particularly 'Nonviolence and Racial Justice' (1957), 'An Experiment in Love' (1958), *Stride Toward Freedom* (1958), 'The Current Crisis in Race Relations' (1958), 'Letter from Birmingham City Jail' (1963), *The Trumpet of Conscience* (1967) and *Where Do We Go From Here: Chaos or Community?* (1967).

Strength to Love [1963] (London: Collins, 1977).

Julia Kristeva

Revolution in Poetic Language [1974], trans. Margaret Waller (New York: Columbia University Press, 1984).

Tales of Love [1983], trans. Leon Roudiez (New York: Columbia University Press, 1987).

In the Beginning Was Love [1985], trans. Arthur Goldhammer (New York: Columbia University Press, 1987).

Black Sun: Depression and Melancholia [1987], trans. Leon Roudiez (New York: Columbia University Press, 1989).

New Maladies of the Soul [1993], trans. Ross Guberman (New York: Columbia University Press, 1995).

(with Catherine Clément) *The Feminine and the Sacred* [1998], trans. Jane Marie Todd (Basingstoke: Palgrave, 2001).

CHAPTER 6

Pagan Humanism
(Nietzsche – Bakhtin – Bataille)

In Shakespeare's *King Lear* (1605), Gloucester characterises the pagan gods in terms of their malicious playfulness: 'As flies to wanton boys, are we to th'Gods;/They kill us for their sport.'[1] The pagan gods can be regarded, from an anthropocentric perspective, as projections of base human characteristics: in *King Lear* human cruelty overpowers kindness, self-aggrandisement makes a mockery of compassion and the violence which reaches its apotheosis in the gouging of Gloucester's eyes is ever more deliriously transgressive of moral boundaries. Seventeenth-century English drama is prone to dramatising extreme violations of conventional morality and the exotic violence frequently accompanying them. Such violations are often associated with a wild, unrestrained Greek or Roman paganism. As Giovanni in John Ford's *'Tis Pity She's a Whore* (1633) prepares to take revenge on his sister for her perceived betrayal of their incestuous relationship, he invokes the classical pagan underworld: 'Be dark, bright sun,/And make this midday night, that thy gilt rays/May not behold a deed will turn their splendour/More sooty than the poets feign their Styx!'[2] Giovanni subsequently enters the final scene of the play 'trimmed in reeking blood', with his sister's heart impaled on the end of his dagger.[3]

A number of the humanisms considered in this book are fairly high-minded: witness the concern in civic humanism for the common good, the ethic of sensitivity to the Other in dialogic humanism, and the appeal in spiritual humanism to both orthodox and unorthodox theologies as moral resources. Pagan humanism, of the kind evoked in *King Lear* and *'Tis Pity She's a Whore*, is different, for 'pagan' here refers to those wild, intemperate aspects of human nature prohibited and denigrated by orthodox religious discourses or self-styled 'civilised' life. Extreme passion, incestuous or otherwise, will out and there is little that 'the laws of conscience and of civil use' can do to prevent it.[4] Prohibitions are artificial, externally imposed rules designed to curb natural passions and instincts; this is one of the arguments from nature employed by pagan humanism.

Although pagan humanism often looks backwards for its inspiration to pre-Christian or pre-modern societies, certain nineteenth- and twentieth-century movements may also be regarded as broadly pagan in orientation. The organicism of Romantic writers like Keats and August Schlegel is one example, although it is the natural spontaneity and often compassionate morality of feeling, as opposed to the ethically transgressive wildness of the untameable body that is mainly privileged. Another example, from the twentieth century, is psycho-analysis. In its emphasis on insurgent bodily drives of the kind described by Kristeva, psychoanalysis can be thought of as a modern 'science' which takes as its object of enquiry the human instincts often associated with paganism. Certain strands of modernism, such as Surrealism, also emphasise deregulated perception as the basis of a more instinctive art. Where spirituality or reason are often placed near the centre of high humanist discourses as part of a moral outlook, the body and transgressive passion are the alternative centres of these versions of pagan humanism. According to Friedrich Nietzsche (1844–1900), discussed as one of the three thinkers in this chapter, the high-mindedness of morality (most often Christian) teaches us to loathe the body: 'On his way to becoming an "angel"', writes Nietzsche sarcastically, 'man has evolved that queasy stomach and coated tongue through which not only the joy and innocence of the animal but life itself has become repugnant to him – so that he sometimes holds his nose in his own presence.'[5] In his evocation of the 'joy and innocence of the animal', Nietzsche praises spontaneity, lack of inhibition and untamed thought. Tamed thought no longer has the pagan power to shock and transgress and it is the concept of the pagan as transgressive to which Nietzsche and the Nietzschean-inspired French thinker Georges Bataille (1897–1962) are especially drawn.

An exuberant Nietzschean irreverence towards sacred truths of all kinds also informs the more recent postmodern paganism of Lyotard. In his dialogue 'Lessons in Paganism' (1989), Lyotard presents a positive image of the pagan as a godless infidel who is not held captive by supposedly sacred truths. According to one of the speakers in the dialogue, the word *pagus* (from which the term pagan is derived) 'was used to refer to the frontier region on the edge of towns'. In such regions, 'you don't feel at home' and 'you do not expect to discover the truth; but you do meet lots of entities who are liable to undergo metamorphoses, to tell lies, and to become jealous or angry: passible gods'.[6] Pagan cultures may have gods, but the gods do not have to be obeyed because 'their word is no more to be trusted than the word of a man'.[7] For Lyotard, as for Nietzsche, truth is just a pious fiction that represses its basis in story and myth. Although the main speaker in 'Lessons' is himself a duplicitous pagan persona (whom we therefore do not have to trust) and, although he is suspi-cious of pious appeals to truth and justice, he nevertheless calls for a 'politics which is both godless and just'.[8] In 'Lessons', stories which are obviously stories are regarded as more just than grand quasi-scientific theories which suppress their fictional status, such as Marxism, because they are based on the egalitarian principle that 'anyone can tell stories'.[9] There is an implied organicist and ethical appeal here to the presumed naturalness of storytelling. The organicism relates to the privileging of instinct in pagan humanism, while the ethical appeal moralises the pagan irreverence and amoral impulsiveness that characterise Nietzsche's work. While the body and the senses are seen by all three thinkers discussed here as subverting the perceived piety of high-minded humanisms, their compatibility with ethical concerns is also sometimes evident. 'Low' and 'high' are, in other words, inverted, so that the conventionally low replaces the conventionally high as a source of moral value. The incestuous Giovanni in *'Tis Pity She's a Whore* himself attempts to invert conventional morality and replace it with his own natural morality by insisting on the instinctive bond – 'one flesh, one love, one heart, one all' – which unites brother and sister.[10] Such a 'moralised' pagan humanism is appealing because its morality appears to be rooted in the rhythms of nature. According to such a perspective, it is surely better to have a morality which indulges rather than renounces the flesh and has nature as its guiding light. One of the most successful examples of a moralised paganism of this kind can be found in the concept of carnival elaborated by the Russian critic Mikhail Bakhtin (1895– 1975). It is for his discussion of grotesque corporeality and the carnivalesque that Bakhtin's work is examined in this chapter.

A third feature of pagan humanist thought, which will be considered alongside Bakhtin's moralised paganism and the transgressive paganism of Nietzsche and Bataille, is its emphasis upon wholeness. In Alice Walker's novel *Meridian* (1976), black American Christian spirituality in the 1960s is contrasted with native American paganism. In a chapter entitled 'Indians and Ecstasy', the female protagonist Meridian's black American great-grandmother, Feather Mae, is described as renouncing 'all religion that was not based on the experience of physical ecstasy – thereby shocking the Baptist church and its unsympathetic congregation – and near the end of her life she loved walking nude about her yard and worshipped only the sun'.[11] Through Feather Mae, Meridian and her father reconstruct the American Indian experience of the 'physical ecstasy' of being at one with nature. Although it may be idealised, American Indian experience here represents a lost wholeness of body and soul and of culture and nature, which, according to Habermas, characterises mythical thought (see Chapter 4). This sense of wholeness is contrasted in Alice Walker's novel with the nomadic and fragmentary existence of Meridian who is shaped by modern American values, with Walker's sympathetic emphasis firmly on pagan and mystical realities. From a similar perspective, ritual is often regarded as a cornerstone of pagan and primitive cultures and as expressive of a sense of wholeness that is no longer available in westernised societies. Bakhtin, Nietzsche and Bataille each testify, in positive and negative ways, to Western experiences of fragmentation. They also articulate, in different ways, a paganist desire for the wholeness of experience expressed by ritual.

Associated as they often are with pre-modern societies, the 'pagan' and the 'primitive' usually overlap, mainly because both concepts have been denigrated by proponents of so-called civilised life. However, as belief in Western progress has waned, slowly in the nineteenth century and then with increased rapidity in the twentieth, so concepts of the primitive have taken on positive value. Whichever version of pagan humanism predominates, it is important to bear in mind the issue of projection: do these thinkers reveal the 'true' nature of primitive cultures or is the primitive an imaginary European construct? In *Meridian*, the eponymous protagonist muses about the possible significance of the Indian burial site that subsequently became part of her father's farm. She questions the possibility of any authentic reconstruction of a culture that has been systematically destroyed.[12] Similarly, in 1935, Walter Benjamin wrote that 'it is precisely the modern which always conjures up prehistory'.[13] The pagan is from this perspective an aspect or invention of modernity itself. Whichever actual historical era the thinkers in this chapter discuss – ancient Greek paganism for Nietzsche, medieval and Renaissance European paganism for Bakhtin, a variety of European and non-European primitive cultures in the case of Bataille – it is important to remember the partly invented nature of the pagan. In each case, paradoxically, we may be in the presence of Europe's own powerful humanist myths about the nature of mythical thought.

Friedrich Nietzsche

'Beneath the twitching convulsions of our cultural life', writes Nietzsche in *The Birth of Tragedy* (1872), 'there lies a wonderful, intrinsically healthy, ancient power, which powerfully stirs itself only at certain glorious moments, before returning to its dreams of a future awakening.'[14] Reacting against the dominance in the late nineteenth century of orthodox Protestant belief, which Max Weber linked to the rise of capitalist social and economic relations, it is the aim of Nietzsche as a pagan humanist to reanimate those ancient, often anarchic human impulses from which modern societies have distanced themselves in the name of supposedly higher moral visions. In *The Birth of Tragedy*, the ancient, revitalising power of the pagan is associated with the Greek god of intoxication, Dionysus. Offset against Apollo, the god of control and order, Dionysus for Nietzsche represents the human urge for the 'blissful ecstasy' of wild abandonment. 'Under the influence of the narcotic potion hymned by all primitive men and peoples', writes Nietzsche, 'or in the powerful approach of spring, joyfully penetrating the whole of nature, those Dionysiac urges are awakened, and as they grow more intense, subjectivity becomes a complete forgetting of the self'.[15] There are three related aspects to this 'forgetting of the self' which are worth distinguishing, because of the way one of them comes to preside over the others as the distinguishing characteristic of the pagan in Nietzsche's writing: first, there is the communal aspect of the 'Dionysiac magic', which, in re-establishing 'the bond between man and man', overcomes our separation from each other; second, there is that sensual, orgiastic aspect of self-forgetfulness which removes the barrier separating normally more restrained human beings from the wilder impulses of their 'inner' nature; finally, there is the seasonal celebration of 'outer' nature, gendered female, which overcomes the separation of 'man' from the natural world. This last rift, which comes about as a result of man's attitude to nature as something to be either feared or manipulated, is repaired in the Dionsysiac festival, for 'alienated, hostile or subjugated nature', writes Nietzsche, 'celebrates her reconciliation with her lost son, man'.[16]

If this expression of paganism seems spiritually healing, then that is because the wild side of the Dionysiac is accompanied by both a communitarian and ecological morality, which reaffirms our closeness to each other and to nature respectively. But elsewhere in *The Birth of Tragedy* and subsequently in Nietzsche's writing, morality does not fare nearly as well, and it is the 'homesickness for the wild', as he refers to the realm of inner nature in the *On the Genealogy of Morals* (1887), that predominates.[17] Thus, in *Beyond Good and Evil* (1886), communitarian morality is undermined: 'how could there exist a "common good"?', asks Nietzsche from the individualistic standpoint of the impulsive free spirit, while an ecological morality based on care for the natural world is replaced by a view of both nature and human nature as rooted in the will to power.[18] However, it is not just particular kinds of morality that are downgraded by Nietzsche, but morality in general which is subverted. Nietzsche notoriously empties morality of its own substance and treats it as a symptom of something else (that tends to vary from book to book). In *Beyond Good and Evil*, for example, Nietzsche prophesies that psychology 'shall again be recognised as the queen of sciences', and morality understood as a symptom of such emotions as 'hatred, envy, covetousness, and lust for domination'.[19] By contrast, in *On the Genealogy of Morals*, history, linguistics and physiology are granted the power to disturb the special status of morality as a transcendent, truth-bearing discourse; history and linguistics will be able to refute the idea that morality remains the same, while physiology will relate morality to the biological make-up of the human organism.

These different angles on morality exemplify Nietzsche's perspectivism. In *On the Genealogy of Morals*, Nietzsche argues that there is no such thing as *the* truth, for there is '*only* a perspective seeing, *only* a perspective "knowing"; and … the *more* eyes, different eyes, we can use to observe one thing, the more complete will our "concept" of this thing, our "objectivity" be'.[20] However, never far away from Nietzsche's different perspectives on morality, is an extreme pagan humanist perspective that regards morality as a husk that masks primordial human impulses. In *Human, All Too Human* (1878), he argues that conventional morality is simply a slavish veneration of custom: 'to be moral, correct, ethical means to obey an age-old law or tradition'.[21] What is perhaps most challenging about Nietzsche is the way that he persistently pushes us beyond the point where we might be able to retrieve a more authentic sense of morality from its merely conventional counterpart. Thus when he claims, in *Beyond Good and Evil*, that morality should be understood as a 'theory of the relations of domination under which the phenomenon "life" arises', we might readily assent to such a perspective, especially when he offers as examples the various ways in which the social morality of a given community may demonise individuals and characteristics deemed 'immoral'.[22] That morality is socially constructed and implicated in questions of social power and control is a commonplace for late twentieth-century poststructuralists, which Nietzsche for one helped to establish. However, to draw attention to those excluded by a socially constructed morality is itself a 'moral' perspective, which motivates us to ask ethically oriented questions about society's so-called morality. But he goes beyond this, by invoking an 'extra-moral' realm in which lies and fictions are somehow more meaningful than the illusions and dead metaphors of conventional religion and morality, and by unsettling all moral perspectives in the name of a repression thesis which holds that morality camouflages baser instincts. 'Fear', writes Nietzsche, 'is the mother of morality', and it is this fear which prevents us from taking ownership of the less palatable subtexts of the moral positions we adopt.[23] Who can say that they have never used morality to control or exclude others, or feel superior, or repress feelings of hatred?

However, to expose these kinds of subtext is still inappropriate as far as Nietzsche at his amoral extreme is concerned, for they once again recoup morality by implying that we have something to feel ashamed about. What this residual feeling of shame fails to grasp is that Nietzsche's Dionysiac abandonment to the wild side constitutes a form of libertarian release – what William James, discussed in the next chapter, would call a moral holiday – from all moral 'hang-ups'. But there is a paradox here in that many of Nietzsche's aphoristic pronouncements, for example that 'the instincts of wild, free, prowling man' consist in 'hostility, cruelty, joy in persecuting, in attacking, in change, in destruction', test our ability to avoid a moral reaction.[24] At the same time, Nietzsche's intoxicating pagan suspension of moral earnestness seems to forbid such a reaction. Nietzsche himself provides us with the wherewithal for various earnest counter-arguments. For example, his perspectivalism, coupled with his relativising sense of history, warn against treating '"man" ... as an *aeterna veritas*, something unchanging in all turmoil, a measure of all things'.[25] This might lead us to the thought that Nietzsche's image of human nature as essentially cruel and rapacious is itself the product of, to use his own words 'a *very limited* time span'.[26] To enlist these kinds of argument raises the issue to be discussed below of the consistency of Nietzsche's thought. But what is of more immediate interest is Nietzsche's paradoxical 'strategy' of simultaneously eliciting and suspending moral judgements.

The paradox stems in part from Nietzsche's consciously cultivated persona as a daredevil. In *Beyond Good and Evil*, Nietzsche announces his intention to venture forth into the 'still almost unexplored realm of dangerous knowledge'. Directly addressing the potentially seasick reader, he then writes: 'Now clench your teeth! Keep your eyes open! Keep a firm hand on the helm! – We sail straight over morality and *past* it, we flatten, we crush perhaps what is left of our own morality by venturing to voyage thither.'[27] Nietzsche thus entices the reader with the alluring prospect of transgressive knowledge. This is a knowing daredevilry, a daredevilry which make us aware of the fact that he and we will be transgressing normal boundaries. And it is this knowing transgressiveness which lends to Nietzsche's writing its excitement and intensity. Nothing would be at risk if morality was not in some way at stake. Nietzsche, in other words, needs morality as a way of creating a sense of risk. The presence of morality intensifies the experience of transgressing it, and it is arguably intensity of experience and feeling which Nietzsche above all else craves.

For this reason, constructing moral arguments against Nietzsche often seems dull and leaden, like talking to someone getting merrily drunk about the harmful effects of alcohol. In one of the many jokes that Nietzsche makes at the expense of moral philosophers, he suggests that they have actually performed a useful function in making sure that morality remains boring:

> May I be forgiven the discovery that all moral philosophy hitherto has been boring and a soporific – and that 'virtue' has in my eyes been harmed by nothing more than it has been by this *boringness* of its advocates; in saying which, however, I should not want to overlook their general utility. It is important that as few people as possible should think about morality – consequently it is *very* important that morality should not one day become interesting![28]

This could be taken as an albeit innocuous example of the pleasure in 'hostility, cruelty, joy in persecuting, in attacking', which Nietzsche claims as natural human instincts that are repressed by morality. A master of the satisfyingly barbed comment, Nietzsche takes considerable delight in deflating people and the truths that they hold sacred. In this cheerful cruelty lies liberation from sanitised manners and morals. There is also a strongly sacrilegious element to Nietzsche's humour. 'Gods', says Nietzsche, 'are fond of mockery: it seems they cannot refrain from laughter even when sacraments are in progress.'[29] The sacrilegious aspect of Nietzsche's laughter is important because it again lends a sense of danger to what he is doing.

If morality is dead and a mere mask for something else, then the 'meaning of life' will be found in living intensely, impulsively and irreverently, in experimenting with as many emotional states as possible, and in rehabilitating those aspects of life that many post-pagan cultures have taught us to loathe. These various features are combined in the image of Dionysus to which Nietzsche returns in *Twilight of the Idols* (1889). There the 'Dionysian state', which for Nietzsche exemplifies aesthetic experience, is described as follows:

> In the Dionysian state ... the entire emotional system is alerted and intensified: so that it discharges all its powers of representation, imitation, transfiguration, transformation, transmutation, every kind of mimicry and play-acting, conjointly. The essential thing remains the facility of the metamorphosis, the incapacity *not* to react ... It is impossible for the Dionysian man not to understand any suggestion of whatever kind, he ignores no signal from the emotions, he possesses to the highest degree the instinct for understanding and divining ... He enters into every skin, into every emotion; he is continually transforming himself.[30]

For Nietzsche, the emotionally intense experience of entering 'into every skin' is epitomised by the Dionysian aspect of pre-Christian pagan culture and has far more 'life' than the life-denying morality, as Nietzsche sees it, that succeeded it.

Reason and the objectivity to which reason is thought to aspire are also subjected by Nietzsche to the same derisory treatment as morality. Nietzsche is a staunchly anti-realist thinker, meaning that he holds that the objective descriptions of reality to which reason aspires only reveal the needs and pretensions to truth of the knower. So, according to Nietzsche, a hard science such as physics is merely 'an interpretation and arrangement ... and *not* an explanation of the world'.[31] Other branches of human knowledge come in for similar criticism. Nietzsche mocks the quasi-scientific aspirations of German philosophy – and philosophy in general – for failing to distinguish between 'finding' and 'inventing'.[32] According to Nietzsche, inventing is actually what all philosophers and scientists do, but they delude themselves into thinking that they have grasped reality itself. A central component of Nietzsche's anti-realist standpoint, which anticipates structuralist and poststructuralist theory, is his emphasis on the role that language plays in constructing our perceptions of reality. 'It is *we* alone', writes Nietzsche, 'who have fabricated causes, succession, reciprocity, relativity, compulsion, number, law, freedom, motive, purpose; and ... we falsely introduce this world of symbols into things and mingle it with them.'[33]

Nietzsche has been claimed as an anti-humanist, anti-Enlightenment thinker because he undermines the proud humanist claim of the rational individual to see past prejudice into the true nature of things. Although this view of the Enlightenment needs qualifying (see Chapters 1 and 4), it can be accepted as a partial truth. But, as this discussion has shown, there is a problem in casting Nietzsche as an unambiguously anti-humanist thinker, when he might be seen instead as redefining the parameters of the human. True, he demolishes faith in the perfectibility of human knowledge by emphasising the role that language and history play in constructing both 'subjects' and 'objects' of knowledge, and his notion of *Übermensch* suggests an overcoming of the human in all its limitations. But he can equally be seen as expanding anthropocentric perspectives, by 'humanising' those 'objective' forms of knowledge which appear to have nothing to do with human impulses. The 'objective man', writes Nietzsche, 'is only an instrument ... accustomed to submitting to whatever wants to be known'. 'Whatever still remains to him of his "own person"', he continues, 'seems to him accidental, often capricious, more often than not disturbing: so completely has he become a passage and reflection of forms and events not his own.'[34] The objective man for Nietzsche is a mere cipher, a recording machine, a slave to what is thought of as already existing. His human instincts are therefore denied. Likewise, his role as a creator of the reality he thinks he is only passively recording is subdued. Nietzsche thus wants to aestheticise science, philosophy and morality, by drawing these activities back into the orbit of human interpretation. There are no givens in Nietzsche's universe, no 'facts of the matter', only human creations of truth and value which vie with one another in an eternal war – called the 'will to power' – for supremacy. The insistence that all knowledge is a product of human interpretation therefore expands, rather than limits, anthropocentric conceptions of the world.

These conceptions, however, can never be fixed by the will to power of any single human subject. In the same passage in which Nietzsche attacks the 'objective spirit', he also takes a sideswipe at the 'subjective spirit':

> However gratefully one may go to welcome an *objective* spirit – and who has not been sick to death of everything subjective ... in the end one has to learn to be cautious with one's gratitude too and put a stop to the exaggerated way in which the depersonalisation of the spirit is today celebrated.[35]

Nietzsche may rail against 'realists' who reduce themselves to automata, but he does not want to replace them with anything so static, dull and fixed as a unified self. For all his antagonism towards so-called truths about the nature of things, Nietzsche does have a theory – or anti-theory – of both objective and subjective reality, based on the way all our notions fail to capture life's flux. Nietzsche thus discards the concept of a static self in favour of an infinite, dynamic subjectivity, which in sublime Romantic style (although with more emphasis than Romantic writers on transgressive bodily instincts) always exceeds its own boundaries. If Nietzsche is inconsistent, then that is because he lives this transgressive subjectivity as part of his pagan humanism. The fragmented, convoluted style of Nietzsche's writing is part of this pagan version of the Romantic sublime, for it suggests an impulsiveness and spontaneity that undermine the leaden coherence of systematic thought.

Mikhail Bakhtin

Like Nietzsche, the Russian thinker Mikhail Bakhtin in *Rabelais and his World* (started during the 1930s, published in 1965) embraces the notion of pagan transgression. The principle of carnival elaborated by Bakhtin involves the overturning of everything that is holy, sacred, official and authoritative in the name of an anti-authoritarian, populist celebration of all things conventionally perceived as low. 'Carnival', writes Bakhtin, 'celebrated temporary liberation from the prevailing truth and from the established order; it marked the suspension of all hierarchical rank, privileges, norms, and prohibitions.'[36] Laughter, clowning, verbal abuse, parody of official truths, grotesque realism, 'free and familiar contact ... among people ... usually divided by the barriers of caste, property, profession and age', eating, drinking and a general emphasis on bodily functions – these elements form part of carnival's rich and varied repertoire of low impulses and energies which subvert the proprieties of normal, official reality.[37] These natural impulses are also linked to seasonal cycles and celebrated in such communal rituals as the rites of spring.

Unlike Nietzsche, Bakhtin throughout *Rabelais and his World* attaches spiritual as well as communitarian value to virtually all of these normally denigrated elements. An example is the 'slinging of excrement and drenching in urine' which Bakhtin identifies as common motifs in François Rabelais' grotesque novel *Gargantua and Pantagruel* (1532–64) and in carnivalesque literature in general. According to Bakhtin, these motifs have their roots in such folk rituals as the 'feast of fools' where 'excrement was used instead of incense' as part of carnival's parodic subversion of official ecclesiastical ceremonies.[38] Such 'debasing gestures and expressions are ambivalent', writes Bakhtin, because their reference to the 'bodily lower stratum' necessarily includes the 'fertilizing and generating stratum' of 'the genital organs'. Therefore, he concludes, 'in the images of excrement and urine is preserved the essential link with birth, fertility, renewal, welfare'.[39] The degradation and abuse endemic to carnival are thus means of renewal. Carnival destroys in order to give birth; it besmirches, mocks, abuses and parodies in order to cast out the old and bring in the new; it dethrones all stultifying, rigid forms of life dictated by official authority and in so doing breathes life into its own liberating principle of 'becoming'.[40]

Bakhtin insists throughout *Rabelais and his World* upon the principle of ambivalence. For ambivalence we could substitute the word 'dialogic', another key concept in his work. Dialogism is a term used by Bakhtin to emphasise the naturally interactive nature of language: 'the word in living conversation', writes Bakhtin in 'Discourse in the Novel' (1934–5), 'is directly, blatantly, oriented towards a future answer-word: it provokes an answer, anticipates it and structures itself in the answer's direction.'[41] The idea of carnivalesque ambivalence can be taken as an example of dialogism, in that one element (the negative, destructive, denigrating element) needs to be seen in conversation with its other element (the positive element of renewal). Once such images as 'the tossing of excrement' are isolated from this ambivalent conversation, then according to Bakhtin they can no longer be properly understood:

> If the positive and negative poles of becoming (death-birth) are torn apart and opposed to each other in various diffuse images, they lose their direct relation to the whole and are deprived of their ambivalence. They then retain the merely negative aspect, and that which they represent (defecation, urination) acquires a trivial meaning, our own contemporary meaning of these words.[42]

Remove the part from the organic whole from which the part originally derived its full meaning and we are left with an only partly understood idiosyncrasy. The question that might be asked of Bakhtin or Rabelais – namely 'why is this man so interested in shit?' – is a question which becomes more insistent once shit is removed from its place in the carnivalesque worldview. It is a question which, in other words, treats the preoccupation with excrement as some kind of psychological aberration. Bakhtin, however, places excrement alongside the various other carnival motifs, of parody and abuse, so that it forms part of carnival's overall cycle of death–birth, destruction–renewal, degradation–elevation, negative–positive.

Elsewhere, Bakhtin suggests that in the seventeenth century 'the men of Rabelais' time grasped the wholeness and order of the Rabelaisian aesthetic and ideological world, the unity of his style, and the harmony of all the elements that composed it, for they were informed by the same world out-look'.[43] The repeated emphasis upon organically related parts which form a complex whole is itself a vital aspect of Bakhtin's concept of the pagan, for it expresses a desire for the lost wholeness associated with a pre-modern mentality that for Bakhtin survived into the Renaissance. The appeal to the lost wholeness of an earthy worldview rooted in bodily instincts and reflected in the cycles of nature is the pagan version of the prelapsarian state imagined by Christianity. Bakhtin contrasts the original wholeness of the carnivalesque world outlook with its subsequent disintegration in post-Renaissance Europe. Rabelaisian carnival survives, according to Bakhtin, but it survives in fragmented or 'watered down' or 'distorted' forms.[44] Carnival paradoxically contributes towards this fragmentation, however, for there is an energy about carnival that contributed to the growth during the Renaissance of historical consciousness.[45] In its this-worldly aspect, in its relativising of established truths, and in its celebration of the incomplete, carnival destroys eternal verities and opens up history to transformation. As part of carnival's dynamism, Bakhtin enlists the Italian scholar Pico della Mirandola's *On the Dignity of Man* (1486), which he treats as a humanist manifesto that shares in common with carnival an emphasis upon the indeterminate – and therefore free – nature of 'man'. 'Pico asserted', writes Bakhtin,

> that man is superior to all beings, including the celestial spirits, because he is not only being but also becoming. He is outside all hierarchies, for a hierarchy can determine only that which represents stable, immovable, and unchangeable being, not free becoming. All the other beings remain forever what they were at the time of their creation, for their nature is ready-made and unchanging; it receives one single seed which can and must develop in them. But man receives at his birth the seeds of every form of life.[46]

Against the conception of human beings locked into a determinate position within a fixed hierarchical order, Bakhtin's Pico affirms the possibility of self-determining human beings who, like the self-fashioning rhetorician discussed in Chapter 1, are free to choose their own nature. Nature is still appealed to – 'man receives at his birth the seeds of every form of life' – but nature paradoxically determines that human beings are free from biological determination. In its joyful embrace of the profane, 'lowly', changeful things of this earth, pagan humanism equates with a buoyant secular humanism, whereby we are left to our own devices, no longer fixed within a set scheme, free to fashion our own history and to transgress the boundaries imposed by systems of authority. The downside of Bakhtin's mainly optimistic attitude to the secular outlook anticipated by carnival is the fragmentation of meaning to which carnival also gives rise. Bakhtin counters carnival's own drive to dismantle settled orders of meaning by showing how the multi-faceted aspects of carnival once formed a distinctive and coherent folk culture. Carnival, then, is at once a 'system' and 'anti-system', coherent and dynamic, a homogeneous worldview that also spells the end of homogeneous worldviews. Bakhtin celebrates the disruptive energies associated with carnival misrule and pagan transgression, but also presents an image of a unified folk culture. In the context of the Stalinist Russia in which Bakhtin lived, carnival can be seen as representing both populist resistance to totalitarianism and a better, non-coercive, more humane form of totality.

Inevitably, Bakhtin's conception of folk culture can, and has been, complicated. Bakhtin's image of 'the people' united by their own distinctive,
colourful and anti-authoritarian subculture is no doubt utopian and possibly
sentimental. As Simon Dentith has pointed out, carnival was used not only to
undermine but to reinforce social hierarchies.[47] Carnival's degradations could
be exercised not just in one direction, by the low upon the high, but in several
directions, by the people upon abject individuals or groups within the category
of 'the people', and by the high upon the low. But then 'complication', necessary as it is to all critical work, is precisely what pagan humanism is keen to
decrease. Not that Bakhtin's *Rabelais and his World* is simple, but its
intellectual complexity is contained by carnival itself, the essence of which can
be fairly easily grasped because it forms a complex but ultimately comprehensible unity. It is at the same time in an identifiable relationship – of opposition
and conflict – with mainstream culture. Bakhtin might therefore have found
his way into Chapter 4 on civic humanism, to provide an example of community based not so much on critical reason as critical ritual. The critique
exercised by carnival is an altogether more visceral, sensual affair than the
'cold rationalism', so-called by Bakhtin himself, of the Enlightenment.[48] To
make social rituals out of eating and drinking is arguably to derive society from
biology, value from fact, in a more immediate way than the abstract process of
reason is able to. Arguing about the need for human sociability is different
from enacting it. Citing Gramsci's concept of myth as a 'concrete phantasy
which acts upon a dispersed and shattered people to arouse and organize its
collective will', Kobena Mercer has suggested that a 'popular and democratic
socialism' needs to 're-mythify socialism or create a new "myth" of socialism
which would be adequate to our needs now and in the future'.[49] Given the co-
option of the carnivalesque (or aspects of it) by the hedonistic gratification of
the senses in consumer capitalism, carnival may not provide the right myth.
But the ability of the carnival rites described by Bakhtin to enact resistance at
the concrete, human level of the senses offers an example of a democratic
socialist myth that counterbalances left-wing intellectualism.

Finally, if carnival has (or had) a critical, counter-cultural edge, then that
edge, as was suggested at the beginning of this section, is largely benign. That
is to say, carnival has a recognisable moral agenda, namely the liberation of
'the people' from authoritarianism and oppression. The degrading, excremental,
abusive aspects of carnival are only trivially or superficially repellent when
taken out of context. In their mythic context, they form one half of a rite of
spring that involves casting out the old and bringing in the new. The excremental is thus part of a wider moral vision based on renewal, freedom and
conviviality. The low, in other words, turns out to be high. However, while it
is possible to rescue Bakhtin for a worthy humanist vision, like Nietzsche (only

more so), the final pagan humanist considered here is far less amenable to such morally uplifting perspectives.

Georges Bataille

In 1936 the French writer and sometime friend of the Surrealists, Georges Bataille, helped to found a secret society called Acéphale, meaning the 'Headless One'. The society was partly the product of Bataille's interest in the excess, sacrificial violence and irrationality that he took to be defining characteristics of the 'primitive'. Because Bataille regards rationality, in the Nietzschean manner, as an artifice masking more elemental urges, 'losing one's head' is a way of reconnecting the self with its primitive underside. The idea of decapitation also suggests Bataille's more general preoccupation with states of physical and psychic disintegration when the boundaries of the self are lost. There is once again a Romantic element present in the notion of a self 'beyond' or 'beside' itself, but for Bataille, as for Bakhtin and Nietzsche, the pagan is the primary source of inspiration. Bataille, however, takes paganism to its extreme, for he is arguably the philosopher of the extreme. A further difference between Nietzsche, Bakhtin and Bataille is that the latter's interest in anthropology and ethnography led him to look beyond the European examples of the pagan invoked by the other two thinkers. Drawing on the work of the French anthropologist Marcel Mauss, Bataille, especially in his book *Eroticism* (1957), adopts an expansive role as a historian of the 'decline' from primitive to civilised societies. As such, his work raises questions about Eurocentric representations, or misrepresentations, of the primitive.

Thirty years or so prior to the founding of Acéphale, in his novel about European colonialism, *Heart of Darkness* (1902), Joseph Conrad had exemplified the conversion from a 'civilised' to a 'primitive' state by describing, via the narrator Marlow, the heads impaled on stakes which encircle Kurtz's house in the African jungle. Marlow's reaction, of horror and fascination, suggest that we are in the presence of something at once strange, terrible and elemental. 'The wilderness', says Marlow, 'had found him [Kurtz] out early ... I think it had whispered to him things about himself which he did not know ... and the whisper had proved irresistibly fascinating.'[50] This way of perceiving the primitive, as a call from the wild reminding us of long-lost origins, is also at the heart of Bataille's primitivism. And like Conrad's Marlow, Bataille fixes upon the excesses of sacrificial violence represented by the practice of decapitation to exemplify the primitive. In line with Nietzsche's and Bataille's own suspicion of the so-called truth to which the rational individual has supposedly privileged access, we need, as indicated earlier, to be aware that the various accounts which Bataille offers of primitive societies may well be Eurocentric constructions of the primitive. In her book, *Gone Primitive: Savage Intellects, Modern Lives* (1990), Marianna Torgovnick draws attention to the way that a universalised, undifferentiated concept of the primitive 'becomes grist for the Western fantasy-mill', and is used, through the 'processing of the other as a version of "our true self"', to stage crises of *Western* identity.[51] Torgovnick's brief discussion of Bataille implicates the French thinker in this neo-colonialist primitivism, which romanticises the primitive in its search for authentic human existence.

Bataille's own appeal to authenticity is built into the methodological points he makes about his book *Eroticism*. Bataille draws attention to the fact that he is writing as a social scientist, with all that that entails in terms of the truth, objectivity and impartial distance to which science has traditionally aspired. But he also draws attention to the realm of 'inner experience' which a strictly scientific analysis might leave out. Bataille wants to be on intimate terms with his subject matter and avoid offering what he calls 'a lifeless accumulation of inert facts'.[52] Like the Romantic humanists discussed in Chapter 1, he wants his objects of knowledge to resonate with his own personal experience, rather than to be at an impersonal remove from him. And just as Romantic writers emphasise the particularity of inner experience at the same time as they attempt to reach outwards, so does Bataille. Waxing semi-autobiographical, Bataille casts himself in the role of a 'loner' attempting to overcome his loneliness: 'I can concern myself with religion', he writes, 'not like a schoolteacher giving a historical account of it, mentioning the Brahmin among others, but like the Brahmin himself. Yet I am not a Brahmin or indeed anything at all; I have to pick my way along a lonely path, no tradition, no ritual to guide me, and nothing to hinder me either.'[53] A fantasy about fusion is being played out here. Bataille does not want to write about the Brahmin from the outside. Like Bakhtin when he writes about carnival or Nietzsche when he embraces the Dionysian principle of oneness, Bataille wants to be on intimate terms with his objects of knowledge, and in so doing fuse his own inner experience with that of human beings in general. The appeal to shared inner experience is also a way of sidestepping reason and intellect. Bataille proceeds intellectually, using argument to persuade his readers, but he is also striving for a more intimate form of connection, based on the emotional resonance which inner experience might have for the reader.

Likewise, when Bataille writes about primitive societies, he tries to connect with the 'inner experience' of primitive ritual. Bataille often introduces a 'we' into his writing about ritual, and uses an emotionally compelling present tense as a way of making the past available to the reader's consciousness. Through his vivid textual recreation of ritual, Bataille wants to be there and us to be there with him. Towards the end of *Eroticism*, Bataille questions the tendency of 'specialised philosophy', epitomised by Hegel, to cut 'ideas off from experience' and to distrust the immediate because the immediate is taken to be an unreliable source of knowledge.[54] Bataille tries to overcome the alienation of abstract specialised thought from concrete experience, and imagining himself being there in the rituals he describes is a way of achieving this. There is even a story, cited by Paul Hegarty, that members of the Acéphale group 'planned to have a human sacrifice'. 'Apparently', continues Hegarty, 'there was a willing victim, but no one willing to be the sacrificer.'[55] It is not surprising, from this perspective, that Bataille wrote erotic/pornographic fiction, such as *The Story of the Eye* (1928) and *Blue of Noon* (1945), for fiction has often been used to render experience vivid and vicarious.

On various levels, then, Bataille seeks to abolish distance. Moreover, the inner experience of ritual and erotic experience are themselves based upon the 'perceived' destruction of an alienating distance between subject and object, inner and outer, self and world. Where critical reason advises us to put sceptical quotation marks around the word 'perceived', as a way of signalling the fact that the perceiver and perceived might not match up, Bataille wants to overcome the distance that such a mismatch implies. And what Bataille wants, we should also want. This is because, according to Bataille, 'we are discontinuous beings, individuals who perish in isolation in the midst of an incomprehensible adventure, but we yearn for our lost continuity'. This continuity, which is described as 'primal', links us 'with everything that is'.[56] For Bataille, this yearning for continuity expresses itself in the form of an unquenchable thirst for transgression. Where Romantic writers tend to treat strong emotion as a sign of either human neediness or mysterious interiority, Bataille takes the former – the desire for continuity with others – to its absolute extreme. The various expressions of human 'togetherness' which this book has examined, in the shape of compassion, *agape* love, sensibility, dialogue, intersubjectivity, folk culture and so forth, are not enough for Bataille, for they are all too tame as compared with the wild abandon of often violent transgression. Anything which transgresses a boundary and takes us out of ourselves – out of our discontinuous existence as separate individuals – is an expression of a yearning for continuity, but the more extreme the better as far as Bataille is concerned, because only in extremity is 'inner experience' fully revealed. Thus death, violence, murder, eroticism, alcohol, trance and obscenity are amongst the experiences which, according to Bataille, take us beyond the limit and satisfy our joyful craving for self-annihilation. In 'The Practice of Joy before Death' (1939), for example, the 'fretful saintliness' of those who 'take refuge in the expectation of eternal beatitude' is contrasted with the 'shameless, indecent saintliness' that is the only way of leading to a 'sufficiently happy *loss of self*'. 'Joy before death', he continues, 'is the apotheosis of that which is perishable, apotheosis of flesh and alcohol as well as the trances of mysticism.'[57]

Although the yearning for continuity survives in attenuated form in 'civilised' societies, it is most forcefully expressed according to Bataille in 'primitive' cultures. Sacrificial violence is often used by Bataille to characterise the primitive, and of sacrifice (in both pagan and post-pagan religious cultures) he writes the following:

> In sacrifice, the victim dies and the spectators share in what his death reveals. This is what religious historians call the element of sacredness. This sacredness is the revelation of continuity through the death of a discontinuous being to those who watch it as a solemn rite. A violent death disrupts the creature's discontinuity; what remains, what the tense onlookers experience in the succeeding silence, is the continuity of all existence with which the victim is now one. Only a spectacular killing, carried out as the solemn and collective nature of religious dictates, has the power to reveal what normally escapes notice.[58]

Here, the sacred, a key term in Bataille's writing, is the transgression of the finite. In this respect, the sacred shares in common with the versions of spiritual humanism discussed in the previous chapter the notion of a beyond. But whereas the sacred for spiritual humanists often implies a concept of a higher reality as a standard against which to measure fallen human values, Bataille, as a pagan, looks 'downwards' rather than 'upwards'. Moreover, unlike Bakhtin (as well as to an extent Kristeva and Benjamin), Bataille does not seek to elevate the low to a high. As Allan Stoekl suggests, 'filth' in Bataille 'does not "replace" God', for that would be simply to substitute 'one hierarchy for another'.[59] He is not so much interested in redeeming humanist value from neglected places, as in annihilating it in the name of an intoxicating nihilism that leads to a glorious freedom from moral responsibility. In the above quotation, he is not concerned with the moral questions posed by 'spectacular killing', but only in the drive towards continuity and annihilation which the ritual reveals.

As a quasi-Marxist thinker, Bataille opposes the unbounded nature of the sacred to the severely restrained and austere nature, as he saw it, of capitalism. Where the 'primitive' in us longs for release, excess and continuity, capitalism and instrumental rationality turn us into servile, rational calculators, mindful only of the utility of 'things'. And as we become obsessed, under capitalism, with how to accumulate, and appropriate the use-value of, more and more things, so capitalism make 'things' of us. 'The slave bound to labor', writes Bataille in *The Accursed Share* (1967), 'is a *thing* just as a work animal is a thing.'[60] The entire ethos of capitalism, for Bataille, is to reduce life's immense 'circulation of energy' to the production and consumption of useful objects, including people as objects.[61] In *The Accursed Share*, the counter-perspective offered by the primitive comes from Bataille's consideration of Aztec culture. Once again, Bataille invokes sacrifice:

> Sacrifice restores to the sacred world that which servile use has degraded, rendered profane. Servile use has made a *thing* (an *object*) of that which, in a deep sense, is of the same nature as the *subject*, is in a relation of intimate participation with the subject. It is not necessary that the sacrifice actually destroy the animal or plant of which man had to make a *thing* of his use. They must at least be destroyed as things, that is, *insofar as they have become things*.[62]

Bataille's affinity with the Surrealists links closely with his concept of sacrifice, for both violate the limits of normal utilitarian perception: surrealism by making strange the things and people it represents; sacrifice by destroying them. In doing so, both reveal the human instinct towards destruction and self-destruction.

Bataille's favourite terms 'excess' and 'expenditure', discussed in his essays collected as *Visions of Excess* (1927–39), also suggest a violent passing beyond the self towards a fusion with a quasi-mystical and eroticised universe. However, his eroticisation of violence and violation (particularly as regards the expenditure of a masculinised libido) sometimes leads him to make some highly questionable, not to say repellent, claims. The following, from *Eroticism*, is an example:

> The act of violence that deprives the creature of its limited particularity and bestows on it the limitless, infinite nature of sacred things is with its profound logic an intentional one. It is intentional like the act of the man who lays bare, desires and wants to penetrate his victim. The lover strips the beloved of her identity no less than the blood-stained priest his human or animal victim. The woman in the hands of her assailant is despoiled of her being. With her modesty she loses the firm barrier that once separated her from others and made her impenetrable.[63]

Are we to conclude from this that a man who violates a woman is doing the woman a 'favour' by releasing her into the infinite, at the same time as he is satisfying his own desire to access the sacred through a transgressive act? Another, related boundary transgression, here, is the treatment of women and animals as virtually interchangeable victims of a predatory male. Bataille may want to dissolve boundaries between perceiver and perceived, self and world, in the name of the primal continuity of all existence, but what these images of violation indicate is a violent and narcissistic absorption of an object by a subject.

The concept of 'sovereignty', another keyword in Bataille's writing, can be related to this issue. There is an ambiguity about Bataille's use of the word, in that it simultaneously recalls and negates (or transgresses) its normal meaning. If sovereignty, in classical humanist terms, suggests the authority and confident self-presence of a powerful individual, then Bataille simultaneously invokes and subverts this meaning, by implying by it a heightened sense of subjectivity, which at the same time involves the loss of a sense of the self as a definable, and therefore servile, object. The ambiguity as to whether sovereignty entails a loss or expansion of subjectivity returns us to Marianna Torgovnick's critique of the narcissistic appropriation of the primitive Other by Western writers. If Bataille's version of the primitive is a Eurocentric construction, then the meaning of sovereignty necessarily veers towards the kind of subjectivism which Bataille is at the same time keen to transgress. Moreover, what Bataille calls the primitive might just as easily be identified as capitalism in its pure form. Although Bataille associates capitalism with utility, the development of capitalism during the twentieth and early twenty-first centuries has arguably borne out Marx's insight discussed in Chapter 1 that capitalism thrives on the very things, namely excess and the transgression of boundaries, thought of by Bataille as capitalism's 'primitive' opposites.[64] Again, then, Bataille's concept of the primitive appears to reveal more about the West than it does about actual so-called primitive cultures.

In *On the Genealogy of Morals*, Nietzsche proposed that all putatively objective knowledge is really subjective, but that the subject, like the object, is itself merely a fiction which should be transgressed. Bataille, himself a devotee of Nietzsche, seems caught in a Nietzschean 'loop' or hall of mirrors, insofar as the notion of a pagan subversion of a civilised self is based upon a Eurocentric construction of the primitive. This might lead to the conclusion that all attempts to rediscover the human, primitive or otherwise, are the products of particular social and historical formations, even as they claim to be looking beyond those formations. A critical humanism always needs to be alert to historically specific constructions of the human masquerading as authentic, but total suspicion of all humanisms would lead to an ethical and political impasse and the abandonment of such ethically evaluative terms as dehumanisation. Bataille does not construct an ethical humanism; indeed, as a thinker who takes certain Nietzschean concepts to their extreme, he attempts to deprive us of the moral high ground which would allow us safe detachment from his excremental view of the human. Nevertheless, Bataille's appeal to a primitive human yearning for indivisibility is dependent upon a notion of alienation. His concept of the primitive may be deeply Eurocentric and his eroticisation of violence and violation deeply masculinist, but the desire to overcome isolation even as it is intensified by looking inwards to the 'real' instinctive self that exists beyond conventional trappings, is common to several of the humanisms examined in this book. However, unlike Bakhtin, who provides an uplifting vision of carnivalesque misrule and leads us back to ideas of human togetherness, Bataille's Nietzschean-inspired emphasis on transgression, destruction and orgiastic self-forgetfulness suggest that what human beings might most want from 'the human', in fact, is its end. Bataille is therefore on the very cusp of the dialogue between humanism and anti-humanism.

The next two chapters will rescue an outward-looking humanism from the abyss to which Bataille the wild paganist takes it. They will also discuss various attempts – some more affirmative than others – to rescue reason and science from the anti-rationalist excesses to which spiritual and pagan humanists are sometimes prone, by suggesting that there is more in common between religion and science than is often acknowledged.

Primary Texts

Friedrich Nietzsche

The Birth of Tragedy [1872], trans. Shaun Whiteside, ed. Michael Tanner (London: Penguin, 1993).

Human, All Too Human [1878], trans. Marion Faber and Stephen Lehmann (London: Penguin, 1994).

Beyond Good and Evil [1886], trans. R. J. Hollingdale (Harmondsworth: Penguin, 1973).

On the Genealogy of Morals and Ecce Homo [1887], ed. Walter Kaufman, trans. Walter Kaufman and R. J. Hollingdale (New York: Vintage, 1969).

Twilight of the Idols and The Antichrist [1889], trans. R. J. Hollingdale (Harmondsworth: Penguin, 1968).

Mikhail Bakhtin

Rabelais and his World [1965], trans. Hélène Iswolsky (Bloomington, IN: Indiana University Press, 1984).

The Dialogic Imagination, trans. Caryl Emerson and Michael Holquist, ed. Michael Holquist (Austin, TX: University of Texas Press, 1981), particularly 'Discourse in the Novel' (1934–5).

Georges Bataille

Visions of Excess: Selected Writings 1927–1939, trans. Allan Stoekl with Carl Lovitt and Donald Leslie Jr, ed. Allan Stoekl (Minneapolis, MN: University of Minnesota Press, 1985).

The Story of the Eye [1928], trans. Joachim Neugroschal (Harmondsworth: Penguin, 1982).

Eroticism [1957], trans. Mary Dalwood (London: Marion Boyars, 1987).

The Accursed Share, 1: Consumption [1967], trans. Robert Hurley (New York: Zone Books, 1991).

CHAPTER 7

Pragmatic Humanism

(James – Dewey – Rorty)

In other chapters we have indicated strong links between European and American humanist traditions, in terms of the nationality of the three primary thinkers or in relation to the cultural context in which humanist ideas were made popular. By way of contrast, pragmatism is a distinctively American tradition that has no European equivalent. With its emphasis on technique and practice, comparisons can be made to nineteenth-century British utilitarianism and early twentieth-century logical positivism, but these links are not particularly helpful for considering the relationship between pragmatism and humanism. Indeed, pragmatism has been often misread as a version of what Adorno and Horkheimer in *Dialectic of Enlightenment* (1944) described as instrumental reason.[1] Where spiritual and pagan humanisms look within before surveying the social world, the two exiled German theorists would see pragmatism as a development of the Enlightenment pursuit of reason in which moral questions are subordinated to social utility. This would put pragmatism at odds with humanism as a method that identifies the means required to achieve a particular goal, without considering the human cost of such a strategy. On this view, according to the critic Peter Lawler, pragmatists believe that all human limitations 'can be overcome through their free and thoughtful mastery of nature'.[2] Although pragmatists do privilege certain types of action, this interpretation overlooks their tendency to focus on questions of meaning and value, rather than devaluing the spirit and reducing the natural world to 'mathematical theorems'.[3] From the early Harvard-based pioneers of the late nineteenth century to the emergence of neo-pragmatism in the late twentieth century, pragmatists not only emphasise the possibility of self-transformation, but also seek to refine a method that can facilitate social and moral change. Without an ethical guiding force, pragmatism can be seen as an empty method that could be misused for self-aggrandisement or social domination on Adorno and Horkheimer's model. But, within a humanist framework, pragmatism is more rigorous than existentialism in offering a way of achieving practical goals and of shifting philosophical parameters from passive 'thinking' to active 'doing'.

Pragmatism derives from the theoretical work of the American logician and mathematician Charles Sanders Peirce, who first used the term 'pragmaticism' in the early 1880s to designate a particular method of looking at reality, purged of the metaphysical baggage that was a feature of nineteenth-century epistemology. The term derives from the Greek *pragma*, meaning action or practice, and from the German *pragmatisch*, corresponding to experimental and purposive action. Peirce attacked traditional metaphysics for being too vague and for not having a rigorous enough approach to empirical problems, calling it a 'puny, rickety, and scrofulous science' that lacks purpose when compared to the scientific project to document reality.[4] As Bruce Kuklick discusses in *The Rise of American Philosophy* (1977), professional philosophy did not exist in America until scientists started to work through the implications of Darwin's challenge to the theory of celestial design in *The Descent of Man* (1871). Evolutionary biology quickly became popular among American thinkers, helping them to dissociate scientific questions from theological issues that hampered a clear understanding of processes in the natural world. Peirce was more directly influenced by the physical sciences than by biology, but, like the American Darwinians, was committed to bracketing off irrelevant metaphysical questions that impeded the pursuit of truth; as Bertrand Russell summarises, Peirce's commitment to 'attain clearness in our thoughts of an object' meant that he needed only to 'consider what conceivable effects of a practical kind the object may involve'.[5] As such, Peirce's work marked a shift from a general theory of knowledge to a specific theory of meaning that helps the inquirer to determine the complex relationships between elements in a system.

This emphasis on developing the most efficient method to achieve a particular goal distinguishes Peirce's contribution to the professionalisation of philosophy and the emergence of pragmatism in late nineteenth-century America, but he is now rarely read outside specialist philosophy courses, partly because he dissociated himself from the type of pragmatism developing in his wake. In contrast to Peirce's specialised vocabulary, two other thinkers associated with the early phase of pragmatism, William James (1831–1910) and John Dewey (1859–1952), are among the most influential figures in American intellectual history, applying Peirce's theory across the spectrum of psychology, science, religion, aesthetics, education and politics.

James's essay 'Philosophical Conceptions and Practical Results' (1898) was his first concerted attempt to develop Peirce's ideas into a practical method for dealing with theoretical problems, which he formulated in *Pragmatism* (1907) and developed in his numerous essays on the subject. Unlike Peirce's focus on laboratory experience, James was unhappy with reductive biological models and deeply humanist in his commitment to understanding the broad sweep of 'the human' in a post-Darwinian intellectual environment. Underpinning James's writings, moving between medicine, anatomy, physiology, psychology, ethics and religion, is his central preoccupation with the idea of selfhood.

He was not interested in the abstractions of classical philosophy (such as Descartes's thinking self), but in the living and embodied self. As a humanist, he wished to move away from the behaviourist model in which creatures (including humans) are determined by instincts and environment, towards the notion of an experiencing self in which the individual retains some sense of free will. While these post-Darwinian ideas fed into James's interest in pragmatic techniques individuals can adopt, Dewey's work focuses more explicitly on public affairs, particularly the ways in which individuals can develop through educational schemes and by participating in communities. James and Dewey were ardent humanists in their belief in the possibilities of personal transformation, and pragmatists in their conviction that individuals should move away from passive philosophical contemplation to active social participation. It is important to distinguish James's and Dewey's pragmatic humanism from another more populist and reactionary strain of American humanism championed by Irving Babbitt and Paul Elmer More in the late 1920s, which engaged only loosely with pragmatism and was geared to affirming Matthew Arnold's high cultural standards.[6] In distinction from this anti-modernist humanism with the mission to rescue America from moral bankruptcy, the discussion below indicates that James and Dewey were both committed to understanding individual and social activity from an ethical perspective, but without assigning human behaviour to a set of universal precepts.

James and Dewey are now established as among the most important thinkers in modern American thought, epitomising the forward-looking ideas of American Progressivism, at its height from the 1890s through to mid-1910s. However, the historian John Patrick Diggins argues in *The Promise of Pragmatism* (1994) that, after its high-point in the first quarter of the twentieth century, American pragmatism had spiralled into free fall when an ageing Dewey was left theoretically ill-equipped to deal with the dark days of the Holocaust and the bombing of Pearl Harbor in 1941.[7] The pragmatic method may be seen as useful for dealing with particular social and domestic problems, such as the economic and political tribulations of the Great Depression in the 1930s, but the historical trauma surrounding Pearl Harbor and the emergence of the Cold War seemed too cataclysmic to be dealt with from a pragmatic perspective. As a consequence, pragmatism became unfashionable from the 1950s through the 1970s, coinciding with the dominance of psychoanalytic and Marxist thought in America and the emergence of poststructuralist ideas in Europe.

Since the 1980s, the renaissance of pragmatism has been stimulated by the likes of Richard Rorty (1931–), Richard Bernstein, Stanley Cavell, Stanley Fish, Hilary Putnam and Cornel West as a revival of a distinctive American intellectual tradition and (for some) as a defence against the dominance of

Continental critical theory. All these thinkers, whether addressing literary ideas (Cavell, Fish), philosophical problems (Rorty, Putnam) or issues of race and democracy (West, Bernstein), can be seen to engage in the search for a pragmatic method amongst the debris of classical philosophy. Cornel West identifies three reasons for this resurgence: first, 'a disenchantment with the traditional image of philosophy as a transcendental mode of inquiry'; second, a theoretical 'preoccupation with the relations of knowledge and power, cognition and control, discourse and politics'; and, third, a humanist drive to retain a notion of agency despite constraints 'that reinforce and reproduce hierarchies based on class, race, gender, and sexual orientation'.[8] The emphasis among these thinkers on the use-value of pragmatism does not represent a return to social technique stripped of human subjectivity, but enables theory to be grounded within the context of lived experience. For James and Dewey, personal or communal experience tends to be the bedrock of their humanism, while neo-pragmatists focus more closely on language, rhetoric and narrative both as the grounds of experience and as tools for 'coping with reality'.[9] As such, the anti-epistemological emphasis of James and Dewey has given way to a more creative set of critical negotiations more applicable to what the critic Morris Dickstein in the late 1990s called 'today's post-ideological' climate.[10]

Rorty has written widely on both Continental theory (particularly Hegel, Heidegger and Foucault) and Anglo-American analytic philosophy, but has returned to James and Dewey as the most important contributors to the development of pragmatism. Rather than always writing in a high academic style, all three thinkers have made concessions to a broader readership to rule against philosophy being seen as a master discourse and to emphasise the importance of pragmatism to everyday life. At times they do rely on abstractions – 'the experiencing self' for James; 'the public thinker' for Dewey; 'the private ironist' for Rorty – but their work often addresses historical and material issues that root their theory in practice. For example, Rorty's most recent writings, his 1997 Harvard Lecture in the History of American Civilization published as *Achieving Our Country* (1998) and his essays collected in *Philosophy and Social Hope* (1999), not only rework pragmatic concepts in a late twentieth-century context, but also focus on the moral development and symbolic survival of America at the beginning of the new millennium: what Cornel West calls 'a conscious cultural commentary' that attempts 'to explain America to itself at a particular historical moment'.[11] This close fusion of pragmatism and American cultural commentary has stimulated some thinkers to criticise Rorty for being too comfortable in his parochial and liberal view, particularly on international issues. Indeed, if the events of Pearl Harbor in 1941 marked the close of the first sixty years of pragmatism, the terrorist bombing of the World Trade Center and the Pentagon in September 2001 may transpire to be the same kind of radical challenge to its second phase. Nevertheless, while James, Dewey and Rorty are not as active in social and humanitarian movements as were Frantz Fanon or Martin Luther King (see Chapters 2 and 5), their pragmatic ideas radiate from a philosophical centre to address issues of personal expression, freedom, equality and human rights in socially valuable ways.

William James

William James was deeply interested in European philosophy, natural science and culture, but he was a profoundly American thinker who bridged the nineteenth-century emphasis on careful empirical research with an early twentieth-century modernist approach to uncertainty and chaos. An early review of James's two-volume *The Principles of Psychology* (1890) describes him as 'a true American for all his European sympathies' and, although he often appears to be an existential thinker in his consideration of 'the "weightless" nature of modern existence', his work retained a forward-looking optimism reflecting his New England sensibility.[12] James lived all but his last ten years in the nineteenth century and as a Victorian polymath shifted his critical attention from medicine, anatomy, physiology and psychology to a developing interest in philosophy, religion and education. However, he was also a very modern thinker in developing a dynamic theory of human activity free from metaphysics and the notion of fixed human essences. While his emphasis on decision-making – 'we must take care to launch ourselves with as strong and decided an initiative as possible'[13] – takes its place alongside nineteenth-century thinkers such as the Scottish essayist Thomas Carlyle's theory of hero-worship and the American president Theodore Roosevelt's emphasis on the 'strenuous life', his reconception of the self as a flexible structure within a constantly changing 'stream of thought' strongly influenced the modernist interest in alternative models of subjectivity. There is enough evidence to claim James as either Victorian or modernist, but he continually grappled with changing conceptions of human existence, both in terms of what distinguishes humans from animal life in *The Principles of Psychology* and in terms of what tools we have available to achieve particular goals in *Pragmatism* (1907). While James shifted between often competing discourses (such as neurology and religion in *The Varieties of Religious Experience*, 1902), his humanist commitment to interrogate the implications, as well as the limitations, of the human remained constant.

The Principles of Psychology is James's most important contribution to the human sciences. He takes 1,350 pages to synthesise the major trends of late nineteenth-century psychology in the light of Darwin's evolutionary theories.

It is not an obviously humanist work, dealing primarily with the functioning of the brain and the complexities of consciousness. However, there is a drive throughout the two volumes to develop a theory that does justice to the multifarious aspects of human experience, taking the reader outside the scientific laboratory to confront the flux of everyday life. The key element in *Principles* that enabled him to shift away from the strictly scientific study of physiology and anatomy to a conception of 'the active self' is his theory of the will. His notion of 'will-as-activity' is subtly different from the attempts of nineteenth-century European philosophers to understand the human will. Taking as his starting point the verb 'to will', James avoided the metaphysical discussion of 'the will' as a fixed psychological faculty. This movement away from an abstract conception of the will did not mean that James wanted to abandon all questions of knowledge; rather that, as a pragmatist, he detects the impossibility of establishing an absolute foundation for knowledge. Even though science had supplanted religion as the dominant explanatory discourse at the turn of the century, James believed strongly that neither science nor religion could furnish individuals with the absolute answers on which they could build their lives. He was heavily influenced by Darwin's evolutionary biology and the theory that human behaviour is largely directed by involuntary instincts, but James maintained his humanist belief that individuals have the capacity to make reasoned choices. Following the pragmatic idea that certain concepts help individuals to achieve particular ends, James advocates 'willing' as a capacity that accounts for otherwise inexplicable phenomena: only a dynamic theory of 'being' can provide individuals with the theoretical impetus to change themselves and positively influence their relationships with others.

A related strain that runs through *Principles* to later essays such as *A Pluralistic Universe* (1909) is his strong connection with Romanticism, which furnished him with a notion of will as a descriptive term. Early Romantic writers often used 'the will' to express a sense of agency and their sensitivity to the inherent design of the natural world. For the poets William Wordsworth and Ralph Waldo Emerson the will is viewed as a positive force which, when exercised creatively, can invoke altruistic feelings for the wider personal, organic and spiritual worlds. However, for both Wordsworth and Emerson a 'higher' guiding force is needed to temper the capricious drive of the will: at the beginning of his narrative poem *The Prelude* (1805) Wordsworth described this as 'the sweet breath of heaven', 'a vital breeze ... blowing on my body', and in his 1841 essay Emerson called it 'the Over-Soul'.[14] As such, the will lies between an innate appreciation of, and sympathy for, the natural world and a guiding force that helps the poets give voice to their experiences. This optimistic and creative view of will contrasts with the Germanic idea that the will is an evil and self-serving force that needs to be checked (as it was for

Arthur Schopenhauer) or that the will to power (for Nietzsche) can overcome the limitations of the self, even if it is at the expense of others. James read Nietzsche avidly (and German Romanticism was a general influence on him), but the spirit of his work is much closer to the New England optimism of Emerson, particularly the idea that individuals have an inner 'force or soul' which directs action within the horizon of human knowledge.[15]

As a scientist James was not content just to use 'the will' as a poetic category, but one that is rooted in material and biological life. In the second volume of *Principles* and in *The Will to Believe* (1897) he describes the activity of the will as a type of reflex that has entered the realm of conscious life, with the potential to override unconscious habits. At moments of difficult decision-making the fluid self, forever changing in the light of new experiences (as described in 'The Stream of Thought' chapter in the first volume of *Principles*), rigidifies into something more substantial to aid self-reflection and facilitate choice between options. This does not mean that James wished to rescue some transcendental sense of selfhood as a therapeutic prop to justify any course of action, but only the kind of self that arises out of previous experiences. To help organise the chaotic flux of experience and make actions meaningful James's theory promotes the belief that by aspiring towards achievable goals, individuals can do more than respond passively to their environment; by keeping one's goals provisional and by avoiding absolutes, aims can be revised in the light of unforeseen changes. Without such a notion of 'willing', humans would be little more than animals in responding to sensory stimuli and following primitive urges for food and shelter. Indeed, he suggests that the belief in a willing self may be a moral question 'whose solution cannot wait for sensible proof'.[16] That is to say, one needs a sense of identity to continue with life without waiting for an irrefutable argument to confirm the existence of the will: to do so would be to give in to inertia or determinism. This theory in which value and meaning emerge as the creative fruit of 'willing' is central to James's humanism.

James wrote two essays in 1905 that deal directly with humanism: 'The Essence of Humanism' and 'Humanism and Truth Once More', collected posthumously in *Essays in Radical Empiricism* (1912). In the first essay he describes humanism not as a theory, but as 'a slow shifting in the philosophic perspective, making things appear as from a new center of interest', which he detects most obviously in Dewey's essays from the late 1890s.[17] He offers his 'own provisional definition of humanism' as a defence against anti-humanist critics who attack the idea of truth without proposing an alternative model of their own.[18] James's definition emphasises the interconnectedness and plurality of experience, which taken 'as a whole is self-containing and leans on nothing'. This view of humanism could be read in two ways: it is secular in the sense that

there is nothing higher than human experience, and it is religious in the sense
that God is not an 'absolute all-experiencer, but simply the experiencer of
widest actual conscious span'.[19] James's view actually reconciles religious and
secular humanisms by dealing with both within the terms of experience: on this
view there is nothing outside of consciousness and sensation, not even God.
Rather than retaining a notion of 'Truth' (with a capital 'T') that transcends the
stream of life, there are only provisional truths that should be modified or
abandoned if future experiences cannot square with them. Developing this idea
in his second essay on humanism, James suggests that we can have degrees of
truth, or a notion of 'the more true', without retaining 'ancient ideals of rigor
and finality'.[20] This strain of humanism is close to James's theory of 'radical
empiricism', which treats even non-empirical phenomena as if they were part
of the empirical world. He argues that we should not just abandon the concepts
of belief, consciousness, imagination and emotion because they cannot be
scientifically tested. If something emerges which falsifies their existence then
James is ready to jettison them as pragmatic concepts, but, until then, by acting
as if such capacities do exist, the individual can achieve a greater range of goals
than physiological activities that are verifiable from an empirical perspective.

The section 'Pragmatism and Humanism' in *Pragmatism* does much the
same work as these two essays in attempting to 'unstiffen' the notions of 'truth'
and 'reality'. James stresses that 'truths are man-made products', reality is
made up of human experiences, and 'all our formulas have a human twist'.[21]
His pragmatic argument is that truth is always being made and is not an all-
encompassing perspective or God's-eye view. This does not mean that we can
rid ourselves of old truths and simply accept anything that we feel means
something at any one moment; indeed, James stresses that the influence of old
truths is 'absolutely controlling' and failure to recognise this 'is the source of
much of the unjust criticism levelled against pragmatism'.[22] He suggests that
we must remain 'loyal' to old truths, but often we encounter new experiences
which encourage a 'rearrangement' of them: thus, truth is what individuals 'do'
when they rearrange experiences into fresh constellations of meaning.[23]
Similarly, rather than reality being a static substratum, the 'skinny outline' of
which can be sketched by empirical means, from a pragmatic view reality is a
'rich thicket' that is 'still in the making, and awaits part of its complexion from
the future'.[24] Just as truth is never entirely objective, James insists that reality is
not simply a subjective fiction with which we can do anything. Instead, reality
is the bedrock of human existence that cannot be overcome by religious belief
or logic; it resists the attempts to mould it in a particular way, and certain
physical and biological forces cannot be overcome by an effort of will. But this
does not mean that individuals are entirely determined by these forces. James's
pragmatism encourages a movement away from determinism towards a

creative reassessment of what there is and what may be in the future: 'it means the open air and possibilities of nature, as against dogma, artificiality, and the pretence of finality in truth'.[25]

Much of James's theoretical work is embedded in the organic metaphors he uses to redescribe certain ideas: he wants to 'unstiffen' theory and describe the 'rich thicket' of reality and 'the river of experience' against the shallow abstractions of science. In *Pragmatism* he extends these metaphors to establish two theoretical temperaments: the 'tough-minded' empiricist, who privileges materialism and tends to be irreligious and fatalistic, and the 'tender-minded' rationalist, who cherishes free will and is both religious and optimistic.[26] Although James gravitates towards the 'tender-minded' pole, he sees pragmatic humanism as bridging the two temperaments as 'a sort of free-will determinism' which respects the commonsense scientific view that there are certain substances that lie beyond the human sphere, but retains the belief that humans can act on and with these substances to create meaning.[27] But, far from human agents being sovereign, chaotic impressions constantly arise to prevent individuals attaining total control over their environment; this would reduce the hidden complexity of experience to the autocracy of the self-determining individual that, from James's humanist perspective, would be philosophically and morally unacceptable.

James's pragmatic humanism is not just theoretical in nature. He was particularly interested in extreme psychic states, alternative religions and the ways in which pragmatic techniques can help individuals suffering from mental and bodily illness (a particular concern with the rise of neurasthenia in the 1890s among the middle classes in America, affecting James's younger sister, Alice, as well as the writer Charlotte Perkins Gilman). In his spiritual and religious writing he does not resurrect a belief in the absolutes of health, reason or God, but emphasises the renewing potential of experience as the 'real backbone of the world's religious life'.[28] Just as in *Principles* he abandoned dogmatic science, in *The Varieties of Religious Experience* James rejects doctrinal thought for its tendency to restrict the range of possible experiences; instead he suggests that for the true humanist 'the world is a double-storied mystery' that always defies absolute clarity of vision.[29] This kind of experiencing traveller wanders through a dense and potentially bewildering universe, but reaps the benefits of creative energies which are undervalued in normal circumstances and which dwell latently in the deeper recesses of the self. Spiritual inspiration can help release these hidden energies to awaken a more strenuous life: like Nietzsche, by tapping into a Dionysian energy source James envisages a self liberated from the rigid structures of egoism or the safe, but shallow, haven of routine. As such, he recommends that we live at maximum energy, stimulated by 'excitements, ideas, and efforts' which can 'carry us over the dam' of apathy or 'chronic invalidism'.[30] This notion of rebellion against social conformity and established categories of illness suggests a higher realm of existence that resists 'intellectual respectability' and 'decorum' for restricting the ends to which humans can direct their energy.[31] While James shows his Nietzschean influence here, where the pair part company is in James's humanist stress on ethical boundaries that the pursuit of intense experiences should facilitate (or certainly should not break), with the individual directed by a strong sense of morality and human compassion.

John Dewey

Following James's death in 1910, the social critic Randolph Bourne hailed John Dewey as 'the most significant thinker in America' for the range of his thought and his 'democratic attitude towards life'.[32] When Dewey himself died in 1952, at the age of ninety-three, his friend and fellow pragmatist Sidney Hook stressed 'the immense and imponderable' impact of his work, fondly recalling 'the warm and husky voice which spoke the liberal conscience of America'.[33] Dewey was not a revolutionary thinker like Nietzsche, nor the leader of a movement like Freud, but he gave pragmatism an institutional legitimacy and provided fresh impetus to James's ideas by applying the pragmatic method to political, social and educational problems. James was a profound influence on the formation of Dewey's philosophy, providing him with a biological theory for understanding the relationship between humans and their environment. James was even complimentary about the new direction Dewey was taking pragmatism, while Dewey recommended chapters of James's *Principles* to his students when teaching at the University of Chicago between 1894 and 1904 (and later at Columbia University).[34] Like James, Dewey forged the transition from Victorian veneration of empirical science to a more nuanced modern approach to human behaviour, while both thinkers stressed experimentalism over a respect for tradition or slavish conformity to procedure. However, whereas James's work focused on the individual and was attentive to the internal phenomena of imagination, emotion and will, Dewey's humanism drew him towards improving social frameworks that would enable individuals to grow morally and help groups to achieve particular goals. Randolph Bourne was later to criticise Dewey openly, but in 1915 commented that Dewey's pragmatism 'challenges the whole machinery of our world of right and wrong, law and order, property and religion, the old techniques by which society is still being managed and regulated'.[35]

As fellow humanists, James and Dewey disliked metaphysics and mistrusted high-level philosophy that removes ideas from their applicability to the living human being. They both conceived of people as active (rather than passive) and as an integrated and organic whole, not divided into mind and body, nor into separate psychological faculties. Although Dewey was a more systematic thinker than James, this emphasis on activity and 'doing' is evident in early essays like 'The Scholastic and the Speculator' (1891), in which Dewey attacked academic scholasticism for its tendency to encourage ivory-tower philosophy divorced from everyday life. He argues that the scholar should not be content to deal with formal problems from an impartial perspective, but 'must throw its fund out again into the stress of life'.[36] Here, and throughout his work, Dewey sought ways to bridge the gap between his role as rigorous philosopher and his belief in the individual's responsibility to find practical ways of dealing with social problems. On this issue, in a review of Dewey's major philosophical work *The Quest for Certainty* (1929), Kenneth Burke argued that Dewey wished to find an alternative to conceiving the universe as 'something like an insect under glass in a museum, and that to know it we must merely go and look at it'.[37] For Dewey, knowledge does not arise through abstract reasoning, but only through experience and an awareness of how organisms interact with their environment. Similarly, rather than accepting philosophical principles as the foundation for future work, Dewey argues for their constant reappraisal: 'It is no longer enough for a principle to be elevated, noble, universal, and hallowed by time. It must present its birth certificate, it must show under just what conditions of human experience it was generated, and must justify by itself its works, present or potential.'[38] In this way, Dewey shared with James a conviction that pragmatism offers a flexible method of inquiry that attends to shifts in experience and explores the gaps between different types of knowledge in order that individuals have room to act.

One of his most accessible essays to chart this shift (and reflecting the general spirit of pragmatism) is his autobiographical essay 'From Absolutism to Experimentalism' (1930), in which he clearly expresses his view that the search for absolute truths and certainty will always be frustrated (a topic also discussed in *The Quest for Certainty*). For Dewey, knowledge should be less about discovering a foundation on which to base a stable and rational worldview and more concerned with working within the flux of experience. He writes about his own development as 'a struggle between a native inclination towards the schematic and formally logical, and those incidents of experience that compelled me to take account of actual material': in other words, a struggle between professional philosopher and experiencing human being.[39] Whereas James gravitated towards organic experience, Dewey was much more ready to concede that procedures were necessary in a developed civil society and he sought a middle way that reconciled a systematic approach with a recognition of experiential change and human needs. This middle way lies at the heart of Dewey's humanism, which he often describes in terms of his belief in 'human nature'. In *Experience and Nature* (1925), Dewey describes human nature in Darwinian terms as the survival and adaptation of the organism, stressing that intelligence and problem-solving arise out of individuals having to respond to and cope with the irregular and unstable aspects of nature. He sees a straightforward path from individuals experimenting with pragmatic techniques as a way of adapting to environmental pressures towards an emergent sense of community in which all members work towards mutually beneficial goals.

Here, though, we can identify a problem with pragmatic humanism, in that personal experiences do not necessarily equip individuals to act in mutually beneficial ways. In order to prevent the individual from being led by self-interest, instinct or whim, the only means to self-fulfillment according to Dewey is a humanistic drive towards the common good: 'what is really good for me *must* turn out good for all, or else there is no good in the world at all'.[40] More than this, in his defence of democracy, *The Public and Its Problems* (1927), Dewey discusses the notion that before individuals can 'learn to be human' they must develop 'the give-and-take of communication' and 'an effective sense of being an individually distinctive member of a community'.[41] To ensure his ideas are not simply packaged as social idealism, he is careful to remind the reader that the persistence of 'the old Adam, the unregenerate element in human nature', means that the notion of a common good is a state that is never finally reached. As a liberal thinker, Dewey remained convinced that, although biology and historical necessity place limitations on human endeavour, this common good should be a constant source of inspiration. While this theory is inherently humanist, balancing individualism with the social good, critics like Neil Coughlan have targeted Dewey's early work for being 'oddly blind to behaviour that was not earnest, methodical, and goal-orientated'.[42] In other words, while Dewey's pragmatism is concerned with the formulation of practical methods which can help individuals strive towards social cohesiveness, his theory of human nature does not really account for sin, waywardness or cultural difference (as elements of spiritual, pagan and civic humanism respectively) which would make some individuals and groups resist working towards the common good. More than anything else, the question of who defines this 'good' remains unanswered in Dewey's work.

Despite this theoretical blind spot, Dewey's pragmatic impulse propelled his mature work away from contemplative analytic philosophy towards formulating theories of action, social involvement and practical politics. Although he remained convinced that intellectuals should have an active and public role, such as his work on 'democratic' educational theory (in which he argued that children should be treated as active human beings whose imagin-ations will never be stimulated by passive book learning[43]), he did not think that intellectuals work best in the service of governments or that they should be directly responsible for social planning. Such pragmatic social policy-making was embodied by the US Brains Trust formed in 1932, which helped to determine F. D. Roosevelt's early plans for lifting the nation out of economic depression following the 1929 Stock Market Crash. Although Roosevelt is often considered to be a pragmatic president (like Jefferson and Lincoln before him), Dewey was critical not just of the imaginative shallowness of the Brains Trust (which tended to subordinate 'the human' to expedient theories of social management), but also of Roosevelt's whole New Deal policy.[44] He felt the New Deal failed to embrace the true spirit of reform liberalism because it lacked 'any defined social philosophy ... which would give direction to this latent idealism'; it needed 'to do something' more than simply regenerate economic growth in order 'to bring about a desired state of society'.[45] This 'latent idealism' lies at the heart of Dewey's pragmatic humanism and his attempt to discover ways of reconciling the roles of intellectual as humanist, political agent and the historically engaged, but disinterested, critical commentator.

Dewey's belief in democracy survived the Depression, so much so that in *Freedom and Culture* (1939) he discusses the democratic ideal in explicitly humanist terms. His liberal beliefs led to his assertion that democracy gives 'freer play' to 'human nature' than do 'non-democratic institutions' and therefore 'has always been allied with humanism, with faith in the potentialities of human nature'.[46] Given that in *Freedom and Culture* Dewey responded to the clash of democratic and totalitarian ideals that led to World War II, his argument that 'the present need is vigorous reassertion' of democratic faith was both timely and pressing.[47] He sees this democratic spirit as most fully expressed in 'the American tradition', but is realistic enough to admit that 'democracy means that humanistic culture *should* prevail', rather than that it necessarily will do so. He argues that only democracy can fully realise 'human potentialities' and looks back to the founding statement of American democratic ideals embodied in the Declaration of Independence as a constant source of inspiration.[48] He fuses the pragmatic method of 'forming' beliefs in the light of experience with the liberal ideal of 'conversation' among responsible individuals as the key for fostering democratic sensibility. For Dewey, the anti-humanist alternative (which, as for Hannah Arendt, was embodied in Nazism) begins with suspicion, intolerance and hostility but ends 'by denying' a particular group of people 'all human qualities': 'the substitution of ballots for bullets, of the right to vote for the lash, is an expression of the will to substitute the method of discussion for the method of coercion'.[49] While it is difficult to argue against this assertion of democratic freedom given the dark days in which Dewey was writing, as Alan Ryan has argued, this argument tends to rely too heavily on the idea 'of a preexisting harmony between human nature and democracy' that may overlook situations in which democracy becomes an ideological veneer or a political slogan to hide a less than democratic reality.[50] Moreover, if the pragmatic method demands attention to short-term and provisional goals, the visionary ideal of democracy may prove illusory and/or harmful to realistic social prospects. Nevertheless, Dewey's emphasis on human interaction and his understanding of democracy as more than a political system, but also 'a moral standard for personal conduct', reveals a thinker whose faith in the better possibilities of the individual runs throughout his work.[51]

As we have seen, although Dewey was not afraid to state his faith in democracy, his brand of pragmatism was worldly and secular in principle, even though his socialist-liberal ideals reveal vestiges of his early Christian faith that he lost in 1891. For example, in his 1934 book on religion, *A Common Faith* (as a variation on the 'common good'), Dewey echoes James in asserting that a rejection of 'supernaturalism' (an umbrella term which includes transcendental Christianity) does not necessarily entail a repudiation of what Dewey calls 'the religious phase of experience'.[52] Dewey wished to dispense with the category of 'religion' altogether because of its anti-empiricism and its preoccupation with metaphysical concerns such as the existence of God, but he wanted to retain the potential of religious experience for nurturing 'the sense of values which carry one through periods of darkness and despair'.[53] While institutional religions legitimate certain kinds of spiritual expression, he argues that they may actually prove to be 'encumbrances that now smother or limit' true religious experience.[54] At this time, Dewey also contributed to the drafting of the *Humanist Manifesto*, signed in 1933 by thirty-four American academics, intellectuals and clergy, that called for a 'candid and explicit humanism' (based on reason, science and democracy) to challenge religious orthodoxy and its limited view of 'human nature'.[55]

These examples suggest that Dewey's work from the 1930s offers a more nuanced view of human nature and a sceptical attitude towards the social organisation of experience (even though he did not totally reject religion and his liberal optimism led him to insist that 'periods of darkness and despair' are only ever temporary). Rather than fleeing the empirical world for a transcendent realm, like James he argued that religious experiences help to enlarge social and moral possibilities by 'bringing about a better, deeper and enduring adjustment in life'.[56] Commitment to a religious life may nurture moral conviction and provide practical knowledge that helps individuals and communities adapt to social demands and strive for more far-reaching goals. Further, although he seems to contradict himself when he argues that the 'scientific method' provides the only means of adapting to the future and the demands of modernity, he is modest in his opinion that science will never relieve us from having to deal with exacting political and ethical problems.[57]

Richard Rorty

As the most famous of the late twentieth-century wave of neo-pragmatists, Richard Rorty has addressed some of the key ideas in James's and Dewey's work and also guided pragmatism away from an emphasis on experience to deal with issues of interpretation and language. Rorty has rarely written explicitly on humanism, but as in his two predecessors there is a humanist strain running through his work, and although he is very sceptical of some concepts, he sees 'nothing wrong' with terms like 'humanism' or 'liberal individualism'.[58] As a professional philosopher at the University of Virginia, Rorty's range of expression may seem more limited than James and Dewey at times. However, although some of his essays demand a reasonably high level of engagement with philosophical ideas and the history of thought, such as his treatise *Philosophy and the Mirror of Nature* (1979) and the essays collected in *The Consequences of Pragmatism* (1982), he has developed a more relaxed writing style to address theoretical issues in more accessible forms in *Contingency, Irony, and Solidarity* (1989) and *Philosophy and Social Hope* (1999), as well as writing on aesthetics, literature and religion. Indeed, in his autobiographical essay, 'Trotsky and the Wild Orchids' (1992) he expresses his 'distrust of intellectual snobbery' which tends to wrap philosophy in highly specialist language accessible only to the technically competent reader.[59] Not only has Rorty given up the 'quest for certainty' (which Dewey dismissed as philosophy's false aim), but he does not believe that philosophy has any 'mission' in a far-reaching sense, nor is it the 'task' of philosophers to confirm or disprove spiritual and moral beliefs. This idea may be interpreted as a concession to the humanity of the reader in which one's private moments 'won't necessarily fit within one big overall account of how everything hangs together', or it may imply that philosophy has been trivialised in an age that tends to privilege technological discourses.[60] Rorty makes the humble claim that he can only offer 'some advice about what will happen when you try to combine or to separate certain ideas, on the basis of our knowledge of the results of past experiments'.[61] This modest pragmatic aim embodies Dewey's notion of the experimenter trying to find a positive way forward, not by dismissing the past but by testing present possibilities against procedures gleaned from experience. While Rorty has inherited some of James's and Dewey's optimism, their sense that 'ideas have consequences' and their intolerance of theoretical absolutes, he is modest when asked what philosophy can and should do.[62]

We will return later to 'Trotsky and the Wild Orchids', but it is worth rehearsing the way in which Rorty's work has moved on from his early rejection of the spectatorial view of truth to more wide-ranging considerations of what philosophy can and cannot hope to do.[63] In *Philosophy and the Mirror of*

Nature, Rorty lays out his early philosophical priorities by arguing that 'the way things are said' is more 'essential' (that is, more useful) as a method of coping with the world, than the empirical project of gathering facts.[64] He wants to dispense with the argument that ideas provide a mirror of the way the world is; like Dewey he abandons theories of representation and knowledge together with the 'desire to find "foundations" to which one might cling' and 'frameworks from which one must not stray'.[65] This abandoning of truth may lead some thinkers to search for an alternative theory to fill the 'vacancy' these foundationalist philosophies leave behind; for Rorty this alternative theory seems to be an interpretative (or hermeneutic) theory of language. However, he is quick to stress that this vacancy should not be filled, arguing that 'hermeneutics is not the name for a discipline, nor for a method of achieving the sort of results which epistemology failed to achieve'; rather it is 'an expression of hope that the cultural space left by the demise of epistemology will not be filled – that our culture should become one in which the demand for constraint and confrontation is no longer felt'.[66] Interestingly, he not only shifts the emphasis from knowledge to interpretation, but also from philosophy to culture. As a 'post-Philosopher', Rorty is hopeful that those who currently 'do' philosophy will reject the role of 'cultural overseer who knows everyone's common ground' and who offers an explanatory master discourse, in favour of the 'informed dilettante' who sees 'the relations between various discourses as those strands in a possible conversation'.[67] The spirit of Dewey hovers over this idea of a rational conversation among consenting beings, but Rorty develops the idea by arguing that such a '*societas*' is formed from 'people whose paths in life have fallen together, united by civility rather than by a common goal'.[68] For Rorty, 'to be fully human' is not to reach agreement with others on common grounds, but to engage in conversations that may lead to 'exciting and fruitful disagreement'.[69]

The way ahead for Rorty is not to wrestle with traditional conceptions of knowledge in the hope of defeating them, but to dissolve certain ideas that make grand truth-claims about the human condition. He introduces the notion of 'redescription' as a way of pushing debates forward, without his needing first to kill off the spectres of tradition. He claims that 'redescribing ourselves is the most important thing we can do', in the sense that we may find 'a new and more interesting way of expressing ourselves, and thus coping with the world'.[70] Any single attempt to theorise the human is no truer than, and cannot be privileged above, any other, it is merely one element 'among the repertoire of self-descriptions at our disposal'.[71] For this reason, Rorty makes a stab at the existentialist notion of the human as a reaction to epistemology; simply to replace the Platonic idea that we have essences with the existentialist idea that 'our essence is no essence' merely replicates the same logic in a different guise.

If it is one of the chief goals of classical philosophy to see the world reflected in an unclouded mirror, then the existential attempt to unclutter the mind by seeking freedom through action can be seen to be as metaphysical as Plato's search for the ideas that lie behind worldly appearances. In Rorty's view, 'to look for a way of making further redescription unnecessary by finding a way of reducing all *possible* descriptions to one ... is to attempt escape from humanity'.[72] The alternative to this pluralistic model would be to find an explanatory discourse (whether drawn from science, religion or ethics) that puts an end to conversation, which for Rorty would lead to the 'freezing-over of culture' and 'the dehumanization of human beings', as tends to happen in totalitarian regimes when the official function of art becomes state propaganda.

In *Philosophy and the Mirror of Nature* Rorty develops Dewey's rationalist emphasis on intelligible conversations that propel debates forward (rather than providing answers), but in his interest in redescription and 'the romantic notion of man as self-creative', he also revives the more dynamic and aesthetic strains of James's pragmatism.[73] The tradition of American liberal thought clearly unites all three thinkers (Rorty actually calls himself a Deweyan at times), but he goes on to claim that pragmatism is not just the offspring of the Anglo-American analytic tradition, but also dovetails with European critical theory: 'James and Dewey were not only waiting at the end of the dialectical road which analytical philosophy traveled, but are waiting at the end of the road which, for example, Foucault and Deleuze are currently traveling.'[74] Linking these thinkers (together with Nietzsche) is 'the sense that there is nothing deep down inside us except what we have put there ourselves, no criterion that we have not created in the course of creating a practice'.[75] This notion of the self as having 'no substrate behind the attributes' refashions James and Dewey as precursors of postmodern thought, in the sense that the self does not exist as an entity, but only comes into being through practical measures.[76] As such, in 'The Priority of Democracy to Philosophy' (1988), Rorty claims that Dewey maintained 'neither the distinction between will and intellect nor the distinction between the self's constituents and its attributes'.[77] It is true that Dewey and James both claimed that the self is always in process of becoming and has no essential core, but neither thinker goes as far as Rorty in invoking a depthless self. For Rorty, theories of the self may simply prove useless or distracting and if we can get along with commonsense views, why then not dispense with the notion of 'the self' or 'the human' altogether?

Rorty actually argues that in certain situations it might prove beneficial to abandon such categories, whereas other occasions may demand that we rely on provisional definitions in order to make things work. The issue is that we do not need first to agree on what 'the self' is or what 'the human' means, before starting to discuss a related topic or to act in a particular way. For example, discussions about democracy, civil rights or religious faith do not need underpinning with a coherent definition of the self, human nature or God: on this view, 'as citizens and social theorists, we can be as indifferent to philosophical disagreements about the nature of the self as Jefferson was to theological differences about the nature of God' when he was helping to formulate The Declaration of Independence.[78] But Rorty's theory does not mean that we must necessarily dispense with such concepts, but only if they prevent us beginning to converse on a given subject. Far from this theory being anti-humanist, Rorty actually moves to a position in which humanity is affirmed through the type of conversation that helps to foster values of attentiveness, sharing, accommodation and tolerance. Writing in the shadow of Dewey's sense that 'the terms "America" and "democracy" are shorthand for a new conception of what it is to be human',[79] Rorty claims that democratic politics should come prior to philosophical rumination (when it is a simple choice between the two), shifting the argument away from asking the question 'what is the self?' to asking 'would not acting out this vision interfere with the ability of others to work out their own salvation?'[80] On this basis, Rorty argues, 'the pragmatic utopia' (which, one suspects, he believes is possible only in America) 'is not one in which human nature is emancipated, but rather one where each has the chance to propose various ways of building a world society'.[81]

While Rorty uses arguments based on common sense as a way of distancing himself from metaphysics, in *Contingency, Irony, and Solidarity* he argues that commonsense thinkers often indulge in intellectual laziness by taking ideas for granted and describing 'everything important in terms of the final vocabulary to which they ... are habituated'.[82] In contrast, he prefers the term 'private ironist' for describing an intellectual who 'has radical and continuing doubts about the final vocabulary' currently used and whose role is to challenge the status quo, playing new descriptions and vocabularies 'off against the old'.[83] Rorty developed this conception of the private ironist through the 1980s: a pluralistic position in which we are surrounded by different vocabularies, some of which are useful in particular situations, but none of which are necessarily better than the others. Rather than accepting Dewey's notion of the 'common good' for which we all must strive, Rorty's notion of competing language games means we should resist final vocabularies – they should always be provisional and flexible – without giving up on the 'common hopes' for a more tolerant and less cruel world.[84] As an ironist, Rorty does not embark on the sceptical path where all vocabularies are treated with suspicion; rather he insists that these language games are personal affairs, admitting that he 'cannot go on to claim that there could or ought to be a culture whose public rhetoric is *ironist*' in which all members are 'continually dubious about their own process of socialization'.[85] Only in a liberal society, he claims, can the gap between private and public be a creative one, encouraging 'greater openness' and 'more room for self-creation' on a personal level, but provoking the individual to have 'imaginative identification' with others by finding 'overlapping words' that enable him or her to notice suffering in other people's lives.[86] Similarly, in 'Trotsky and the Wild Orchids' he claims that we should avoid collapsing everything – private tastes, public roles and moral priorities – into one coherent frame of reference, and resist subordinating human concerns to a non-human principle such as reality or moral law. Dewey's democratic community cannot be achieved by explanation, only through the individual's obligation to 'sympathize with the pain of others'.[87]

Although Rorty does not like words like 'mission' because they are too idealistic, his essays written in the late 1980s and 1990s in *Philosophy and Social Hope* contain glimmers of latent idealism. For example, in 'The Humanistic Intellectual: Eleven Theses' (1989) he considers that the purpose of the humanities should be to expand an individual's 'moral imagination' and 'to enlarge their sense of what is possible and important'.[88] In order to achieve this, the vocation of the humanist intellectual is 'to instil doubts in the students about the students' own self-images, and about the society to which they belong'.[89] He claims that in the 1980s (with the influence of poststructuralism) the humanities became 'self-obsessed, 'ingrown' and 'over-philosophized', leading to stagnation and the policing of subject areas in universities, whereas his vision of the humanities is one in which they change 'fast enough so that they remain indefinable and unmanageable', an ideal situation that can only be brought about, he claims, through 'good old-fashioned academic freedom'.[90] Rorty is quick to admit that he believes his country is 'in decline' and is 'in danger of losing its soul', that Dewey's vision of America has been lost with the emergence of an 'overclass' in which only the top 20 per cent live in protected social spaces in which liberal values can be preserved.[91] He does not see America as the template for a just society (he actually promotes the revitalised global role of the United Nations), but suggests that a certain American temperament – pragmatic and forward-looking – means that 'the possibilities of a utopian future' are more likely to flourish there than elsewhere.[92] In developing Dewey's democratic ideals and James's emphasis on personal qualities, Rorty has begun to promote 'fraternity' as the key for overcoming inequality and injustice, rather than a rights-based social philosophy. These ideas are certainly both pragmatic and humanist. However, in his essay 'Looking Backwards from the Year 2096' (1996) – written five years before the terrorist attacks on New York and Washington – he remains perplexed how this 'principle of fraternity' can be formulated without reducing it to a meaningless abstract model.[93] Perhaps, he suggests, the only way fraternity could be both 'an inclination of the heart' and a means for authentic social cohesion is by not expecting too much of the future, of maintaining 'our chastened mood, our lately learned humility'.[94]

Primary Texts

William James

The Will to Believe and Other Essays in Popular Philosophy [1897] (New York: Dover, 1956).
The Varieties of Religious Experience: A Study in Human Nature [1902], ed. Martin E. Marty (London: Penguin, 1985).
Pragmatism [1907], ed. Bruce Kuklick (Indianapolis, IN: Hackett, 1981).
Essays in Radical Empiricism [1912] (Lincoln, NB: University of Nebraska Press, 1996).
The Moral Equivalent of War and Other Essays, ed. John K. Roth (New York: Harper & Row, 1971).

John Dewey

Experience and Nature [1925] (New York: Dover, 1958).
The Public and Its Problems (New York: Holt, 1927).
The Quest for Certainty [1929] (New York: Capricorn, 1960).
A Common Faith [1934] (New Haven, CT: Yale University Press, 1991).
Freedom and Culture [1939] (New York: Capricorn, 1963).

Richard Rorty

The Consequences of Pragmatism: Essays 1972–1980 (Brighton: Harvester, 1982).
Contingency, Irony, and Solidarity (Cambridge: Cambridge University Press, 1989).
Objectivity, Relativism, and Truth (Volume 1 of *Philosophical Papers*) (Cambridge: Cambridge University Press, 1991).
Truth and Progress (Volume 3 of *Philosophical Papers*) (Cambridge: Cambridge University Press, 1998).
Philosophy and Social Hope (London: Penguin, 1999).

CHAPTER 8

Technological Humanism
(Foucault – Baudrillard – Haraway)

The English Romantic poet William Blake's painting *Newton* (c. 1795) offers one of the most powerful meditations on the promises and dangers of science. Blake depicts the body of the mythologised Isaac Newton emerging organically from a rocky cliff as he crouches down to make an accurate mathematical drawing with his callipers. The dominant reading of the painting suggests that while scientific rationalism has the capacity to measure the natural world, it does so by reducing nature to mathematical formulae that imprison the human spirit. Blake's attack on static Newtonian mechanics in favour of Romantic dynamism was perhaps unfair on Newton, who actually believed the universe is made up of both matter and spirit; not until the eighteenth century with scientific materialists like Julien Offrey de la Mettrie in *L'Homme machine* (1747) was Newton's dualism assigned to a study of a single underlying substance by which everything else could be explained. While Newton directed his attention to the formulation of physical laws that explain the movement of matter and the workings of nature, post-Newtonian science has commonly been attacked for disregarding human experience or for attempting to reduce ineffable phenomena like emotions and imagination to raw matter. The scientific revolution in seventeenth-century Europe was crucial for accelerating the shift from a religious cosmology to a secular humanist worldview and, in its applied forms, in laying the groundwork for the industrial revolution that would radically alter the sphere of social relations. While the exactitude of science has often been viewed as the enemy of human creativity, the counter-view of scientific knowledge as a 'majestic procession' suggests, as Bryan Appleyard states, that 'science is *the* human project. It is what we are intended to do. It is the only adventure.'' Appleyard argues that there has always been a hard edge to materialist science (often called scientism), but we need to distinguish this from moderate scientific practices that are more amenable to the realm of human experience and do not try to reduce it to precise formulae. Scientific theory may not have the same world-shaking impact it had in the mid-sixteenth century when Nicolaus Copernicus refuted the dominant Ptolemaic view of the universe as geocentric (and elaborated by Galileo and Kepler), but the marriage between science and technology as its 'materialised practice' has historically held an increasingly profound sway over human life.[2]

The notion that science provides the only viable framework in the secular humanist search for truth is exemplified in George Sarton's introduction to the updated edition of the important collection *Science, Religion and Reality* (1955, first published in 1925). Sarton claims that science is:

> the whole body of systematised and objective knowledge; it is very incomplete and very imperfect, but it is indefinitely perfectible. The quest for truth fulfills one of the highest human purposes; moreover, it is the only human activity that is truly cumulative and progressive. The science of today is definitely and measurably better (closer to the truth) than that of yesterday.[3]

While Sarton recognises the limits of science when faced with an 'infinitely larger' universe, and that scientists tend to rely on thinkers from other disciplines to ask 'the bigger questions' underpinning scientific research, he concurs with the general mid-twentieth-century opinion that science and technology offer a kind of secular salvation that promises 'freedom from scarcity, want, and the arbitrariness of natural calamity'.[4] The focus in the post-war years, particularly in the USA and France, was not only on science increasing the quality of life in the invention and manufacture of time-saving appliances, but also its role in a broader project guided by technocrats and geared to overcoming human limitations through prototypes of the first robots and huge investments in space exploration. Given the threat of nuclear annihilation in the Cold War years, the development of technology was seen by many in the West as the only way in which global peace could be preserved, even though for critics like Norman Mailer it only served to trivialise or even to violate human life: Mailer argued that we, as frail human beings, might 'be doomed to die as a cipher in some vast statistical operation in which our teeth would be counted, and our hair would be saved, but our death itself would be unknown, unhonored, and unremarked.'[5] This tension between technology as the liberating handmaiden of science in its search for truth and technology as assigning humanity to the dustbin of history dominated debates in the second half of the twentieth century.

As we discussed in Chapter 4, Jürgen Habermas has argued that since the general collapse of religion and metaphysics in the nineteenth century, three distinct 'spheres' of science, morality and art have emerged, each prone to being guarded by 'special experts'.[6] Although Habermas claimed that in an ideal communicative world these spheres would talk to each other without collapsing their boundaries, since the mid-twentieth century 'arts versus science' debates have raged, with thinkers like C. P. Snow, F. R. Leavis, Julian Huxley, Jacob Bronowski and, more recently, Richard Dawkins arguing passionately for the primacy of either art or science. However, with the acceleration of biotechnological research in the 1980s and 1990s science has arguably placed itself in debate with the other spheres, at the same time as it threatens to overwhelm them. Indeed, as early as 1948 the pioneering chemist and inventor of the cinematograph Auguste Lumière claimed that

> it would be impossible to deny that the discoveries of Science always have affected Humanity's material progress ... Formal proof of this is found in the fact that these discoveries have permitted the existence of man to be prolonged to the point that the average life span has tripled since the beginning of our century.[7]

Lumière's comment seems homely when compared with current projections of dramatically increased life expectancy in developed countries (estimates in 2002 suggest around a hundred days per year added to life expectancy), suggesting that the duration of a 'human life' will need to be radically modified to contend with the likelihood of more years after the age of fifty than prior to it. Ethical debates concerning the quality of life in an ageing demography often reflect on the ways in which biotechnology may augment organic life to such an extent that in 'old age' the label 'human' may no longer be applicable. As the Human Genome Project promises to unlock the secrets of our genetic make-up, the Visible Human Project attempts to translate the human body into digital codes, and neurological scientists move closer to explaining how consciousness arises from physical matter, so these fields of research threaten to destroy the myth that each human being has a core of unique individuality that can neither be explained nor replicated. Catherine Waldby claims in *The Visible Human Project* (2000) that 'these "Human Projects" present themselves as new ways to map and know the human, yet [they] imply a disconcerting threat to any idea of the human as a stable, knowable "species", an organic integrity whose limits can be positively specified'.[8] The dangers of completing such genetic and neurological maps often appear to weigh heavier on the layman than the benefits, because they project human life into an unknowable future in which technology is so sophisticated that no ordinary individual will be able to cognitively map it. In the hands of specialists, technocrats and corporations, biotechnology is a frightening prospect, threatening to replace the 'natural' limits of human life with a more menacing type of obsolescence.

In 'The Question Concerning Technology' (1954) Heidegger claimed that it is impossible to unthink science or to leave behind technology once it has been introduced; consequently 'we remain unfree and chained to technology, whether we passionately affirm or deny it'.[9] Heidegger defines technology in instrumental terms as both a pragmatic tool and, in distinction from Habermas' theory of the separation of the spheres, as defining the whole realm of 'human activity'.[10] Basic tools like hammers and complex computerised operating systems each require technical mastery, but they are also resources that we have 'to hand' to transform the arena of human activity. Realising that scientists often overlook profound questions about the nature of technology (defined as the machinery which allows an activity or process to happen), Heidegger emphasises the often neglected aesthetic dimension of *techne*, from the Greek *tekhnē* meaning art or skill. *Techne* implies a 'bringing-forth' or disclosure of something new that had previously been concealed: the revelation of a truth previously beyond the horizon of human thought. While technological revelation and transformation are often linked to the humanist idea of progress, Heidegger stresses that we may be masters of tools but do not 'have control over unconcealment itself', nor can we determine their precise sphere of applicability, nor the ethical consequences of such application.[11] On this basis technology is both human and unhuman: on the one hand it provides tools which widen the sphere of human experience and, on the other, technology is simply a hybrid from the world of objects, or a system of components arranged to process abstract data – we may have the ability to manipulate such machines, but they remain fundamentally alien from us. While technology may liberate us from repetitious and dehumanising tasks, the exponential growth of technology threatens the death of the human or, at least, a radical historical transition into 'the posthuman'.[12]

We will leave a full discussion of 'posthuman' and 'inhuman' for the Conclusion as terms that are inseparable from the spectre of an ultra-technologised future. Nevertheless, this chapter engages with broadly posthuman concerns by focusing on three influential figures who have dealt with the dangers and benefits of technology: the French social theorists Michel Foucault (1926–84) and Jean Baudrillard (1929–), and the American historian of science and feminist Donna Haraway (1944–). As we discussed in the Introduction, Foucault and Baudrillard have been frequently recruited as anti-humanist thinkers for their apocalyptic declarations, such as Foucault's poetic claim that the human face has all but been washed away by the encroaching tide of history and Baudrillard's dystopian view that in a cybernetic age we have simply become copies of copies for which the original has been lost. However, while both thinkers have their apocalyptic anti-humanist sides, they also reveal strong humanist impulses – Foucault in his later writings on the 'technologies of the self' and Baudrillard in his work on the relationship between art and technology – that make them into much more interesting figures for assessing the ongoing tensions between humanism and anti-humanism. If, as we have claimed throughout the book, the two terms are locked in a continuing dialectic, it is perhaps most fully evident in Foucault's and Baudrillard's ambivalent relationship to humanism. While the impact of radical cultural theory continues to give currency to theories of the 'death' of the author, the 'death' of representation and the 'death' of originality in art and literature, digital technologies continue to invent new spaces – many of them invisible cyberspaces – that offer to extend infinitely the range of creative practices, just as they threaten the stability of the human. For example, despite his endless accounts of reality's decline into mass-mediated simulation, in the 1990s Baudrillard has modified his negative readings of technoculture with the unexpected suggestion that certain forms of mechanical reproduction, such as photography, may well regenerate human value. As such, Foucault concentrates on self-empowerment and 'technologies of the self' as a means to resist institutionalised power; Baudrillard looks back with a fond modernist eye to the mechanical medium of photography; and other critics praise digital technology as a form of 'quasi-spiritual technological utopianism' that optimistically revives the pronouncements of the new media guru Marshall McLuhan in the 1960s (despite McLuhan's reservations about technology), particularly his claim that 'the computer holds out the promise of a technologically engendered state of universal understanding and unity, a state of absorption in the logos that could knit mankind into one family and create a perpetuity of harmony and peace.'[13]

While Foucault and Baudrillard stand at the high point of Continental theory where anti-humanist and humanist ideas are finely balanced, in the 1990s Donna Haraway has addressed the fields of biotechnology and bioinformatics that look set to dissolve the dialectic by transforming the intellectual infrastructure on which it rests. As Catherine Waldby claims, these forms of biotechnics are self-propagating and 'do not work at the service of some pre-existing hierarchy of human subject/human species but rather work over any such hierarchy, modifying and upsetting existing sets of historical terms in [their] articulation'.[14] The likelihood that we are, or will soon all become 'theorised and fabricated hybrids of machine and organism' (or cyborgs) motivates Haraway's inquiry into the ontological, ethical and gender implications of biotechnics.[15] Biotechnology is not just a resource to be coordinated between hand and eye, but has the capacity to transform the parameters of the human body into a potentially unrecognisable form. Neither Baudrillard nor Haraway favours the 'death of …' theories that are often associated with them, and, while critics like Neil Badmington use 'posthuman' to identify a historically distinct period coinciding with the rise of biotechnics, Waldby discerns in Haraway's account of the cyborg a commitment to 'the human as a point of origin' that reinvokes humanism just as it appears to surpass it. Claiming that in the world of technoscience 'the lines among human, machine, and organic nature are highly permeable and eminently revisable', at the end of her 'Cyborg Manifesto' (1985) Haraway states, 'though they are both bound in the spiral dance, I would rather be a cyborg than a goddess'.[16] As we discuss below, her personal choice here between goddess and cyborg matters less than this image of a 'spiral dance' for illustrating the intertwining of humanist and anti-humanist discourses and their relation to technology.

Michel Foucault

Michel Foucault dealt with the concept of technology most explicitly in his work from the late 1970s and 1980s, but it is worth beginning the discussion by returning to his anti-humanist proclamations of the 1960s and 1970s and his highly critical view of humanism as an expression of 'the ideology of Western civilization in its most repressive and decadent phase'.[17] The popular image of Foucault is as an outspoken opponent of modern society and of the repressive social controls that developed in the nineteenth century in the form of hospitals, clinics, prisons and educational institutions. Although they often wear a mask of benevolence, to Foucault's mind these repressive institutions have increasingly bound individuals into networks of power and coercion. In his complex study of the systems of Western thought, *The Order of Things* (1966), he describes a clear epistemological break between what he calls the 'classical order' of the seventeenth and eighteenth centuries and the 'modern order' that began at the end of the eighteenth century, arguing that fixed conceptions of human nature contributed to the rise of scientific normalisation and social discrimination as powerful discourses of modernity. Rather than taking the line that humanism was at its zenith in the mid-eighteenth century and has been in decline ever since, he argues that the Enlightenment was a point of historical change which laid the ground for the discourse of 'man' becoming the 'self-evident ground for our thought' for modern thinkers.[18] Marking the 'point of departure' of this discourse in Kant's attempt to understand 'what constitutes the humanity of human beings' in his three *Critiques*, Foucault argues that the human-centred enquiry of modernity became an 'inevitability', but now appears to be approaching its end.[19] If humanist thought was 'inevitable' in the nineteenth and much of the twentieth century, then 'man's disappearance' occurs when the quest to understand 'the human' has exhausted itself (although this view seems premature in the light of recent biotechnological and genetic research). Foucault actually sees the demise of humanist discourse as liberating, arguing that the 'void left by man's disappearance ... does not create a deficiency' but 'the unfolding of a space in which it is once more possible to think'.[20] Like Nietzsche, who saw the 'death of God' as the unprecedented opportunity for the individual to surpass him or herself, Foucault sees this moment as the liberation from 'man' as fixed essence, as the anchor of knowledge and as a transcendental ideal: in short, 'all these warped and twisted forms of reflection' which he answers 'with a philosophical laugh'.²¹

On this view, the word 'man' is simply a label that is very close to its sell-by date, a convenient fiction that is now a dead metaphor. Certainly in the last third of the twentieth century it has become a major inconvenience for thinkers like Foucault, Derrida, Barthes and Deleuze in their attempt to 'unthink' humanism and approach theoretical issues from a radically different perspective. But while Foucault seemed to have buried humanism in favour of a historicised study of the systems of Western thought, in his important late essay 'What is Enlightenment?' (1984) he returned to reconsider its implications. Realising that the Enlightenment and humanism are often elided with each other, in this essay he is keen to differentiate between the two terms. He describes the Enlightenment as 'a set of events and complex historical processes' that 'includes elements of social transformation, types of political institution, forms of knowledge, projects of rationalisation of knowledge and practices, technological mutations that are very difficult to sum up in a word, even if many of these phenomena remain important today'.²² By way of contrast, he claims that humanism is 'something different entirely': a recurring 'set of themes' that are always tied to value judgments' and that serve 'as a critical principle of differentiation'.²³

Where *The Order of Things* and *The Archaeology of Knowledge* call for an escape from the prison-house of a humanism defined as 'the search for a total history, in which all the differences of society might be reduced to a single form', in 'What is Enlightenment?' Foucault takes a more modulated position.²⁴ Noting that humanism has been open to many mutations and distortions – Christian, theocentric, suspicious, Marxist and existentialist humanisms, or used in the name of National Socialism and Stalinism – he argues that 'the humanistic thematic is in itself too supple, too diverse [and] too inconsistent to serve as an axis for reflection'. He contrasts this kind of malleability with 'the principle of a critique and a permanent creation of ourselves' that he sees at the heart of the Enlightenment project. Although he does not explicitly follow this line, his claim that humanism and the Enlightenment are locked 'in a state of tension' reflects the idea that humanist and anti-humanist thought are the flipsides of the same discourse. Although Habermas has criticised Foucault for being too harsh on institutions of modernity, the two agree that the principle of critique is Enlightenment's saving grace.²⁵ Without the notion of a permanent, self-questioning critique humanism becomes essentialist, transcendental and uncritical; yet without a working notion of 'the human', what Kant calls *Menschheit*, critique may dissolve into world-weary cynicism, or frees itself from humanist inquiry only to see humanism reappropriated elsewhere in the name of a particular technology of power.

Foucault's critique of humanism derives from his theory that after the Enlightenment 'the human' becomes the starting point of enquiry and establishes all the parameters of what it is possible to know. He argues that the relatively new human sciences (psychology, sociology and literary analysis) are predicated on modes of enquiry derived from their more empirical scientific counterparts (biology, economics and philology), with all these fields of enquiry sanctifying 'the human' as the end point of knowledge. While humanism often posits the infinite resourcefulness of humans and celebrates scientific progress for its promise to free individuals from necessity, Foucault argues that humanism actually offers only the illusion of sovereignty, freedom and self-empowerment. Worse than this, the rhetoric of humanism is often used as a way of delimiting the repertoire of techniques available to individuals or restricting the possibility of acting in non-prescribed ways: as Jon Simons writes, on this view 'humanism is ... a series of doctrines which tie us to our subjectivities and to particular notions of personhood' that 'prevent us from attaining maturity and bind us to the authority of the forces that limit us'.[26] Similarly, while science may open the door to a broader spectrum of knowledge, for every moment of scientific progress Foucault detects a 'strange regression' into ever more pervasive forms of social domination, political surveillance and debilitating governmentality.[27] In an increasingly technolo-gised world it becomes more and more difficult to identify coercion and false consciousness within the machinery of relations that seems to define our subjectivity. For example, 'technologies of health' are not just confined to the contents of a doctor's medical bag or the chemical technologies that refine medication. Foucault would use 'technology' in the widest possible sense to refer to 'all the diverse means, projects and devices' in the realm of medical and pharmaceutical governmentality that give value to certain kinds of health and that diagnose, treat, administer to and make patients out of individuals.[28] On this level, Donna Haraway reads Foucault's concept of bio-power to mean all those 'practices of administration, therapeutics, and surveillance of bodies that discursively constitute, increase, and manage the forces of living organisms'.[29]

Foucault was very attentive to the ways in which the power/knowledge nexus controls an individual's body, particularly in relation to health and sexuality. Taking the metaphor of Jeremy Bentham's nineteenth-century design for a prison, the Panopticon, in which total surveillance of the inmates was possible, Foucault's idea of a 'carceral society' in which individual freedom is limited by marshalling space and regulating behaviour was central to his writings in the mid–1970s. In its most punitive forms, such governmental power can 'expose, mark, wound, amputate, make a scar, stamp a sign on the face ... in short, seize hold of the body and inscribe upon it the marks of power', but in modern Western society it works more often in a confining manner to impose restrictions on freedom in return for certain civil liberties.[30] Noticing that such a history has not yet been written, Foucault calls for a study of the total 'physics' of power, including the 'optics' of observation, the 'mechanics' of discipline and the 'physiology' of 'corrective interventions that are ambiguously [both] therapeutic and punitive'.[31] In the nineteenth century, scientific theory gave (sometimes spurious) justification to the labelling and control of certain 'abnormal' conditions such as madness, idiocy, delinquency, perversion and onanism, with technology developed to limit, confine or cure those who threaten, or are seen as a threat to, the power–knowledge nexus. The hospital, for example, is a 'place of observation, of diagnosis, of clinical and experimental identification, but also of immediate intervention' against disease, the control of hygiene and the internment of the sick.[32] On this model, science and technology become the theory and practice of controlling particular modes of behaviour and of delimiting freedom. While on the one hand Foucault claimed he was afraid of humanism presenting 'ethics as a universal model for any kind of freedom', on the other hand he wishes to rescue the (albeit limited) notion of human rights from the technological forces of unfreedom that are central to his vision of a carceral society policed by pernicious forms of knowledge and power.[33]

The enquiry into the limits of knowledge was central to Foucault's anti-humanism (what he calls a 'limit-attitude'[34]), but a stronger humanist current is apparent in his early interest in existentialism and then resurfaces again in explicit reference to a more positive conception of technology in his writings from the late 1970s and early 1980s. Rather than subjectivity being simply defined as subjugation to technologies of social power, in the incomplete multi-volume *The History of Sexuality* (1976–84) he outlines 'etho-poetic' rules of conduct that can help the individual to become his or her own subject. Like Nietzsche and Arendt, Foucault searches for the antidotes to the unfreedom of the modern world in Classical thought (although he rarely makes these historical parallels explicit), looking back to the Stoic technique of *askesis* as 'an exercise of oneself in the activity of thought'.[35] His theory of 'technologies of the self' is bound up in this practice of *askesis*, not as a 'disclosure of the secret self' or the laying bare of the unconscious, but an active remembering.[36] He describes it as the

> progressive consideration of self, or mastery over oneself, obtained ... through the acquisition and assimilation of truth ... It is a set of practices by which one can acquire, assimilate, and transform truth into a permanent principle of action. *Aletheia* becomes *ethos*. It is the process of becoming more subjective.[37]

Rather than seeing technology simply as machinery or an interface with the 'outside world' that requires manipulation, Foucault (like Heidegger) emphasises the notion of *techne* as the mastery of a set of techniques and practices that enable individuals to become, at least to some extent, self-determining. 'Technologies of the self' thus becomes a powerful metaphor for an ethics of living in which 'the self' is in a constant state of construction and does not need to refer back to any fixed notion of human nature. Foucault argues that an individual has 'not an immortal soul but many mortal ones' which are 'unable to be mastered by the powers of synthesis'.[38] We cannot 'find ourselves' by synthesising these technologies or by resurrecting a grand unified narrative of humanity; rather, in line with his theory of *techne*, freedom from pernicious technologies can be achieved by replacing humanist 'sovereignty' with the notion of an actively constructed self (or selves), constantly made and remade piecemeal by means of techniques like *askesis*.

Foucault is careful to distinguish 'technologies of the self' that enable individuals to 'transform themselves in order to attain a certain state of happiness, purity, wisdom, perfection, or immortality' from an existentialist notion of self-becoming (discussed in Chapter 2), because he sees in Sartre a nostalgia for an essentialist self: 'we should not have to refer the creative activity of somebody to the kind of relation he has to himself, but should relate the kind of relation one has to oneself to a creative activity'.[39] Rejecting this limiting notion of a 'somebody' to which 'creative activity' occurs, we are left with a set of techniques that are not predicated on the notion of a core self. Foucault certainly proceeds with more care than Sartre but, as Jon Simons argues, he remains bound to a neo-Romantic notion of an aestheticised self that is somehow free from debilitating forms of subjugation.[40] Moreover, as Lois McNay notes, his image of an 'unencumbered self' disregards any 'fundamentally embedding structures' that may prevent certain transformations taking place, be they in terms of biology, psychology, economics, race or gender.[41]

Although Foucault emphasises stoic self-discipline over aesthetic expressiveness, it is not difficult to detect hints of Romantic humanism in his valorisation of key terms: aestheticisation, invention, possibility, transgression and the notion of beginning again. Indeed, mainly because he does not stress social relatedness as much as a civic-minded thinker like Hannah Arendt (whose theory of improvisation is discussed in Chapter 2), there seem to be less reason why Foucault's re-technologised self cannot attain the kind of dubious sovereignty that he sees as the chief weakness of classical humanism. We will return to these problems later in the chapter, but it is important to stress again that the force of Foucault's criticism is directed at a grandiose humanism that often hides threatening technologies of power behind the mask of benign universalism. However, although he claimed 'that there are more secrets, more possible freedoms, and more inventions in our future than we can imagine in humanism as it is dogmatically represented on every side of the political rainbow', it is this dogma of which he is most critical. Indeed, in his later writing in the early 1980s Foucault seemed to be moving toward identifying certain techniques that would activate an agonistic, situated and self-critical humanism.[42]

Jean Baudrillard

Where Foucault concentrates on technologies that have developed in the 'modern age', Jean Baudrillard's critical attention has been firmly focused on postmodern technologies and developments in visual media, information processing and digital culture in the late twentieth century. Both thinkers are concerned about the dehumanising potential of technology, but it can be argued that they develop a neo-humanist position that sustains a notion of agency. While the poststructuralist dismantling of individuality, truth, clarity and meaning drives the anti-humanist thrust of their work, critics like Graham Coulter-Smith have argued this is countered in Baudrillard by 'predominantly humanist Marxian notions of alienation and reification, or at least hyper-realised versions of those ideas'.[43] On this view, not only does Baudrillard's anti-humanism 'become less an alternative to humanism than a means of intensifying the humanistic critique of technological society', but it also allows him to preserve a more enabling understanding of technology.[44] While Baudrillard maps out the ways in which postmodern society has eroded a certain conception of the human, he also examines the transformation of social relations in an attempt to devise strategies in which technology can remain at the service of human agency, or in which human agency can accommodate itself to technology. Just as Foucault argues that 'there are times in life when the question of knowing if one can think differently than one thinks, and perceive differently than one sees, is absolutely necessary if one is to go on looking and reflecting at all', so Baudrillard moves between the strategies of critique, reversibility, irony and circularity to transcend simplistic distinctions between individuality, nature, culture and technology.[45] Rather than remaining aloof from mass culture like Adorno, one strategy would be to immerse oneself in mass-mediated technology with the hope that familiarity with it would reduce what the novelist Don DeLillo describes in *White Noise* (1984) as 'its narcotic undertow and eerie diseased brain-sucking power'.[46] As we shall see, there are risks of losing the self entirely in technology but, as Baudrillard discusses in his writings from the late 1990s, in the face of this risk perhaps we can rescue agency by becoming cultural practitioners, rather than just consumers.

In *Simulations* (1983) Baudrillard plays his most familiar anti-humanist card by arguing that if, under late capitalism, it is now impossible to distinguish between reality and representation, then 'the whole [social] system becomes weightless; it is no longer anything but a gigantic simulacrum: not unreal, but a simulacrum, never again exchanging for what is real, but exchanging in itself, in an uninterrupted circuit without reference or circumference'.[47] In this 'uninterrupted' world of simulacra human agency seems to disappear entirely, leaving us adrift in 'the cool universe of digitality'.[48] Locating the simulacrum in post-war consumer culture, Baudrillard claims that Foucault's modern image of the all-seeing eye of the Panopticon no longer has currency. Taking television as his symbol of mass-mediated technology, he argues that 'the eye of TV is no longer a source of an absolute gaze' in which the individual is scrutinised and controlled; rather, it is a 'system of deterrence, where the distinction between active [gaze] and passive [subject] is abolished'.[49] By this he means that the viewer and screen mutually implicate, and dissolve into, each other: 'you' may have a remote control but 'are always already on the other side' of the screen.[50] Baudrillard replaces modern notions of subject, focal point and meaning with postmodern concepts of 'pure flexion or circular inflection … secret virulence, chain reaction, slow implosion and simulacra of spaces'.[51] This shift can best be illustrated by two brief literary examples. The first is from DeLillo's pre-postmodern novel *Players* (1977) in which the TV-viewer Lyle has a degree of control over the images he absorbs. As he sits 'eighteen inches from the screen he turned the channel selector every half minute or so, sometimes more frequently', simply enjoying 'jerking the dial into fresh image-burns' as 'the tactile-visual delight of switching channels took precedence … transforming even random moments of content into pleasing territorial abstractions'.[52] Practising a 'discipline like mathematics or Zen', Lyle remains at least partially in control of the speed of images as he switches between channels, while 'seeing identical footage many times was a test for the resourcefulness of the eye'. Contrast this mode of resourceful interaction in which viewer and screen are distinct with William Gibson's futuristic cyberpunk novel *Neuromancer* (1984), in which the protagonist's identity is subsumed entirely in the flow of images in his head: 'in the bloodlit dark behind his eyes, silver phosphenes boiling in from the edge of space, hypnagogic images jerking past like film compiled from random frames. Symbols, figures, faces, a blurred, fragmented mandala of visual information.'[53] In Gibson's description the medium and the message have become identical (to use Marshall McLuhan's terms), imploding the distinctions between subject and object and between life and film into what Baudrillard calls 'a nebula' that is 'indecipherable into its simple elements, indecipherable as to its truth'.[54]

Simulacra and hyperreality are the most readily identifiable concepts in Baudrillard's thought, but he has also dealt with other aspects of technology. For example, in his first book *The System of Objects* (1968) he identifies the principle of automatism, 'supra-functionality' and the prominence of gadgetry

as the ideals of post-war technology.[55] Although humans may design, manufacture and operate machines, Baudrillard argues that 'automatism means a
wondrous absence of activity' that pushes us into a passive relationship to
technology.[56] Rejecting the 'two cultures' argument in which the logic of
science is seen as alien to human experience, he claims that 'automatism' is not
the opposite of 'personalisation' but the very extension of it into the realm of
objects. The robot is the classic example of synthesis of 'man and the world',
embodying both the 'absolute functionality' of the ultra-rational machine and
the 'absolute anthropomorphism' of man-made-machine.[57] Early robots were
laughably primitive in their crude replication of human behaviour ('its body is
metallic, its gestures are discrete, jerky and unhuman') but a more
sophisticated machine that behaves with 'truly human fluidity' presages a
posthuman world (as the science-fiction writer Isaac Asimov predicted), in
which the robot's slave-like function and impoverished existential state
(without emotions, will or libido) will be finally transcended. The paradox for
Baudrillard is that there is an inbuilt 'fatality' in 'world-mastering technology'
that transforms it from a useful tool into a self-sustaining entity that has the
capacity to supersede its maker.[58] Fifty years after the first operational robots,
intensive research into intelligent machines and developments in biological
and genetic engineering give substance to Baudrillard's vision. At this juncture
'man' will no longer be the homunculus running the machine but, to use his
metaphor, he will be the old master outpaced by the runaway slave. Following
the Marxist position in which technological transformation is seen as the
'fundamental mechanism of capitalist accumulation', the danger for Baudrillard is not in technology *per se*, but the capitalist order that gives manufactured
objects their fragility and ephemerality and, to his mind, simultaneously
prevents moral growth keeping pace with technological development.[59] Pursuing this argument under the subheading 'A New Humanism?', he distinguishes
between 'freedom of being' that 'pits the individual against society' and
'freedom of ownership' that often unknowingly serves the purpose of capitalism, where liberty degenerates into the precarious freedom to choose between
manufactured objects and to 'project one's desires into commodities'.[60]

One of Baudrillard's techniques of resisting capitalist momentum is what he
calls in *The Ecstasy of Communication* (1987) the 'artificial ecstasy' of im-
mersing the self into technology. This strategy may seem like 'an abdication
before this new power of objects', but he argues it does not augur the death of
the self, only 'a mode of disappearance' in which the subject reappears as
object.[61] The fusion of body and technology in such a 'fatal strategy' would
mean that we no longer talk of subject and object, flesh and metal, lymph and
plastic, but in terms of digital processes in which 'we no longer exist as
playwrights or actors but as terminals of multiple networks'.[62] Rather than

bemoaning the fact that the human body as biologically conceived has become superfluous, the disappearance of bodily limits ushers in a schizophrenic state in which we become overexposed to 'the transparency of the world'.[63] In this uncertain state Baudrillard identifies the benefits and the dangers of giving the ecstatic self over to technoculture: this free-floating condition is at once a liberation from subjectivity (defined as subjugation to power), but also perilously close to 'a pure absorption and resorption surface of the influent networks' in which 'man becomes eminently vulnerable to science'.[64] Not only would the human form disappear into this network, so too, crucially, will thought 'be favorably replaced by a better system, a cerebro-spinal bubble, freed of all animal and metaphysical reflexes'.[65]

Baudrillard's language in *The Ecstasy of Communication* is more suggestive of this condition than explanatory, but he has developed these ideas more accessibly in relation to visual technology. Extending Foucault's theory of surveillance, he has argued in the 1990s that not only are we subject to visual technology that films, replicates, replays and distorts our image, but 'our whole life has taken on a video dimension' to the extent that we have 'swallowed our microphones and headsets' and carry a 'virtual camera' in our head.[66] This may suggest an increase in our sensory range, but with the ubiquity of the image – including CCTV, virtual reality, digital recording, reality television and iconic branding – in advanced capitalist countries, what once may have taken the form of 'police control' now appears as little more than entertainment or 'advertising promotion'.[67] Virtual reality is no longer a discrete zone but has eroded the boundaries between reality and simulation to such an extent that humans have become virtualised, living in a visually over-stimulated climate in which it is all but impossible to frame images in terms of economic production.[68] In this climate even technological hardware is hidden by an enveloping 'mediatized space' that completes the 'technical trans-figuration of the world'.[69] Rather than a passing phase in the ongoing process of social change, Baudrillard sees this stage of technological supremacy as an end point without any 'hope of salvation, revelation, or even apocalypse' that simply accelerates 'the process of declining ... towards a pure and simple disappearance'. On this account technology has found its home in the world and human beings have become the aliens. However, crucially, Baudrillard goes on to argue that this vision of a 'perfectly autonomous world' may never transpire because it would entail the complete removal of the human being, which he understands as 'a dangerous imperfection'. It is precisely the biological messiness and genetic unruliness of human life, in alliance with the 'evil genius for dysfunctions, electronic viruses and other perverse effects', which undermines the notion of technological perfection and leaves the possibility that we may wreck the machine by accident.[70] Developing his ideas from *The Ecstasy of Communication*, Baudrillard identifies in this overexposed climate traces of the human that testify to its technological afterlife, detecting in the 'signs of defect, or imperfection' evidence of 'our species' signature in the heart of an artificial world'.

The tension between the celebration of the disappearance of the human into technology and the preservation of critique weaves throughout Baudrillard's writing, almost as if the two impulses emanate from the same source. His more recent work on photography might suggest that he is in nostalgic retreat from an accelerating digital technology in favour of a cultural form that the artist can control, but he continues to describe the process of taking pictures as an escape from the self into the enigmatic world of objects. Although he likes moments of deceleration when culture slows down or momentarily stops, he is also interested in the 'rapid' and 'spontaneous' act of taking a photograph that he compares to the kind of automatic writing that had fascinated the French Surrealists in the 1920s.[71] Following his claim 'I've never photographed faces, portraits or human beings', the majority of images included in his exhibition Strange World: Photographs 1986–1995 held in Leicester in 1998 focus on random objects and are largely devoid of human forms.[72] He does not see photography as an art of interpretation but of capturing objects that irradiate emptiness and a lack of meaning which can intrigue, captivate, excite or even wound the viewer. In a 1993 interview Baudrillard revised his opinion of technology by claiming that it may prove to be 'an instrument of magic or of illusion' and a positive 'way of playing with reality'.[73] Here, he does not repudiate his earlier critical view of technology (or his theory, after Heidegger, that reality and representation have imploded), but attempts to find another starting point to deal with what he calls the 'emptiness' of both subject and object: 'technology can be seen as a whole domain within which the subject thinks they can seize the world, transform it, interpret it and so on, but from which the world escapes'.[74] As we discuss further in the Conclusion, Baudrillard does not resurrect heroic artistry or human sovereignty in the guise of photography, but elaborates the way that objects can delicately invoke 'a certain sensibility, and certain forms of joy', which in turn suggests that just as the subject disappears it magically reappears in the realm of sensation.

Donna Haraway

Just as Foucault and Baudrillard have their popular faces as the outspoken apostles of anti-humanism, so Donna Haraway is most often associated with the figure of the cyborg, a 'hybrid of machine and organism' that presages the demise of humanism and the end of humanity as we know it.[75] Androids and cyborgs had appeared in science-fiction stories and horror films even before

1960 when two American scientists Manfred Clynes and Nathan Klein coined the term 'cyborg' as an abbreviation for 'cybernetic organism', meaning a mechanical and electrical system that resembles, and functions as, a human being. Haraway's interest in the cyborg grew out of her eclectic academic grounding in zoology, philosophy and literature and a largely sympathetic response to the 'creativity of natural scientific inquiry' that derives more from the scientific pragmatism of Charles Sanders Peirce than from European techno-sceptics like Heidegger.[76] With the publication of her signature essay 'A Cyborg Manifesto: Science, Technology, and Socialist-Feminism in the Late Twentieth Century' in 1985, Haraway synthesised a number of currents from the physical and human sciences, industry, medicine, science fiction, reproductive theory and an early form of queer theory in an attempt to recruit the cyborg as a conceptual tool for rethinking the relationship between humanism and technology. As a mythical hybrid the cyborg seems the obvious successor to the tired myth of the human, providing 'a condensed image of both imagination and material reality' that she believes are 'the two joined centres structuring any possibility of historical transformation'.[77] Whereas Foucault and Baudrillard at their most provocative appear to hold little hope for the survival of humanity, Haraway claims that the confusion of once-stable boundaries between nature and technology offers certain pleasures and does not rule out the possibility of individuals acting responsibly in the careful reassembly of these categories.

From a millenarian perspective the technologically enmeshed cyborg is the 'awful apocalyptic *telos* of the "West's" escalating dominations of abstract individuation', but for Haraway it also offers freedom from constraining humanist stories of 'original unity, fullness, bliss and terror' that she sees as the major structuring narratives of psychoanalysis and Marxism.[78] The cyborg is not an 'antihuman' creature (she assigns 'the domain of the antihuman' to the European philosophical tradition of negativity towards science and technology[79]), and might in fact prove to be a redemptive figure for a wounded and struggling humanity. Craig Klugman has argued that there are two pervasive myths surrounding the cyborg: the first myth is that of 'replacement' in which damaged body parts are exchanged to restore human capacities and return individuals 'to something approaching former functioning', and the second myth is that of 'enhancement' in which the 'cybernetic implant allows an individual to do things that were not possible before'.[80] While technology may promise to restore the beleaguered human organism to its former glory, it also fulfils the Promethean yearning for enhanced and superhuman powers. Haraway sees the cyborg as a liminal creature at the intersection of these two potent myths, a trickster figure that reconfigures possible futures, and a symbol of reversibility in which humanist and anti-humanist discourses can easily flip over into each other. She argues that as the 'illegimate offspring of militarism and patriarchal capitalism', the cyborg has the potential to overcome rigid distinctions between man–woman, nature–technology, public–private and reproduction–replication, but the figure also embodies certain technologies of the self – 'partiality, irony, intimacy, and perversity' – that echo Baudrillard's and Foucault's search for alternative strategies of social engagement. Haraway is certainly critical of traditional and repressive humanisms, but she also retains humanist notions of agency, commitment and critique as essential techniques for survival in an ultra-technologised world.

Haraway's interest in technoscience stems from what she describes as 'the implosion of science and technology into each other in the past two hundred years', but she concurs with Baudrillard in arguing that this tendency is most evident since the 1960s in the development of digital and genome techno-logies.[81] She emphasises the networks of power that accompany the spread of technoscience and sees that 'social relations of domination are built into the hardware and logics of technology'.[82] However, in her second book *Primate Visions* (1989) Haraway argues that the history of technology cannot simply be read 'as a tale of evil capitalists in the sky conspiring to obscure the truth', but also of 'committed Progressives struggling to dispel darkness through research, education, and reform'.[83] Like Foucault she sees power as being agonistic: at once controlling, reifying and commodifying, but also providing a usable resource for resisting, denouncing and transforming technologies of power. Technoscience should be treated from a microcosmic level, less as a monolithic imposition on human freedom and more as a 'heterogeneous cultural practice that enlists its members in … ordinary and astonishing ways'.[84] The power of technology lies both in its hardware and the way it has taken on mythical proportions within humanist and anti-humanist narratives, either as a redemptive path to social utopia or as a dark dystopian chasm that awaits us in the near future. Taking the poststructuralist position that 'facts' and 'truths' are simply sub-stories of a grand scientific master narrative, Haraway claims that the fields of biology and sociobiology that most interest her are themselves imbricated with stories of 'origins, natures, and possibi-lities'.[85] The reason why the cyborg is such a potent image of the future-human is because it embodies the hope that the species can adapt quickly enough to survive in what, from an old-fashioned humanist perspective, seems like a radically alien environment. While the cyborg is sometimes depicted as a successor to the human, or a mutant survivor in a posthuman future, it has elsewhere been used as way of affirming humanist values. For example, in James Cameron's sci-fi film *Terminator II* (1991) set in 2029, the futuristic terminator-cyborg (Arnold Schwarzenegger) learns the importance of human emotion to such a degree that the mother figure Sarah Connor (Linda Hamilton) exclaims at the end: 'If a Terminator can learn the value of human life – maybe we can too.' It is easy to dismiss such representations as pure fantasy or wishful thinking, but they have an intricate and troubling link to those scientific and technological discourses that purport to be immune from storytelling.

Haraway has a slightly different take on modernity to Foucault and Baudrillard, focusing centrally on the intensification of technoscience in the twentieth century for transforming discourses relating to 'brain, chip, gene, fetus, race, database, and ecosystem'.[86] Taking the position that the opposition between science and humanism is actually an illusion, in her recent book, *Modest_Witness@Second_Millennium* (1997), she looks back to the 'hopeful, but fatally flawed, biological humanism' of the mid-twentieth century (roughly from the late 1930s to the 1970s) that made links between geographical variations, population shifts and genetic changes to posit a humanism 'that emphasised flexibility, progress, cooperation, and universalism'.[87] She includes figures like the British biologist Julian Huxley and the American systematist Ernest Mayr in a group of mainly scientific thinkers that attempted to uncouple an understanding of human nature from essentialist theories of 'race, blood and culture' that had taken on such frightening proportions in the Nazis' Final Solution.[88] Arguing that science and politics formed 'the tightest possible weave' during the Cold War years, Haraway identifies in UNESCO's statements on race at the beginning of the 1950s a scientific-humanist discourse of 'universal brotherhood' that invalidated the 'race-and-culture tie' of biological theory. The tenor of UNESCO's statements were reflected in a major photographic exhibition The Family of Man held at the Museum of Modern Art, New York in 1955, in which over 500 photographs (selected from two million images) from 68 countries celebrated the diverse panorama of life across lines of race, culture, gender and age. The curator Edward Steichen claimed that the exhibition was 'a mirror of the universal elements and emotions in the everydayness of life ... a mirror of the essential oneness of mankind throughout the world', and the American poet Carl Sandburg described it as humanism with a face, 'a drama of the grand canyon of humanity'.[89] Although the humanist sentiments of the exhibition – together with the quotations that accompany the images from the Bible, Shakespeare and Blake to Joyce, Pueblo Indians and the Charter of the United Nations – are infinitely preferable to the racist implications of earlier biological and eugenic theory, Haraway reads the humanism of these photographic texts critically, arguing that the purported celebration of diversity actually degenerates into statements about the importance of family, heterosexual relationships, lineage and child-rearing. Even though she admits that she is susceptible to the emotional appeal of the images in The Family of Man exhibition (that she deems to be 'less sanitised' than many expression of 1990s multiculturalism), the discourses of unity, harmony, cooperation and what she calls 'the multiplication of same-ness' characterise and, to her mind, jeopardise the humanist impulses behind the exhibition.[90]

Haraway's view of sociobiology as a form of 'hyperhumanism' has led her to mount a feminist challenge to what she sees as the masculinist myth of 'human fulfillment' and the ultimate sociobiological goal to acquire 'accurate knowledge of the requirements of human design and redesign'.[91] The notion of the fulfilment of 'man' seems to Haraway to be simply a perpetuation of the humanist narrative of self-creation and mastery over nature: what she calls the myth of Man the Hunter. She argues that this view dominated post-war thought in America and Europe (exemplified by the universalist declarations of the United Nations and UNESCO in the 1950s) and remained unchallenged until the mid–1970s when the rival myth of Woman as Gatherer 'emerged from a contentious marriage of Euro-American feminism and biological humanism'.[92] This feminist counter-narrative is a clear example of Haraway's interest in stories that 'explore the theme of identity on the margins of hegemonic groups' and 'attempt to deconstruct the authority and legitimacy of dominant humanist narratives by exposing their partiality'.[93] The focus of Second Wave feminists on the complex relationship between sex and gender (which cannot simply be taken as biological givens) provided a robust cultural and scientific challenge to the powerful myth of biological humanism in the 1970s. Haraway sees that a similar, but perhaps more complex, 'dismantling' of myths surrounding science and technology is needed at the turn of the millennium, particularly in relation to gender and sexuality.

Whereas Baudrillard envisages little more than a gigantic threat in the 'fluidity' of sophisticated intelligent machines (which he links closely to the 'liquidity' of late capitalism[94]), feminist thinkers like Haraway, Teresa de Lauretis and Sadie Plant see the 'fluidity of identity' to be potentially liberating for women, especially if it is indexed to 'a new tactile environment in which women artists can find their space'.[95] Plant argues that the heterogeneous spaces created by technoculture help to undermine the fixity of patriarchal discourse, offering fresh opportunities and a rejuvenated sense of mobility for women. Asserting that there is 'more to cyberspace than meets the male gaze', Plant claims that the cyberfeminist 'virus' that began in the early 1990s has the potential to help women overcome their secondary role as 'a deficient version of a humanity which is already male' and enable them to 'discover their own post-humanity'.[96] Rather than 'post-humanity' here auguring the death of the human, the term seems to be little more than the gendered pronouncement of a critical and self-reflexive humanism. Similarly, when Haraway chooses the role of 'cyborg' over that of 'goddess' at the end of her 'Cyborg Manifesto', she invests in the new myth of techno-hybridity to replace older myths that tend to assign women to the category of nature: if the goddess is dead (and perhaps for very good reasons), then the cyborg may be an enabling myth that invents new creative roles out of old binaries. Just as Foucault asserted that discourse is one of the key instruments of power but is also a potent means to contest power, so Haraway argues that the 'marked body' can also become a 'self-activating body' transforming 'female/colonised/laboring/animal bodies' into potential citizens.[97] In essence, Haraway's post-gender perspective is an attempt to step beyond a totalising definition of sex that, as the French feminist Monique Wittig claims, 'grips our minds [and bodies] in such a way that we cannot think outside it ... we must destroy it and start thinking beyond it if we want to start thinking at all'.[98] Although Haraway admits the goddess and cyborg are tightly bound in a 'spiral dance' (implying that the goddess is not exactly dead), the cyborg is a usable myth that opens up new experiences by dismantling and 'queering' the biological category of sex.

The cyborg is not the only creature drawn from technoscience that Haraway has discussed. From her earlier work on primates and simians to her fascination in the mid-1990s with the Janus-faced post-gender FemaleMan© and the manufactured transgenic OncoMouse™ (a hybrid creature, like Dolly the sheep cloned in 1997, that passes on transplanted genes to the progeny), Haraway has returned to stories that explore the origins, limits and possible futures of humans.[99] Rejecting the binary oppositions that structure the arts versus science debates, she is interested in complex relationships between terms that complicate binary oppositions: nature–culture–science, world–humanity–technology and primate–human–cyborg. Working at the interface of these discourses, she is keen to develop strategies for dealing with the fact that 'the fleshy body and human histories are always and everywhere enmeshed in the tissue of interrelationship where all the relators aren't human'.[100] Taking a more modulated, and more intensely committed, position towards the creative aspects of technology than have Foucault and Baudrillard, Haraway's humanist vision (although she does not label it as such) is of a modest and 'more adequate, self-critical technoscience committed to situated knowledges' which can heal the long-standing rift between arts and sciences; scientists need to recognise their responsibility for a world culture, but so too should non-scientists realise that the relationship between humans and machines will continue to be shaped by science.[101] Indeed, as Godfrey Reggio's *qatsi* film trilogy, *Koyaanisqatsi* (1983), *Powaqqatsi* (1988) and *Naqoyqatsi* (2002), reveals in its three-pronged exploration of ecology, humanity and technology, it is the responsibility of the global community (and particularly in the West) to realise that the mountains of e-waste that have been accumulating since the 1980s and the industrial threat to the environment may be the ultimate humanist questions that we have to deal with, not by turning our back on science, but by looking to different forms of technology to those that currently exist.[102] On this point Foucault, Baudrillard and Haraway would agree that technology is both a threat and a promise from which it is impossible to turn away.

Primary Texts

Michel Foucault

The Order of Things [1966], trans. unidentified collective (London: Routledge, 1970).

Power/Knowledge: Selected Interviews and Other Writings, 1972–77 [1977], ed. Colin Gordon (Brighton: Harvester, 1980).

Technologies of the Self: A Seminar with Michel Foucault, ed. Luther Martin et al. (London: Tavistock, 1988).

Ethics: Subjectivity and Truth, ed. Paul Rabinow, trans. Robert Hurley et al. (London: Penguin, 1994).

Jean Baudrillard

The System of Objects [1968], trans. James Benedict (London: Verso, 1996).

Simulations, trans. Paul Foss et al. (New York: Semiotext(e), 1983).

The Ecstasy of Communication [1987], ed. Sylvère Lotringer, trans. Bernard and Caroline Schutze (New York: Semiotext(e), 1988).

Jean Baudrillard: Art and Artefact, ed. Nicholas Zurbrugg (London: Sage, 1997).

Donna Haraway

Primate Visions: Gender, Race and Nature in the World of Modern Science [1989] (London: Verso, 1992).

Simians, Cyborgs and Women: The Reinvention of Nature (London: Routledge, 1991).

Modest_Witness@Second_Millennium.FemaleMan©_Meets_OncoMouse™: Feminism and Technoscience (New York: Routledge, 1997).

How Like a Leaf: An Interview with Thyrza Nichols Goodeve (New York: Routledge, 2000).

Inhuman, Posthuman, Transhuman, Human

A number of Jean Baudrillard's photographs from his 1998 exhibition Strange World depict scenes that have been recently vacated by a human subject. One image (Paris, 1985) shows a crumpled blue pillow on an unmade bed casting a dark shadow on a deeper blue wall; another (Paris, 1986) depicts a reading lamp and notebook on a red table with the corner of a picture frame and half-open window, through which streams of bright sunlight cast blunt shadows on the wall; and yet another (Florida, 1986 and the signature photograph for the exhibition) portrays the white bonnet of a parked car in front of an expanse of turquoise wall cut vertically by the faint lines of a door and the base of a thick dark telegraph pole.[1] In each image a human subject is implied, but is notable by his or her absence: the bed has recently been slept in; the notebook, lamp, picture and open window all have human functions; and the car either contains a driver (outside the photographic frame) or has recently been parked. There are darker images in the exhibition such as a battered and sunken car (St Clément, 1988) and some disused steps flanked by ancient statues (Rome, 1994), suggesting a world in which human agency has been entirely extinguished or absent for some time, but the more domesticated images depict objects that remain in the service of human life or have somehow established a life of their own that surpasses their use value. The enigmatic and quasi-surreal features of Baudrillard's photographs invite readings from two very different perspectives. An anti-humanist reading of the images would suggest that the object-world has established a kind of sealed autonomy that eradicates the need for (or possibility of) human intervention; and yet, as discussed in the last chapter, Baudrillard is also interested in the way in which the subject disappears into the object-world but re-emerges transformed as traces, emotions and subterranean currents that attest to the continuation of the human on another level. Even a subjectless photograph implies a hidden relationship with a viewer: he or she is always outside the frame of the picture but may be imprisoned, teased, puzzled or wounded by the image. While Baudrillard's photographs can certainly be approached in terms of 'the inhuman' (the objects stripped of their human function), 'the posthuman' (in which we witness a post-historical world) or 'transhuman' (the banal objects transcend their human value to speak to a broader condition of 'things'), in each instance we are still forced to speak about the images with reference to a lost, absent or transformed humanity.

Baudrillard would resist the label of humanist for its (assumed) optimism about social progress and (also assumed) uncritical attitude towards human capability, but, as we discussed in the last chapter, a certain spirit of humanism animates his work. Where his photographs take us beneath, beyond or behind the human is not only in the absence of a human subject, but in their cold colours and eerie silences, as if he is suggesting that we can no longer see clearly nor breathe comfortably. If this 'strange world' is inhuman it is an inflection of what Fredric Jameson has called a 'new depthlessness' and a 'waning of affect' in the late twentieth century, leaving the viewer existentially impoverished and starved of 'real' human contact.[2] To exemplify this cultural shift from modern depth to postmodern depthlessness Jameson contrasts Vincent Van Gogh's much-discussed painting *A Pair of Boots* (1887) with Andy Warhol's silkscreen reproduction *Diamond Dust Shoes* (1980). Where the intensity of the brushstrokes in Van Gogh's painting conveys the hard work and intensive wear the peasant's boots have undergone, Warhol's depthless reproduction depicts a photographic negative of a row of women's shoes, which Jameson describes as:

> a random collection of dead objects hanging together on the canvas like so many dead turnips, as shorn of their earlier life world as the pile of shoes left over from Auschwitz or the remainders and tokens of some incomprehensible and tragic fire in a packed dance hall.[3]

Even though there is no human subject in either work, Jameson argues that Warhol's image 'no longer speaks to us with any of the immediacy of Van Gogh's footwear' because we cannot recreate the 'whole larger lived context' that informs the image. For example, Heidegger describes Van Gogh's painting as belonging to an 'undefined space' in which 'the toilsome tread of the worker' nevertheless stares forth from 'the dark opening of the worn insides of the shoes'.[4] It is clear that in Van Gogh's case a human story is much easier to recreate than it is from Warhol's mass reproduced image. This tempts Jameson to read the aesthetic differences between the two images as a parable of the 'death of the world of appearance' in late twentieth-century culture and the 'commodity fetishism of a transition to late capital'.[5] On this count, if we talk about the human in the context of late capitalism it is likely to be as a packaged commodity or a fetishised simulacrum that is marketed as a vague (and possibly vacuous) marker of progress, authenticity and optimism. It is easy to see in the cases of Marilyn Monroe or Michael Jackson the way in which their humanity has become 'commodified and transformed into their own [star] images', but the intensification of visual culture in the late twentieth century has made commonplace the kind of packaged image that claims the name of the human only to empty it out. However, where Baudrillard's photographs and Jameson's reading of Warhol's silkscreen can intervene in this familiar post-modern story is that, paradoxically in the case of Warhol, they invite us to go behind the flat image to behold the vacancy and eeriness within. As examples of 'existential inscapes', these images 'open up' to reveal traces of human stories, whether it is the recent sleeper in Baudrillard's unmade bed, the shoes left over from Auschwitz, or the fire in the dance hall.

Another equally familiar story about late twentieth-century and early twenty-first-century global culture is that eclecticism and cultural hybridity throws us (the participant and consumer) into a seemingly inevitable state of cultural relaxation. Jean-François Lyotard tells us 'it's time to relax' now that 'eclecticism is the degree zero of contemporary general culture'.[6] In such a state of relaxation intense emotions seem to have no place and the owner of Van Gogh's *A Pair of Boots* seems to speak to a forgotten epoch of painful labour. However, as with all stories, this is only a partial narrative that speaks to a universalised 'we', but on closer inspection reveals an economic fault line ('the realism of money') between those who have the capacity to consume eclectically and those who have little exposure and even fewer resources (what Fanon calls 'a world inhuman in its poverty').[7]

Against this logic of mass consumerism Lyotard pits a notion of the sublime that emerges, or can emerge, in those fugitive moments, as with Baudrillard's photographs or Barnett Newman's abstract paintings (which Lyotard discusses in *The Inhuman*), when the intensity of sensory bombardment and speed of images briefly decrease. Rather than offering a complete break from the past, Lyotard detects that the 'lack of reality' in contemporary culture is prefigured in Nietzsche's nihilistic philosophy and Kant's theory of the sublime. Usually associated with visual perception, as we discussed in Chapter 1, the sublime speaks to a human awareness of the immeasurably large (the Romantic grandeur of the Alps) or infinitesimally small (Walt Whitman's blade of grass) as experiences that induce 'powerful and equivocal' emotions of 'both pleasure and pain'.[8] Lyotard explains the sublime as those moments 'when the imagin-ation in fact fails to present any object which could accord with a concept' such as 'the world', 'the simple', 'the absolutely great' and 'the absolutely powerful'. We can have ideas about each of these terms but not 'the capacity to show an example of it' because they refer to 'unpresentable' experiences.[9] While con-temporary culture may erode our awareness of, or decrease the opportunity to experience, these sublime moments (where eclecticism becomes a kind of cultural flattening), Lyotard and Baudrillard are both interested in the reve-lation of 'the human' as something that we can have an idea about, but which

exceeds thought and ultimately cannot be presented. On this reading, we can
speak about the human in poststructuralist terms as an 'absent presence', or an
unpresentable concept that goes under different guises, some versions of which
appear to undermine it. If, as Lyotard and Jameson assert, the master narratives of modernity – rationalism, Marxism, psychoanalysis, humanism – no
longer have currency because they can no longer speak in their totality, we are
left to make sense of a plurality of 'travelling' stories that contain traces of these
master discourses that now criss-cross in bewildering ways. But just as George
Grosz's image *Travelling People* (see frontispiece) transforms the human only
to retain it, so terms such as anti-human, inhuman, posthuman and transhuman
remain bound up in human stories. These terms may be used to contest or
refute such stories but they nevertheless, to recall Kate Soper's description,
continue to 'secrete' forms of humanist rhetoric. As we discuss below, while
the panoply of rival terms that emerged in the 1990s seems to transcend
humanist concerns, the stories they tell continue, perhaps inevitably, to reveal
traces of humanism.

Inhuman

There have been so many announcements of the demise of humanism in the
1980s and 1990s that the attempt to resurrect it as a meaningful and critical
category may seem belated or futile. As part of an alternative vocabulary
drawn from postmodern and poststructuralist discourses, terms like inhuman,
posthuman and transhuman not only attest to a movement beyond humanism,
but to a more tense attitude to those aspects that are given the name of the
human. This is not surprising when humanism has often been used as a benign
mask to hide a politically motivated agenda, whether it is in the name of what
Noam Chomsky variously describes as 'international financial arrangements,
trade agreements, control over technology [or] material and human resources',
or what William Spanos identifies as the crisis in liberal humanist education in
post-Vietnam America, in which he argues the 'principle of disinterested
inquiry is in fact an agent of disguised power'.[10] To take a recent example, in
February 2003 Tony Blair used the rhetoric of humanism as propaganda to
justify morally the need for military action against Iraq, arguing at the Labour
Party Conference in Glasgow that 'ridding the world of Saddam Hussein
would be an act of humanity. It is leaving him there that is inhumane.' It is easy
to unmask debased or dubious humanisms with historical hindsight, particularly when they are invoked to hide the barbarity of National Socialism or
Stalinist Communism, but it is less easy with current discourses such as the
humanitarian goals to which Western powers, particularly the USA and UK,
claim they are committed as they tackle the rise of nationalism, ethnic warfare

and international terrorism. As a leftist thinker, Chomsky argues that the 'new humanism' in the West, which claims its ethical commitment to 'humanitarian intervention', in fact masks an imperialist militarism that dresses up strategic intervention as the preservation of basic human rights. Chomsky argues that 'humanitarian intervention is [now] an orthodoxy, and it's taken for granted that if we do it, it's humanitarian. The reason is because our leaders say so'; but if we look closely, according to Chomsky, we will find 'that virtually every use of military force is described as humanitarian intervention'.[11]

What seem to be benevolent foreign policies, such as the American-led offensive against the Iraqi invasion of Kuwait in the early 1990s and NATO's intervention in Yugoslavia in the mid-1990s, can be exposed as having other, more self-interested, agendas. For example, Chomsky argues that George Bush Sr actually supported repression in Kuwait, and the bombing in Yugoslavia was designed to 'lead to a very sharp escalation of atrocities and had nothing to do with humanitarian goals'.[12] Although Chomsky is arguably too hasty in reading all claims of humanitarian intent as devious political strategies, Michael Ignatieff comments in his book on the Balkan conflict *Virtual War* that 'wars waged in the name of values invariably turn out to be more controversial than wars waged for interests'.[13] This type of dispute stems from the fact that values are precarious to maintain across national, ideological and ethnic borders, and appeals to universal human rights will nearly always be compromised in the arena of international politics; as Edward Said noted in the early 1980s, 'our bankruptcy on the once glamorous question of human rights alone is enough to strip us of our title to humanism'.[14] On this line of argument, not only is it hard to find positive uses of the term 'humanitarianism' (especially with the United Nations seemingly losing its direction in the early twenty-first century), but Chomsky argues that 'humanitarian' might actually be an 'empty' category.[15] He does not deny that proletariat, anti-apartheid and women's movements (to which we might add gay rights and the green movement, together with ethical pressure groups such as Human Rights Watch and Amnesty International) have made profound differences to social and political relations, but Chomsky nevertheless maintains that nation states rarely act for humanitarian ends, if at all. Ignatieff is more nuanced in his approach, arguing that although the aim of military interventions in the post-Cold War era have been to minimise the cost to human life (in the form of 'precision violence'), the very '"right" of these forces to intervene' has been contested by countries outside the West, notably former communist countries like the Soviet Union and China.[16] The question that Chomsky and Ignatieff raise is whether we should jettison the idea of humanitarianism as another form of false consciousness, or maintain it as a valuable goal despite devious and inhumane uses. Ignatieff maintains a degree of faith in the term despite its political misuses, but the pair agree that if the rhetoric of humanitarianism is part of the arsenal of an 'idealistic New World bent on ending inhumanity', it may simply result in re-establishing an inhuman (and inhumane) regime by another name.[17]

Lyotard has theorised this notion of the inhuman more coherently than any other twentieth-century thinker, arguing at the beginning of his essay collection *The Inhuman* (1988) that too often humanism puts 'a certain value' in the human that 'has no need to be interrogated'.[18] On this account humanism 'has the authority to suspend, forbid interrogation, suspicion, the thinking which gnaws away at everything'. Rather than the naïve belief-system that it sometimes presents itself as, humanism is often at the service of a power politics that invests in related terms like 'the human', 'humanity', 'human nature' and 'humanitarianism' for particular ends. Lyotard claims that human-ism is much more than 'simply a marketing operation' to stop us thinking, but an attempt to bolster up knowledge and truth in the face of an uncertain future. Taking the hypothesis that human beings are 'in the process of ... becoming inhuman', Lyotard pursues a series of thought experiments to interrogate the rhetoric and logic of humanism. He is careful to separate two versions of the inhuman. The first version is wholly negative, the 'inhumanity of the system which is currently being consolidated under the name of development' (whether it is military, economic or ideological inhumanity), but the second version preserves a more positive image of 'a mind haunted by a familiar and unknown guest which is agitating it, sending it delirious but also making it think'.[19] For an uncritical and uncontested humanism, this second notion of the inhuman works to turn the light on in the darkroom of contemporary culture, as Julia Kristeva would describe it.[20]

Rather than outlining an inevitable drive towards the future, Lyotard links the psychoanalytic term 'anamnesis' to this second version of the inhuman as a mode of 'thinking back' to work through past problems, or what Paul Harris calls 'restless seeking'.[21] Harris argues that Lyotard's position 'revolves around the necessary blind spots that emerge in thought's tangled reflections on its own nature', allowing us to perceive 'those nebulous opacities that hinder a desire to formulate any systematic model'.[22] If social development does not gradually increase the store of collective wisdom but actually encourages a culture of 'active forgetting' to justify the prevailing order, then anamnesis would be a vital technique for rescuing those still usable elements of human-ism. Lyotard argues that listening with a 'third ear' to the echoes of the human from the past can provide us with a resource for living in the present and for challenging the inhuman elements of any new social order.

Given Lyotard's view that humanism in its classical form asserts the belief that 'humanity is something that ought to be freed', it is perhaps not surprising that he is interested in those aspects of the human which it is hard to escape from or to fully grasp: childhood, paganism, and the stranger within the self.[23] To take one example, while the child may be seen as 'eminently human because its distress heralds and promises things possible', classical humanists would agree that childhood is a state that must be overcome before we can become fully human.[24] This logic of overcoming can be seen in a number of thinkers discussed in this book, but others (notably the Romantics) would put more faith in childhood as a value in itself, arguing that we are always in danger of forgetting or losing the past in struggling to be free of it. For this reason Lyotard argues that the 'unharmonizable' and unruly elements of childhood may actually provide a resource against corrosive forms of inhumanity. In his 1990 essay 'The Grip', for example, Lyotard challenges those critics who claim his theory of anamnesis and interest in childhood are retrograde, claiming that they are vital resources for resisting the dubious master narrative of progress and development. He asks the question 'which man, or human, or which element in the human is it that thinks of resisting the grip of development?', and answers it by focusing on the 'remainder, the element that all the memory data banks forget' that attests not simply to human survival or making life bearable, but to 'the uncertain and slow resource' of active, resisting agency.[25]

If we are to discover a third way – a critical humanism that splits the difference between those humanists that proclaim the human as fully present and those that see an infinite malleability in the human – then it is by contesting the 'inhumanity of the system' with the more positive version of the inhuman: that which Lyotard sees as deriving from pre-rational childhood and the kind of primitive aesthetic expression that can never be fully commodified.[26] Perhaps it matters less if we defend either one of the terms 'humanism' or 'inhuman' as having more critical weight or contemporary relevance, than it does if we abandon Lyotard's notion of two competing discourses stemming from the same source (what Fanon called an 'untidy dialectic') in favour of simple binary oppositions (human versus inhuman) or neat synthesis (the one triumphing over the other).

Posthuman

A similar tension between different inflections of the same term is evident in the discourse of the posthuman that, as we discussed in the last chapter, has dominated debates in science, culture and ethics since the early 1990s. As with the inhuman there are a number of different stories to tell about the posthuman, particularly as it concerns the nascent future unfolding in the present. One story would take posthumanism as a periodising term that follows on from the discourse of humanism in the same way that the post-war period would follow on from wartime conflict. In this case, as Lyotard describes it, 'the "post-"

indicates something like a conversion: a new direction from the previous one'.[27] The posthuman would thus follow after Foucault's description of 'the modern age' and its obsession with human knowledge, as a period in which the ambition and optimism of humanism are finally left behind, or what Ernesto Laclau would call the lowering of ontological pretensions.[28] This view suggests that a posthuman period is more realistic and has fewer expectations about the world and its inhabitants. But it is difficult to determine the beginning of such a period – maybe it began with the rise of oppositional cultural movements in the late 1960s or with the fall of the Berlin Wall in 1989 – and either account tells only a partial story. Another perspective on the posthuman actually raises our ontological pretensions by envisaging a futuristic cyborg with enhanced powers of strength, mobility, intelligence and communication, and living out to its biotechnological conclusion the classical humanist vision of the self-reliant and masterly individual, but with a slight twist because humans would no longer exist. The twist, of course, casts a shadow over such an optimistic story, with technoscience becoming so sophisticated and autonomous that it will surpass its need for human operators: to quote Lyotard, 'technoscientific development [now] seems to proceed of its own accord, with a force, an autonomous motoricity that is independent of ourselves [and] does not answer to demands issuing from man's needs'.[29]

One notable debate, 'A Posthuman Future', in which posthuman issues were discussed in relation to biotechnology, was staged at the Institute of Ideas in London in May 2002. Including a range of scholars from different disciplines, the central debate involved the medical and scientific writer Gregory Stock (biotechnology advisor to Bill Clinton in the 1990s) pitted against the political theorist Francis Fukuyama (a member of the Republican think-tank in the 1980s). Stock's bright liberal vision of a posthuman future was contrasted to Fukuyama's more cautionary approach to biotechnology. Stock takes a neo-Darwinian approach to human evolution, arguing in *Redesigning Humans* (2002) that 'we are on the cusp of profound biological changes, poised to transcend our current form and character on a journey to destinations of new imagination'.[30] He maintains that it would be strange to argue that the current stage of human development is the last, particularly when genetic research has made it possible to intervene in the 'natural' cycle of genetic transference through embryo selection, *in vitro* fertilisation and cloning. He sees great promise in the fact that genetic intervention and 'human self-design' will take us past the current biological order 'into a highly selective social process that is far more rapid and effective at spreading successful genes than traditional sexual competition and mate selection'.[31] Maintaining that human beings have always manipulated their environment and designed tools to increase their chances of survival, Stock sees the realm of biotechnology as the next logical step.

He tries to sidestep the posthuman spectre of the cyborg as something alien and threatening (despite questionable reports in December 2002 of successful human cloning), by arguing that techniques like germline engineering will reinforce human continuity, making us 'more human' by increasing the chances of living a healthy life. Although Bryan Appleyard questioned the very notion of an 'improved' human being in the Institute of Ideas discussion, rather than using anti-humanist rhetoric in which humanity is seen as coming to an end or already deceased, Stock sees the turn of the millennium as a period of natality (to recall Arendt's term), when we move out of childhood 'into a gawky, stumbling adolescence' and begin to learn how to manage our new powers 'wisely'.[32] According to Stock, turning away from the promise of germline engineering to skilfully manipulate gene pools 'would be to deny our essential nature and perhaps our destiny ... such a retreat might deaden the human spirit of exploration, taming and diminishing us'.[33] Instead of a bright posthuman future then, turning our backs on the possibilities of biotechnology may lead to the loss of cherished humanist values such as the dignity of spirit and the power of the imagination to envisage possible futures.

Against Stock's thoughtful optimism, Fukuyama focuses on the political implications of biotechnology that Stock tends to brush over in favour of the self-regulation of the free market. In *Our Posthuman Future* (2002) Fukuyama outlines the need to instigate moral and political control over technoscience, with international legislation needed to restrict or ban further research into cloning. Whereas Stock sees great promise in the genetically controlled future, Fukuyama sees biotechnology as offering the same kind of 'threat' that Aldous Huxley envisaged in *Brave New World* (1932) and George Orwell in *1984* (1949), arguing that the possibility of reshaping 'what we are will have possibly malign consequences for liberal democracy'.[34] Fukuyama envisages three possible scenarios: the first in which a pharmaceutically sophisticated future would mean that 'negative' personality traits such as addiction or depression would be eradicated; the second in which stem cell research pushes age expectancy up dramatically; and the third in which parents would pay to screen embryos in order to determine their children's genetic make-up. He sees dangers in all three scenarios: the first in which we would limit our emotional range for a permanent Prozac high; the second in which the implications of human ageing have not (or perhaps cannot) be sorted out; and the third which has monstrous implications for those children who are no longer considered fully human because their parents could not afford to elevate their IQ or enhance socially advantageous characteristics. While Fukuyama maintains his faith in capitalism as the best possible economic and political model there is, he thinks that biotechnology will alter the parameters of 'human nature', and thereby lead to a class war in which the rich can buy an enhanced posthuman future, while the poor will be left struggling in a subhuman backwater. Whereas Stock betrays the naïve ethics of his relaxed vision with comments like 'if biological manipulation is indeed a slippery slope, then we are already sliding down that slope now and we may as well enjoy the ride', Fukuyama remains uptight and vigilant lest human nature is tampered with too much and with potentially disastrous ethical and political consequences.[35] Rather than a posthuman world being 'free, equal, prosperous, caring, compassionate ... with better health care, longer lives, and perhaps more intelligence', Fukuyama sees it as being 'far more hierarchical and competitive ... in which any notion of "shared humanity" is lost'.[36]

It is easy to suggest that Stock's vision is too optimistic and Fukuyama's too cautionary, but the fact that both thinkers return to key humanist issues about human nature, freedom of choice, responsibility and 'shared humanity' indicates that any debate about a posthuman future condition is intimately bound up with humanist concerns. This theory would concur with Lyotard's claim that even though ecological and humanitarian disasters wait on the horizon, human stories will not cease until the actual 'disappearance of earth' when 'there won't be any humanness' left or any living creatures to worry about it.[37] There is a general truth in Lyotard's account of the continuation of the human, but Neil Badmington has suggested there is always something deficient in humanism: that it 'never manages to constitute itself; it forever rewrites itself as posthumanism. This movement is always happening: humanism cannot escape its "post-".'[38] Our argument in this book – that humanism is always shadowed by its negation – actually accords with Badmington's assertion that humanism rewrites itself as posthumanism, but it is also possible to go further by arguing that 'if humanism cannot escape its "post-"', then neither can posthumanism escape its humanist anchor. Even in a radically transformed future on the free-market biotechnological model that Stock describes, humanist concerns seem certain to recur along with the ethical implications discussed in previous chapters. But there is the danger of intellectual laziness in this edifying claim. Even if we maintain a belief in a future-humanism it does not mean that regulating biotechnology will be any easier to implement and sustain on a global basis. If posthumanism refuses 'to take humanism for granted', then neither should a critically engaged humanism rest on its laurels or assume it can take for granted its own future.[39] On this reading we can, following Catherine Waldby, see the posthuman as 'a particular kind of critical moment' in the mutating but nevertheless identifiable discourse of humanism.[40]

Transhuman

Transhuman is a category of a slightly different order than inhuman and posthuman and their corresponding 'isms', a category that Keith Ansell Pearson claims has taken on a 'viral life' of its own in the 1990s.[41] New Age cults like the web-based The Extropy Institute (www.extropy.org) see the transhuman as a term that refers to those who are actively preparing themselves for a posthuman future (by means of simple exercises, or calorie restriction, taking food supplements, using mnemonics to improve brain power, or investing in artificial intelligence or cryonics), suggesting that the transhuman is always in service of the posthuman. Although the founders of The Extropy Institute see transhumanism as the philosophy that 'humanity can strive to higher levels, physically, mentally and socially', it is actually a more complex and ambiguous idea than that. Along with commonplace terms like translation and transformation and more theoretically dense terms such as transcultural, transpolitical, transsexual and transgenic (some of which Baudrillard discusses in *The Transparency of Evil*, 1990), transhuman can suggest either a movement across the borders of the human, causing such a radical change that the original cannot be reformed, or a deliberate transgression of parameters. Alternatively, rather than maintaining a tight grip on human knowledge, the transhuman could be used to describe a more inclusive condition that incorporates human beings, but moves outwards to address much broader zoological, ecological and cosmological issues, or it could refer to the recreation of humans by means of transgenic and transsexual modification. Transhuman does not have explicitly negative connotations, in the way that the inhuman is often closely related to inhumanity and the posthuman implies a potentially tragic laying waste of the human, but there are nevertheless subtler ethical and civic implications. Positioned against a classical humanism that claims its freedom from history and purity from cultural contamination, the transhuman condition is characterised by an admixture of elements that cannot be sorted out into their constitutive parts, ushering in a world of hybrids that can no longer be classified in terms of genus, sex, ethnicity, nationality or ideology.

The transhuman is arguably more flexible than the other terms we have discussed, suggesting an ongoing process of self-perpetuating change along the lines that Deleuze and Guattari describe in *A Thousand Plateaus* (1980) with their theory of the rhizome. While transgenic manipulation and transsexual operations require elaborate processes carried out by skilled humans (at least at present), Deleuze and Guattari describe a 'transsemiotic' order that is brought about by the rhizomatic transformation of 'one abstract semiotic into another' that breaks free of the first and in which no intervention is required on the part of a 'translator' or other human agent.[42] Drawing their examples from the experiences of 'sleep, drugs, and amorous rapture', to subtle changes in religious beliefs and the metamorphosis of English lyrics in African-American work songs, they envisage a transformative plane that is not under the aegis of individuals, scientists, governments or any other form of authority. Because it is impossible to control such change and we can never be sure what to 'make a rhizome with and don't know which subterranean stem is effectively going to make a rhizome', Deleuze and Guattari invite the reader to experiment, arguing that only a restless experimentation will bring about new forms: 'you can start it in a thousand different ways; you will always find something that comes too late or too early, forcing you to recompose all of your relations of speed and slowness … and to rearrange the overall assemblage.'[43] This trans-human reassemblage does not mean experimenters should reassert their authority or individually make a claim to 'own' the process, but by carefully identifying compatible borderlines they might help to facilitate new forms.

On one level *A Thousand Plateaus* seems to recommend techniques for mobilising a new experience of the human, but Deleuze and Guattari (recalling Levinas in Chapter 3) are also haunted by the human face as at once the most recognisably human aspect and also the most inhuman, revealing a 'horror story' behind the skin.[44] From a certain perspective the face becomes a death mask revealing both the finitude of the human and the unfathomable void within. When faced with this void, as Deleuze and Guattari claim, perhaps art is the only transhuman 'tool for blazing life lines', but also for sweeping us toward what cannot be represented: 'the realm of the asignifying, asubjective, and faceless'.[45] This invitation to aesthetic free play is similar to Lyotard's call for a renewed avant-garde in giving expression to the inhuman (the stranger within who challenges the inhumanity of the system), but there are other more worrying implications to transhuman free play, particularly in the fields of theology and science. Orthodox religions would admit certain transformations as central to their doctrines – the paradox of God as the three-in-one Father, Son and Holy Ghost, or the Buddha as a multiplicity of forms – but pious believers would want to warn against unnatural transformation such as the human becoming 'pig, ox, or wolf' or cold-blooded creatures, which, outside the realm of metaphor, would be morally and spiritually disastrous.[46] Even the American Indian belief in which the interchangeable shape shifting of tribe and buffalo derives from a deep spiritual source ('the buffalo is more than an animal … our lives are bound to it'), would be challenged if other, less dignified, human–animal alliances or transformations were to take place.[47] And, in the realm of science, particularly biotechnology and cosmetic surgery, although certain transformations would be viewed as having humane ends (the recon-struction of a child's face after a severe accident), other practices may have adverse consequences (the multiple surgery to Michael Jackson's face has made it virtually fall apart), while others may catalyse a rhizomatic chain of effects which it is difficult or impossible to stop (the 'slippery slope' of biotechnology that Gregory Stock describes).

The transhuman is closely bound up with posthuman technoscience in respect to the way in which one order of being is, often irreversibly, manipulated into another to create a hybrid form. Rather than a late twentieth-century occurrence, Catherine Waldby actually sees this logic of translation as a dimension of scientific modernity, particularly 'all those technological practices which amplify the contacts between humans and the nonhuman realm of organisms and technics, and which assume and promote an interchangeability between human, animal and technological organs'.[48] As Stock and Fukuyama discussed in their 'A Posthuman Future' debate, the ethical and political ramifications of such a project are often overlooked, or only reluctantly acknowledged, by the scientific community. But perhaps the two thinkers are too quick to dismiss the value of a reinvigorated humanism for working through these potential problems. Waldby is right in her claim that this biotechnological culture of hybridity is 'increasingly demanding public conceptualisation beyond the terms of humanist bioethics', but only if we maintain the stereotyped view that humanism is still locked in its classical form and that it does not like – or cannot cope with – change, travel and transformation.[49] An immobile and aloof humanism seems ill equipped to say anything meaningful about the fields of biotechnology, cybernetics or virtual reality with their in-built concepts of self-propelling mutability. But it might be the case, again, that the bad name of humanism derives from a limited conception of it, by stereotyping it as interested only in depth rather than surface, concerned with truth and not stories, and committed to reason and the search for knowledge over any other kind of desire. If, as we suggested in respect to the posthuman, the transhuman is seen as another moment within the ongoing discourse of humanism, then we may be able to better address issues related to technoscientific practices.

As a critical moment within humanism, the transhuman does provide a resource to engage with a rapidly changing semiotic world in which technology and digital culture have given birth to what seem to many to be a secret language with its own syntax. To recall Baudrillard in *The Ecstasy of Communication* (quoted in the Introduction), if 'we are in a system' in which familiar metaphors of 'body' and 'soul' no longer have currency, then it also seems that political commitment and social agency also seem to have been emptied of meaning. One story about the transhuman is that the actual and ideological barriers of the Cold War years have crumbled (with the fall of the Berlin Wall), leaving a wide-open space for globalisation where 'concepts like *global village*, [in] which the old binary system of walls and divisions retained the force of a paradox or oxymoron, [have been transformed] into tensionless commonplaces'.⁵⁰ While Martha Nussbaum sees such a world as generating new discussions that are necessary if 'effective solutions to pressing human problems are to be found', this does not seem very far from the apolitical cultural relaxation that Lyotard worries about or what William Spanos identifies as the complicity between some forms of Western humanist education and the industrial-military complex.⁵¹ And, for every liberal like Bill Clinton who sees a 'world of expanding freedom', opportunity, 'growth in diversity' and a 'common humanity' (even after September 11), there are conservative critics such as the British philosopher Roger Scruton who want to reinforce the boundaries of the sovereign nation state as a 'constraint' on 'the process of globalization, so as to neutralise its perceived image as a threat from the West to the rest'.⁵²

However, another interpretation of the transhuman in which the combination of elements throws up surprising new tensions can actually regalvanise notions of agency. The Canadian journalist and economist Naomi Klein has discussed in her critique of corporate branding, *No Logo* (2000), the way in which recent political demonstrations have emerged spontaneously from discrete and multi-situated interest groups. She detects an 'anticorporate attitude … emerging among young activists' in which eco-warriors, feminists, 'ethical shareholders, culture jammers, street reclaimers, McUnion organizers, human rights hacktivists, school-logo fighters and Internet corporate watchdogs' have collectively contributed to anti-capitalist demonstrations on both sides of the Atlantic (in Latin as well as North America) and in Australasia since the end of the 1990s.⁵³ Fanon would surely approve of such alliances that cut across national, ideological, linguistic and ethnic boundaries, as we discussed in Chapter 2. The anti-capitalist demonstrations which began at the Seattle World Trade Organization Summit in November 1999, that seemed to emerge spontaneously and without need for leaders, have been coordinated largely via the Internet as a transhuman space for virtually undetectable communication between the protestors.

Klein identifies the question of 'what values will govern the global age' as the key for mobilising these 'largely subterranean movements' against democracies that have compromised or obfuscated human rights issues and that many see as having ceased to be 'responsive and participatory' and in collusion with powerful transnational corporations.⁵⁴ What is of most value to Klein is that globalisation is not just about single currency in Europe or equitable trade laws or relaxing into culture or having the economic resources to 'wear Paris perfume in Tokyo' (as Lyotard describes it), but 'an intricate process of thousands of people tying their destinies together [through the Internet] simply by sharing ideas and telling stories about how abstract economic theories affect their daily lives'.[55] This would be an example of Deleuze and Guattari's rhizomatic transformation in which the stories proliferate, reterritorialising virtual and real spaces alike. It may be, as Baudrillard and Lyotard suspect, that the Internet is not the safe transhuman space that Klein describes (with its fill of corporate logos, sales gimmickry, US-biased advertising and the risk of new forms of paedophilia), but Klein seems sure that, to wrestle a metaphor back from Microsoft, it can create meaningful 'windows' that open out onto fresh opportunities to renew human contact.[56] Against the hubristic posthuman story of a limitless technological future, Klein tells a more modest and immanent transhuman story about dissent and protest stemming from the impact of globalisation on lives throughout the world. If globalisation actually puts up new fences to restrain individuals just as it promises to pull others down, so Klein discerns windows of freedom through which we can breathe deeply and sense new humanist possibilities.

Notes

Texts listed in the Primary Texts sections at the end of each chapter are referred to in shortened form in the following notes.

Introduction: Towards a Critical Humanism

1. Terence Hawkes, 'General Editor's Preface', in Catherine Belsey, *Critical Practice* (London: Methuen, 1980), pp. vi–vii.
2. Roger Eaglestone, *Ethical Criticism: Reading After Levinas* (Edinburgh: Edinburgh University Press, 1997), p. 4.
3. Matthew Arnold, *Essays in Criticism: First and Second Series* (London: Dent, 1964), p. 302. Lionel Trilling, *Beyond Culture: Essay on Life and Literature* (London: Secker & Warburg, 1966), p. 168.
4. René Wellek, 'Literary Criticism and Philosophy', *Scrutiny*, 5(4) (1937), 376. F. R. Leavis, *The Great Tradition* (London: Chatto & Windus, 1948), p. 10.
5. Belsey, *Critical Practice*, p. 7.
6. Iain Chambers, *Culture After Humanism: History, Culture, Subjectivity* (London: Routledge, 2001), pp. 2–3.
7. Ibid., p. 2.
8. Richard Kearney, *Dialogues with Contemporary Continental Thinkers* (Manchester: Manchester University Press, 1984), p. 32.
9. Zygmunt Bauman, *Life in Fragments* (Oxford: Blackwell, 1995), p. 2.
10. Immanuel Kant, 'An Answer to the Question: "What is Enlightenment?"', in *Kant's Political Writings*, ed. Hans Reiss, trans. H. B. Nisbet (Cambridge: Cambridge University Press, 1970), p. 54.
11. Quoted in Tzvetan Todorov, *On Human Diversity*, trans. Catherine Porter (Cambridge, MA: Harvard University Press, 1993), pp. 66–7.
12. Jean Baudrillard, *The Ecstasy of Communication*, trans. Bernard and Caroline Schutze (New York: Semiotext(e), 1987), p. 19.
13. Ibid., p. 51.
14. Ibid., p. 50.
15. Edward Said, *The World, The Text, and the Critic* (London: Vintage, 1983), p. 275.
16. Said, *Culture and Imperialism* (London: Vintage, 1993), p. 408; p. 394.
17. Alain Finkielkraut, *In the Name of Humanity: Reflections on the Twentieth Century* (London: Pimlico, [1996] 2001), p. 90.
18. Frantz Fanon, *Black Skins, White Masks* (London: Pluto, [1952] 1986), p. 217.
19. Theodor Adorno, *Minima Moralia*, trans. E. F. N. Jephcott (London: New Left Books, [1951] 1974), p. 65. For a different reading of Adorno and the Frankfurt School as critics of humanism see Martin Jay, 'The Frankfurt School's Critique of Marxist Humanism' (1972), in *Permanent Exiles: Essays on the Intellectual Migration from Germany to America* (New York: Columbia University Press, 1985), pp. 14–27.

20. Gayatri Chakravorty Spivak, *Outside in the Teaching Machine* (New York: Routledge, 1993), p. 27.
21. Desiderius Erasmus, *Praise of Folly*, trans. Betty Radice (Harmondsworth: Penguin, [1509] 1971), p. 156.
22. Peter Brooker, 'Introduction: Reconstructions', in *Modernism/Postmodernism*, ed. Peter Brooker (London: Longman, 1992), p. 5.
23. Publication details of these and other examples are given in the General Bibliography.
24. Michel Foucault, *The Order of Things*, trans. unidentified collective (London: Tavistock, [1966] 1970), p. 387.
25. Kate Soper, *Humanism and Anti-Humanism* (London: Hutchinson, 1986), p. 128.
26. Roland Barthes, 'The Death of the Author', in *Image–Music–Text*, trans. Stephen Heath (London: Fontana, 1977), p. 146.
27. Ibid., p. 142.
28. Finkielkraut, *In the Name of Humanity*, p. 37.
29. Another example is Derrida's account of the spectres in Marx's writing and the spectres of Marx in contemporary thought: Jacques Derrida, *Specters of Marx*, trans. Peggy Kamuf (New York: Routledge, 1994).
30. Todorov, *On Human Diversity*, p. 390.
31. Chambers, *Culture After Humanism*, p. 4.

Chapter 1 Romantic Humanism

1. John Keats, 'To John Hamilton Reynolds. *Sunday 3 May 1818*', in *The Letters of John Keats*, 4th edn, ed. Maurice Forman (London: Oxford University Press, 1952), p. 141.
2. August Schlegel, *On Dramatic Art and Literature*, Lecture 22, in *Romantic Criticism:1800–1850*, ed. R. A. Foakes (London: Arnold, 1968), p. 58.
3. Keats, *Letters*, p. 143.
4. For discussion and qualification of this perception see Marshall Brown, 'Romanticism and Enlightenment', in *The Cambridge Companion to British Romanticism*, ed. Stuart Curran (Cambridge: Cambridge University Press, 1993), pp. 25–47.
5. Keats, *Letters*, p. 143.
6. Roy Porter, *Enlightenment: Britain and the Creation of the Modern World* (London: Penguin, 2000), p. xxi.
7. Foucault, 'Nietzsche, Genealogy, History', in *The Foucault Reader*, ed. Paul Rabinow (London: Penguin, 1991), p. 87.
8. Arthur F. Marotti, '"Love is not Love": Elizabethan Sonnet Sequences and the Social Order', *English Literary History*, 49 (1982), 398.
9. See also Achsah Guibbory, '"Oh, let me not serve so": The Politics of Love in Donne's *Elegies*', *English Literary History*, 57 (1990), 811.
10. Bertolt Brecht, 'A Short Organum for the Theatre', in *Brecht on Theatre*, 2nd edn, trans. John Willett (London: Methuen, 1974), p. 193.
11. Ibid., p. 188.
12. Charles Taylor, *Sources of the Self* (Cambridge: Cambridge University Press, 1989), p. 175.
13. For discussion of the relationship between modern feminism and Romanticism, see chapter 3 of Pauline Johnson, *Feminism as Radical Humanism* (Boulder, CO: Westview Press, 1994), pp. 47–67.
14. For further discussions of Renaissance humanism see *The Cambridge Companion to Renaissance Humanism*, ed. Jill Kraye (Cambridge: Cambridge University Press, 1996).

15. Stephen Greenblatt, *Renaissance Self-Fashioning* (Chicago: University of Chicago Press, 1980), p. 162.
16. Shakespeare, *Hamlet*, II, ii, 304–8.
17. Ibid., II, ii, 249–50.
18. Ibid., I, ii, 76–86.
19. For further discussion of representations of individualism in Renaissance drama see Andy Mousley, *Renaissance Drama and Contemporary Literary Theory* (Basingstoke: Macmillan, 2000), pp. 66–73, 95–100 and 174–83.
20. Katharine Eisaman Maus, *Inwardness and Theater in the English Renaissance* (Chicago: University of Chicago Press, 1995), p. 5; p. 7.
21. Martha C. Nussbaum, *Upheavals of Thought: The Intelligence of the Emotions* (Cambridge: Cambridge University Press, 2001), p. 473.
22. Ibid., p. 272.
23. Sigmund Freud, *The Interpretation of Dreams*, trans. James Strachey (London: Penguin, [1900] 1991), p. 367.
24. Shakespeare, *A Midsummer Night's Dream*, ed. Harold Brooks (London: Methuen, [1595] 1979), IV, i, 215.
25. Shakespeare, *Macbeth*, I, i, 42.
26. Ibid., I, vii, 60–71.
27. Ibid., V, v, 24–8.
28. Alan Sinfield (ed.), *New Casebooks: Macbeth* (Basingstoke: Macmillan, 1992), p. 6.
29. Shakespeare, *Othello*, I, i, 155–7.
30. Ibid., I, iii, 384–8.
31. Shakespeare, *King Lear*, V, iii, 322–3.
32. The stimulus for these ideas is Terry Eagleton, *The Ideology of the Aesthetic* (Oxford: Blackwell, 1990), pp. 219–26.
33. Marx, *Capital*, p. 167.
34. Ibid., p. 381.
35. Ibid., p. 127.
36. Ibid., p. 356.
37. Ibid., p. 354.
38. See Aristotle, *The Politics*, rev. edn, trans. T. A. Sinclair (London: Penguin, 1981), pp. 81–2; and Aristotle, *Ethics*, rev. edn, trans. J. A. K. Thompson (Harmondsworth: Penguin, 1976), pp. 183–6.
39. Aristotle, *The Poetics*, trans. Stephen Halliwell (London: Duckworth, 1987), pp. 37–42.
40. Marx and Engels, *The Communist Manifesto*, p. 82.
41. Ibid., p. 83.
42. Ibid., p. 86.
43. Percy Shelley, *A Defence of Poetry*, in *Shelley's Poetry and Prose*, ed. Donald Reiman and Sharon Powers (New York: Norton, 1977), p. 505.
44. Immanuel Kant, *The Critique of Judgement*, trans. James Meredith (Oxford: Clarendon, [1790] 1952), p. 104; p. 92.
45. Lyotard also draws on Romantic concepts of the sublime in his characterisation of postmodernism (see Chapter 5 and the Conclusion).
46. Marx, *The Eighteenth Brumaire of Louis Bonaparte*, p. 11.
47. Ibid., p. 13.
48. Cixous, 'The Laugh of the Medusa', p. 338.
49. Shakespeare, *Hamlet*, I, v, 174–5.
50. Cixous, 'The Laugh of the Medusa', p. 338.

51. Cixous and Clément, 'Sorties', in *The Newly Born Woman*, p. 87.
52. Ibid., p. 86.
53. Ibid., p. 86.
54. Ibid., p. 86.
55. Cixous, 'The Laugh of the Medusa', p. 345.
56. Cixous and Clément, 'Sorties', pp. 92–3.
57. Ibid., p. 93.
58. Cixous, 'Castration or Decapitation?', p. 323.
59. Cixous and Calle-Gruber, *Rootprints*, p. 43.
60. Ibid., p. 44.
61. Ibid., p. 33.
62. Ibid., p. 31.
63. Ibid., pp. 52–3.
64. Shakespeare, *A Midsummer Night's Dream*, V, i, 17.
65. Cixous and Calle-Gruber, *Rootprints*, p. 53.
66. Ibid., p. 52.
67. Ibid., p. 52.

Chapter 2 Existential Humanism

1. Jacques Derrida, *Margins of Philosophy*, trans. Alan Bass (London: Harvester, 1982), p. 114.
2. Ibid., p. 115.
3. Robert Young, *Colonial Desire: Hybridity in Theory, Culture and Race* (London: Routledge, 1995), p. 161.
4. Søren Kierkegaard, *The Sickness Unto Death*, trans. Alastair Hannay (London: Penguin, 1989), p. 43.
5. Derrida, *Margins of Philosophy*, p. 116.
6. Neil Badmington (ed.), *Posthumanism* (London: Palgrave, 2000), p. 144.
7. Sartre, *Existentialism and Humanism*, p. 28.
8. Fanon, *The Wretched of the Earth*, p. 251.
9. Alain Robbe-Grillet, *Snapshots and Toward a New Novel*, trans. Barbara Wright (London: John Calder, 1965), p. 81.
10. See Christina Howells (ed.), *The Cambridge Companion to Sartre* (Cambridge: Cambridge University Press, 1992), pp. 178 ff.
11. Sartre, *Existentialism and Humanism*, pp. 23–4.
12. Ibid., p. 25; p. 24.
13. Ibid., p. 25.
14. Ibid., p. 28.
15. Ibid., p. 29.
16. Ibid., p. 30.
17. Sartre, *Being and Nothingness*, p. 544. For Kierkegaard's influence on Sartre see William McBride's essay 'Sartre's Debts to Kierkegaard', in *Kierkegaard in Post/Modernity*, ed. Martin J. Matustik and Merold Westphal (Bloomington, IN: Indiana University Press, 1995), pp. 18–42.
18. Sartre, *The Wall and Other Stories*, trans. Lloyd Alexander (New York: New Directions, 1975), p. 16.
19. Sartre, *Existentialism and Humanism*, p. 36.
20. Sartre, *Being and Nothingness*, p. 516.
21. Ibid., p. 54.

22. Sartre, *Nausea*, pp. 25–6

23. Sartre, *Existentialism and Humanism*, p. 55.

24. Ibid., p. 56.

25. William McBride argues in his essay 'Sartre and Marxism' that the French thinker made an error in linking existentialism with humanism because it threatens to undermine his Marxist commitment, but McBride admits that it is less an idealisation of human beings and more a 'radical social criticism' that characterises the common ground between existentialism and Marxism: Paul Arthur Schlipp (ed.), *The Philosophy of Jean-Paul Sartre* (La Salle, IL: Open Court, 1981), pp. 627–8.

26. Sartre, *Existentialism and Humanism*, p. 6.

27. Martin Heidegger, *Basic Writings*, ed. David Farrell Krell (London: Routledge, [1978] 1993), p. 225.

28. Ibid., p. 248.

29. Heidegger, *Being and Time*, trans. John Macquarrie and Edward Robinson (Oxford: Blackwell, 1962), p. 21; p. 23.

30. Sartre, *Being and Nothingness*, p. 639.

31. Heidegger, *Being and Time*, p. 154.

32. Sartre, *Existentialism and Humanism*, p. 45.

33. Ibid., p. 44.

34. Heidegger, *Being and Time*, p. 155.

35. Derrida, *Margins of Philosophy*, p. 136.

36. Sartre, *The Words*, trans. Irene Clephane (London: Hamish Hamilton, 1964), p. 211.

37. Arendt, *The Human Condition*, p. 10.

38. Ibid., p. 10.

39. Carol Brightman (ed.), *Between Friends: The Correspondence of Hannah Arendt and Mary McCarthy 1949–1975* (London: Secker & Warburg, 1995), p. 172; p. 176. See Parekh Bhikhu, *Hannah Arendt and the Search for a New Political Philosophy* (London: Macmillan, 1981), pp. 46–7 for a discussion of her position on Sartre's existentialism. There is a case to suggest that Arendt is closer to the spirit of Camus: see Jeffrey Isaac, *Arendt, Camus and Modern Rebellion* (New Haven, CT: Yale University Press, 1992), particularly pp. 68–104.

40. Arendt, *Between Past and Future*, p. 29; p. 35.

41. Ibid., p. 9.

42. Ibid., p. 9.

43. Ibid., p. 11.

44. Ibid., p. 14.

45. Ibid., p. 13.

46. Ibid., p. 14.

47. Ibid., p. 4.

48. Ibid., p. 146.

49. Ibid., p. 5; p. 148.

50. Arendt, *The Origins of Totalitarianism*, pp. 299–300. Richard King argues that *Origins* represents 'an extended intervention in the post-war debate about humanism' between Heidegger and Sartre: Richard H. King, 'Hannah Arendt', in *From Kant to Lévi-Srauss: The Background to Contemporary Critical Theory*, ed. Jon Simons (Edinburgh: Edinburgh University Press, 2002), p. 226.

51. Arendt, *Between Past and Future*, p. 264. Heidegger also discusses education in 'Letter on Humanism', *Basic Writings*, pp. 224–5.

52. Arendt, *Between Past and Future*, p. 265.

53. Ibid., p. 266.

54. Ibid., p. 267.
55. Ibid., p. 268.
56. Ibid., p. 280.
57. Ibid., p. 90.
58. Ibid., pp. 151–2.
59. Ibid., p. 153.
60. Arendt's discussion of relatedness owes a great deal to Heidegger's theory of 'Being-in-the-world-with-Others', but in 'What is Existenz Philosophy?', *Partisan Review*, 18(1) (1946), 35–56 she criticises Heidegger for retreating into Being and for not dealing with the implications of a democratic public space. See Seyla Benhabib, *The Reluctant Modernism of Hannah Arendt* (London: Sage, 1996), pp. 47–56.
61. Arendt, *Origins of Totalitarianism*, p. 39.
62. Sartre, *Anti-Semite and Jew*, trans. George J. Becker (New York: Shocken Books, [1946] 1948), p. 27.
63. Nigel Gibson (ed.), *Rethinking Fanon: The Continuing Dialogue* (New York: Humanity Press, 1995), p. 12.
64. See David Macey's biography *Frantz Fanon: A Life* (London: Granta, 2000), pp. 126–7 and pp. 163–4 for a discussion of Sartre's influence on Fanon.
65. Fanon, *The Wretched of the Earth*, p. 266. Fanon, *Black Skins, White Masks*, p. 10; p. 232.
66. Lewis R. Gordon, *Fanon and the Crisis of European Man* (New York: Routledge, 1995), p. 10.
67. Ibid., p. 11.
68. Fanon, *The Wretched of the Earth*, p. 252. Fanon, 'Racism and Culture' (1956), in *Toward the African Revolution*, p. 46.
69. Sartre's Preface to Fanon's *The Wretched of the Earth*, p. 22.
70. Ibid., p. 22; p. 7.
71. Fanon, *Black Skins, White Masks*, p. 10.
72. Richard C. Onwuanibe, *A Critique of Revolutionary Humanism: Frantz Fanon* (St Louis, MO: Warren H. Green, 1983), p. 2.
73. Fanon, *Black Skins, White Masks*, p. 16; p. 13.
74. Fanon, *The Wretched of the Earth*, p. 84.
75. Sartre, *The Communists and Peace*, p. 55.
76. Fanon, *The Wretched of the Earth*, p. 33.
77. Ibid., p. 27.
78. Arendt claims that Sartre goes further in advocating violence in his Preface to *The Wretched of the Earth* than Fanon actually does: Arendt, *On Violence*, p. 12.
79. Fanon, *The Wretched of the Earth*, p. 117; cited in Arendt, *On Violence*, p. 14.
80. Fanon, *Black Skin, White Masks*, p. 18.
81. Stuart Hall, 'Negotiating Caribbean Identities', *New Left Review*, 209 (January/February 1995), 8. Fanon, *The Wretched of the Earth*, p. 31.
82. Fanon, *The Wretched of the Earth*, p. 30.
83. Ibid., p. 253. Gibson (ed.), *Rethinking Fanon*, p. 431. Fanon's dialectic is 'untidy' because he does not seek a totalising position and also because there is something loose and, at times, not fully coherent about his position, as L. Adele Jinadu notes in reviewing Fanon's critics in *Fanon: In Search of the African Revolution* (London: KPI, 1986), p. 230.
84. See Homi Bhabha's Foreword to *Black Skin, White Masks* in the 1986 Pluto Press edition; reprinted as 'Remembering Fanon: Self, Psyche, and the Colonial Condition' in *Rethinking Fanon*, ed. Gibson, pp. 179–96.

85. Gibson (ed.), *Rethinking Fanon*, p. 410.
86. Ibid., p. 22.
87. For a discussion of nationalism and national culture see Fanon, *The Wretched of the Earth*, pp. 45–54 and pp. 166–99.
88. R. Radhakrishnan, *Diasporic Mediations: Between Home and Location* (Minneapolis, MN: University of Minnesota Press, 1996), pp. 190–1.
89. Fanon, *The Wretched of the Earth*, p. 165.
90. Ibid., p. 251.
91. Onwuanibe, *A Critique of Revolutionary Humanism*, p. 13.
92. Gibson (ed.), *Rethinking Fanon*, p. 443.
93. Fanon, *The Wretched of the Earth*, p. 41.
94. See, for example, T. Denean Sharpley-Whiting, *Frantz Fanon: Conflicts and Feminisms* (Lanham, MD: Rowman & Littlefield, 1998).
95. June Jordan, *Civil Wars* (Boston: Beacon Press, 1981), p. 53. Jordan's essay 'Black Studies: Bringing Back the Person' (1969) echoes Fanon on the role of revolutionary violence: 'We do not deride the fears of prospering white America. A nation of violence and private property has every reason to dread the violated and the deprived. Its history drives the violated into violence and, one of these days, violence will literally signal the end of violence as a means': p. 48.

Chapter 3 Dialogic Humanism

1. Quoted in Peter Dews, *Logics of Disintegration: Post-Structuralist Thought and the Claims of Critical Theory* (London: Verso, 1987), p. 45.
2. Freud, *Complete Psychological Works*, Volume 1, p. 295; pp. 307–11.
3. Freud, *Complete Psychological Works*, Volume 15, p. 168; p. 87.
4. Adam Phillips, *Terrors and Experts* (London: Faber and Faber, 1995), pp. 8–17.
5. Tony Davies, *Humanism* (London: Routledge, 1977), p. 60.
6. Soper, *Humanism and Anti-Humanism*, p. 125.
7. Judith Ryan, *The Vanishing Subject: Early Psychology and Literary Modernism* (Chicago: University of Chicago Press, 1991), p. 21.
8. For a discussion of these views see Martin Halliwell, *Romantic Science and the Experience of Self* (Aldershot: Ashgate, 1999) pp. 70–155.
9. Freud, *Historical and Expository Works on Psychoanalysis*, p. 358.
10. Ibid., p. 290; p. 287.
11. Ibid., p. 290. Freud's search for appropriate metaphors can be seen in *The Interpretation of Dreams* (1900) in his various uses of 'pictographic script', 'picture-puzzle' and 'rebus', and his analogy between the 'mystic writing-pad' and the 'perceptual apparatus' of the mind in his essay 'A Note on the "Mystic Writing Pad"' (1924).
12. Freud addresses these charges implicitly through the figure of the 'Impartial Person' and explicitly in his 1927 Postscript to the essay in relation to 'one of our high officials' of the International Psychoanalytic Association, with whom Freud discussed the charges: Freud, *Historical and Expository Works*, p. 355.
13. Ibid., p. 320.
14. Ibid., p. 321.
15. John Carroll, *Humanism: The Wreck of Western Culture* (London: Fontana, 1993), p. 173.
16. Freud, *On Metapsychology*, p. 278; p. 283.
17. Ibid., p. 284.

18. Ibid., p. 285.

19. Walter Lippmann, *A Preface to Morals* (New Brunswick: Transaction Books, [1929] 1982), pp. 180–1.

20. Freud describes another version of the *fort-da* game in which the child uses 'a full-length mirror which did not quite reach to the ground, so that by crouching down he could make his mirror-image "gone"': Freud, *On Metapsychology*, p. 284. This example may suggest the boy is retreating into a narcissistic world at the expense of the mother or, as Lacan later argued, merely an instance when the child is coming to terms with a specular image of himself from the chaos of the first months of life.

21. Irigaray, *The Irigaray Reader*, p. 9.

22. Irigaray, *This Sex Which is Not One*, trans. Catherine Porter and Carolyn Burke (Ithaca, NY: Cornell University Press, [1977] 1985), p. 69.

23. See, for example, Jacques Lacan, *The Four Fundamental Concepts of Psychoanalysis*, trans. Alan Sheridan (New York: Norton, 1978), p. 205.

24. Irigaray, *The Irigaray Reader*, p. 88.

25. Freud, *New Introductory Lectures on Psycho-analysis*, 3rd edn, trans. W. J. H. Sprott (London: Hogarth, 1946), p. 202.

26. Irigaray, *Je, Tu, Nous: Toward a Culture of Difference*, p. 11.

27. Herbert Marcuse, *Eros and Civilization* (London: Ark, [1956] 1987), p. 5.

28. Irigaray, *Sexes and Genealogies*, trans. Gillian C. Gill (New York: Columbia University Press, [1987] 1993), p. 99.

29. Ibid., p. 99.

30. Carolyn Burke et al. (eds), *Engaging With Irigaray: Feminist Philosophy and Modern European Thought* (New York: Columbia University Press, 1994), p. 64.

31. Irigaray, *An Ethics of Sexual Difference*, p. 7.

32. Irigaray, *Je, Tu, Nous*, p. 19.

33. Irigaray, *An Ethics of Sexual Difference*, p. 5; p. 7.

34. Ibid., p. 117.

35. Ibid., p. 9; p. 18. See also Irigaray, *Democracy Begins Between Two*, trans. Kirsteen Anderson (London: Athlone, 2000).

36. Irigaray, *An Ethics of Sexual Difference*, p. 12. Irigaray, *This Sex Which is Not One*, p. 79.

37. Irigaray, *An Ethics of Sexual Difference*, p. 13.

38. Ibid., p. 14.

39. Ibid., p. 16.

40. Ibid., p. 127.

41. Ibid., p. 129.

42. Irigaray, *Je, Tu, Nous*, p. 16. Irigaray, *I Love To You*, p. 26.

43. Irigaray, *I Love To You*, p. 10. For a discussion of Irigaray on utopia, see Margaret Whitford, *Luce Irigaray: Philosophy in the Feminine* (London: Routledge, 1991), pp. 9–24.

44. Levinas, *Humanisme de l'autre homme*, p. 95, translation by Colin Davis in *Levinas: An Introduction* (Cambridge: Polity, 1996), p. 124.

45. Levinas, *Otherwise than Being*, p. 127.

46. Derrida, *Writing and Difference*, trans. Alan Bass (London: Routledge, 1978), p. 96.

47. Levinas, *Otherwise than Being*, p. 59.

48. Martin Buber, *I and Thou*, trans. R. G. Smith (Edinburgh: T. & T. Clark, [1923] 1987), p. 15.

49. Ibid., pp. 15–16.

50. Levinas, *Outside the Subject*, p. 10.

51. Ibid., p. 17.
52. Ibid., p. 19; p. 17.
53. Levinas, *The Levinas Reader*, p. 25.
54. Ibid., p. 76.
55. Simon Critchley, *Ethics–Politics–Subjectivity* (London: Verso, 1999), p. 185.
56. Ibid., p. 185.
57. Levinas, *The Levinas Reader*, pp. 82–3.
58. Ibid., p. 83.
59. Irigaray, *The Irigaray Reader*, p. 179.
60. Derrida, *Writing and Difference*, p. 101.
61. Irigaray, *To Be Two*, p. 25.
62. Ibid., p. 26.
63. See Edward Said, *After the Last Sky: Palestinian Lives*, photographs by Jean Mohr (London: Faber and Faber, 1986) and Paul Gilroy, *The Black Atlantic: Modernity and Double Consciousness* (London: Verso, 1993).

Chapter 4   Civic Humanism

1. Aristotle, *The Politics*, p. 198; p. 59.
2. Ibid., p. 61.
3. For a discussion of the Aristotelian tradition in relation to the liberal individualism thought to have fragmented it, see Alasdair MacIntyre, *After Virtue*, 2nd edn (London: Duckworth, 1985).
4. Aristotle, *Ethics*, trans. J. A. K. Thompson (Harmondsworth: Penguin, 1976), p. 209.
5. For discussion of the intensifying conflicts in modernity between commerce and citizenship see J. G. A. Pocock, *Virtue, Commerce, and History: Essays on Political Thought and History* (Cambridge: Cambridge University Press, 1985) and his discussion of civic humanism in *Politics, Language and Time: Essays on Political Thought and History* (London: Methuen, 1971).
6. For a discussion of the importance of civic humanism in the English Renaissance see Markku Peltonen, *Classical Humanism and Republicanism in English Political Thought 1570–1640* (Cambridge: Cambridge University Press, 1995), particularly pp. 1–53.
7. Philip Sidney, *A Defence of Poetry*, ed. Jan Van Dorsten (Oxford: Oxford University Press, [1595] 1966), p. 29.
8. Martin Davies, 'Humanism in Script and Print in the Fifteenth Century', in *The Cambridge Companion to Renaissance Humanism*, ed. Kraye, p. 47; p. 60.
9. Taylor, *Sources of the Self*, p. 186.
10. Immanuel Kant, 'An Answer to the Question: "What is Enlightenment?"', in *Kant's Political Writings*, ed. Hans Reiss, trans. H. B. Nisbet (Cambridge: Cambridge University Press, 1970), p. 54.
11. Ibid., p. 55.
12. For further discussion of the concept of the public sphere, including comparison and contrast between Kant, Habermas and Kristeva, see Noëlle McAfee, *Habermas, Kristeva and Citizenship* (Ithaca, NY: Cornell University Press, 2000), particularly pp. 166–74 for a critique of the abstraction implied by the concept of public interest.
13. Kant, *Political Writings*, p. 55.
14. Mary Wollstonecraft, *A Vindication of the Rights of Woman*, p. 47.
15. Ibid., p. 12.
16. Ibid., pp. 160–1. For further discussion of Wollstonecraft's religious views see Barbara Taylor, 'The Religious Foundations of Mary Wollstonecraft's Feminism', in *The*

Cambridge Companion to Mary Wollstonecraft, ed. Claudia L. Johnson (Cambridge: Cambridge University Press, 2002), pp. 99–118.

17. Wollstonecraft, *Vindication*, p. 53.
18. The genesis for this notion of balancing inward and upward movements is Charles Taylor's discussion of Augustine in *Sources of the Self*, pp. 127–42.
19. Wollstonecraft, *Vindication*, p. 54.
20. See, for example, Mary Jacobus, 'The Difference of View', in *The Feminist Reader*, ed. Catherine Belsey and Jane Moore (Basingstoke: Macmillan, 1989), pp. 54–5.
21. Wollstonecraft, *Vindication*, pp. 60–1.
22. Wollstonecraft, *The Wrongs of Woman*, p. 73.
23. Wollstonecraft, *Vindication*, p. 30.
24. Ibid., p. 30.
25. Ibid., p. 116.
26. Ibid., p. 30.
27. Ibid., p. 30 for the association of childhood with caprice.
28. Ibid., p. 66.
29. Ibid., p. 67.
30. Habermas, *Theory of Communicative Action*, Volume 1, p. 47.
31. Habermas, *Theory of Communicative Action*, Volume 2, p. 159.
32. Habermas, *Communicative Action*, Volume 1, p. 52.
33. Ibid., pp. 52–3.
34. Habermas, *Communicative Action*, Volume 2, pp. 397–8.
35. Habermas, 'Modernity – An Incomplete Project', p. 132.
36. Habermas, *Communicative Action*, Volume 1, p. 340.
37. Ibid., p. 287.
38. Ibid., p. 286.
39. Habermas, *Communicative Action*, Volume 2, p. 305.
40. For critical discussion of Habermas' concept of reason see Georgia Warnke, 'Communicative Rationality and Cultural Values', in *The Cambridge Companion to Habermas*, ed. Stephen White (Cambridge: Cambridge University Press, 1995), pp. 120–42 and Tracy Strong and Frank Sposito, 'Habermas's Significant Other', ibid., pp. 263–88.
41. Habermas, *The Philosophical Discourse of Modernity*, p. 315.
42. Ibid., p. 302.
43. Habermas, *Communicative Action*, Volume 1, pp. 100–1.
44. Hall et al. (eds), *Culture, Media, Language*, pp. 269–75.
45. Ibid., pp. 273–4.
46. Hall, 'The Toad in the Garden', pp. 69–70.
47. Hall and Held, 'Citizens and Citizenship', p. 177.
48. Ibid., p.176.
49. Ibid., p. 174.
50. Ibid., p. 183.
51. Ibid., p. 175.
52. Quoted in Zygmunt Bauman, 'From Pilgrim to Tourist – or a Short History of Identity', in *Questions of Cultural Identity*, ed. Stuart Hall and Paul du Gay (London: Sage, 1996), p. 35.
53. For Hall on the National Health Service see 'Learning from Thatcherism', in *The Hard Road to Renewal*, pp. 271–83.
54. Hall, 'Cultural Studies and its Theoretical Legacies', p. 277.
55. Ibid., p. 278.

56. Hall, 'Cultural Studies and the Centre', p. 46.

57. Hall, 'The Toad in the Garden', p. 54.

58. Ibid., p. 53.

59. Hall, 'Cultural Studies and its Theoretical Legacies', p. 277.

60. Hall, 'New Ethnicities', in *Stuart Hall: Critical Dialogues in Cultural Studies*, p. 446.

61. Hall, 'What is this "Black" in Black Popular Culture', in *Stuart Hall: Critical Dialogues*, p. 473.

62. Hall, 'The Formation of a Diasporic Intellectual', in *Stuart Hall: Critical Dialogues*, p. 493.

63. Hall, 'New Ethnicities', p. 444.

64. Hall, 'The Formation of a Diasporic Intellectual', in *Stuart Hall: Critical Dialogues*, p. 490.

65. Ibid., p. 490.

66. Hall, 'Cultural Studies and the Centre', p. 19.

67. Raymond Williams, *Keywords*, rev. edn (London: Fontana, 1988), p. 89.

68. Hall, 'Cultural Studies and the Centre', p. 20.

69. Francis Mulhern, *Culture/Metaculture* (London: Routledge, 2000), p. 151. See also Ian Hunter, 'Aesthetics and Cultural Studies', in *Cultural Studies*, ed. Grossberg et al., pp. 347–72.

70. Mulhern, *Culture/Metaculture*, pp. 173–4.

71. Ibid., p. 174.

72. For further discussion of the problems and possibilities of participatory citizenship in postmodern culture see David Buckingham, *The Making of Citizens: Young People, News and Politics* (London: Routledge, 2000).

Chapter 5 Spiritual Humanism

1. See, for example, Friedrich Nietzsche, *Human, All Too Human*, trans. Marion Faber and Stephen Lehmann (London: Penguin, [1878] 1994), pp. 97–100.

2. Mikhail Bakhtin, *Rabelais and his World*, trans. Hélène Iswolsky (Bloomington, IN: Indiana University Press, [1965] 1984), p. 364.

3. The Catholic philosopher Jacques Maritain discusses anthropocentric and theocentric humanisms in *Integral Humanism* (1934–5), reprinted in *Integral Humanism, Freedom in the Modern World, and A Letter on Independence*, ed. and trans. Otto Bird (Notre Dame, IN: University of Notre Dame Press, 1996).

4. King, *Strength to Love*, p. 75.

5. Ibid., p. 106.

6. King, 'The Most Durable Power', in *A Testament of Hope*, p. 11.

7. Benjamin, 'Theses on the Philosophy of History', in *Illuminations*, p. 256. Derrida makes use of Benjamin's concept of weak messianism in *Specters of Marx*, trans. Peggy Kamuf (New York: Routledge, 1994), p. 55.

8. Benjamin, 'Franz Kafka', in *Illuminations*, p. 129.

9. King, *The Trumpet of Conscience*, in *A Testament of Hope*, p. 643.

10. Jean-François Lyotard, 'The Sublime and the Avant-Garde', in *The Inhuman: Reflections on Time*, trans. Geoffrey Bennington and Rachel Bowlby (Cambridge: Polity, [1988] 1991), pp. 89–107. Lyotard, *The Postmodern Condition*, trans. Geoffrey Bennington and Brian Massumi (Manchester: Manchester University Press, [1979] 1984), p. 82.

11. For further discussion of the relationship between negative theology and postmodern theorists, such as Derrida, see Rowan Williams, 'Hegel and the Gods of

Postmodernity', in *Shadow of Spirit: Postmodernism and Religion*, ed. Philippa Berry and Andrew Wernick (London: Routledge, 1992), pp. 72–80.

12. John Peacocke, 'Heidegger and the Problem of Onto-Theology', in *Post-Secular Philosophy*, ed. Phillip Blond (London: Routledge, 1996), p. 192.

13. Carl Raschke, 'Fire and Roses, or the Problem of Postmodern Religious Thinking', in *Shadow of Spirit*, ed. Berry and Wernick, p. 104.

14. Ibid., p. 104.

15. Benjamin, 'Surrealism', in *One Way Street*, p. 237.

16. As an example of the anti-theological strain in Benjamin's work see 'The Work of Art in the Age of Mechanical Reproduction', in *Illuminations*, pp. 219–53. For further discussion of Benjamin's concept of profane illumination see Margaret Cohen, *Profane Illumination: Walter Benjamin and the Paris of Surrealist Revolution* (Berkeley, CA: University of California Press, 1993), pp. 1–15.

17. Benjamin, 'Theses on the Philosophy of History', p. 265.

18. For discussion of Benjamin's concept of time see Andrew Benjamin, 'Time and Task: Benjamin and Heidegger Showing the Present' in *Walter Benjamin's Philosophy: Destruction and Experience*, ed. Andrew Benjamin and Peter Osborne (London: Routledge, 1994), pp. 216–50 and especially pp. 233–9 for Benjamin's theologised concept of time.

19. Benjamin, 'Theses on the Philosophy of History', p. 266. For discussion of Benjamin's Judaism, see Irving Wohlfarth, 'On Some Jewish Motifs in Benjamin', in *The Problems of Modernity*, ed. Andrew Benjamin (London: Routledge, 1989), pp. 157–215.

20. Benjamin, 'Theses on the Philosophy of History', p. 256.

21. Ibid., p. 258.

22. Benjamin, 'Karl Kraus', in *One Way Street*, p. 278; p. 286.

23. Benjamin, 'Theses on the Philosophy of History', p. 263.

24. Ibid., p. 263; p. 265.

25. Ibid., p. 256.

26. Ibid., p. 256.

27. Benjamin, 'The Work of Art in the Age of Mechanical Reproduction', in *Illuminations*, pp. 219–53.

28. Benjamin, 'On Some Motifs in Baudelaire', in *Illuminations*, p. 188.

29. Ibid., pp. 189–90.

30. Ibid., p. 189.

31. Ibid., p. 165; p. 167; p. 169; p. 161; p. 180; p. 181.

32. Ibid., p. 193.

33. Ibid., p. 191.

34. Benjamin, *Charles Baudelaire*, p. 79.

35. Benjamin, 'On Some Motifs in Baudelaire', p. 176.

36. For a fuller discussion of the aesthetic and ethical implications of Surrealism see chapter 3 of Martin Halliwell, *Modernism and Morality: Ethical Devices in European and American Fiction* (Basingstoke: Palgrave, 2001), pp. 69–87. For further discussion of Benjamin's interest in Surrealism see Peter Osborne, 'Small-scale Victories, Large-scale Defeats: Walter Benjamin's Politics of Time', in *Walter Benjamin's Philosophy*, ed. Benjamin and Osborne, pp. 62–9.

37. Benjamin, *Charles Baudelaire*, p. 80.

38. Rainer Rochlitz, *The Disenchantment of Art: The Philosophy of Walter Benjamin*, trans. Jane Marie Todd (New York: Guildford Press, 1996), p. 169.

39. Ibid., p. 150.

40. Benjamin, *Charles Baudelaire*, p. 165.

41. Ibid., p. 176.

42. Hannah Arendt, 'Introduction', in *Illuminations*, pp. 48–9.

43. King, 'The Most Durable Power', in *A Testament of Hope*, p. 11.

44. King, *Strength to Love*, p. 79.

45. Ibid., p. 80.

46. King, 'Letter from Birmingham City Jail', in *A Testament of Hope*, p. 297.

47. King, *Strength to Love*, p. 97.

48. King, 'Letter from Birmingham City Jail', p. 294.

49. See, for example, 'Pilgrimage to Nonviolence', in *A Testament of Hope*, p. 37.

50. King, *Strength to Love*, p. 16.

51. King, 'Nonviolence and Racial Justice', in *A Testament of Hope*, p. 7.

52. King, 'The Power of Nonviolence', in *A Testament of Hope*, p. 13. King criticises Fanon in *Where Do We Go from Here?: A Testament of Hope*, pp. 596–7.

53. King, 'The Current Crisis in Race Relations', in *A Testament of Hope*, p. 88; p. 87. See also Kenneth L. Smith and Ira G. Zepp Jr, *Search for the Beloved Community: The Thinking of Martin Luther King* (Lanham, MD: University Press of America [1974] 1986).

54. King, 'The Current Crisis in Race Relations', p. 87.

55. King's dual emphasis on 'the sacred' and 'the scriptural' positions him against many of the African-American thinkers included in Anthony B. Pinn's anthology *By These Hands: A Documentary History of African American Humanism* (New York: New York University Press, 2001). Compared to thinkers like Frederick Douglass and Richard Wright (ardent critics of the Christian church), Zora Neale Hurston and Alice Walker (who verge on pagan mysticism), and Huey Newton (who advocated a political movement away from the God concept), King seems too close to Christian orthodoxy to be called a humanist, but his exclusion from Pinn's anthology is striking given his critical understanding of the relationship between religion and the world, between individualism and communal experience. Norm Allen calls for a more rigorous engagement with the 'humanistic ideals' of these, and other, African-American thinkers to fully assess the impact of humanism on the thought of religious leaders like King: Norm R. Allen (ed.), *African-American Humanism: An Anthology* (Buffalo, NY: Prometheus, 1991), p. 10.

56. Quoted in Peter J. Ling, *Martin Luther King, Jr.* (London: Routledge, 2002), p. 144.

57. For further discussion of King's critics see Richard H. King, *Civil Rights and the Idea of Freedom* (Athens, GA: University of Georgia Press, 1996), pp. 89–91.

58. Keith Miller, 'Alabama as Egypt: Martin Luther King, Jr., and the Religion of Slaves', in *Martin Luther King, Jr., and the Sermonic Power of Public Discourse*, ed. Carolyn Calloway-Thomas and John Louis Lucaites (Tuscaloosa, AL: University of Alabama Press, 1993), pp. 18–32.

59. John Patton, '"I Have a Dream": The Performance of Theology Fused with the Power of Orality', in *Martin Luther King*, ed. Calloway-Thomas and Lucaites, p. 117; p. 122.

60. Robert Harrison and Linda Harrison, 'The Call from the Mountaintop: Call-Response and the Oratory of Martin Luther King, Jr.', in *Martin Luther King*, ed. Calloway-Thomas and Lucaites, p. 163.

61. Richard King, *Civil Rights and the Idea of Freedom*, p. 95.

62. King, *Where Do We Go From Here?*, in *A Testament of Hope*, p. 578.

63. King, 'An Experiment in Love', in *A Testament of Hope*, p. 18.

64. Ibid., p. 19.

65. Ibid., p. 19.

66. Ibid., p. 19.

67. Ibid., p. 18.
68. King, '*Playboy* Interview', in *A Testament of Hope*, p. 374. Reinhold Niebuhr discusses the tensions and compatibilities between religion and humanism in his 1952 lecture 'Christian Faith and Humanism' given at the Union Theological Seminary, New York. He claims that Christianity is humanist in that 'it regards man in his individual existence and in his historical responsibilities as significant' and he even admits that at times humanism offers a more enriching view of culture than orthodox Christianity. But he goes on to discuss the 'incompleteness of man', which is often overlooked by humanism, and argues that social problems cannot simply be overcome by a secular humanist emphasis on 'more power, more wisdom, more intelligence'.
69. King, *Strength to Love*, p. 13.
70. For a differently inflected discussion of concepts of agency and determinism in King's work, see Richard King, *Civil Rights and the Idea of Freedom*, pp. 121–4.
71. King, *Strength to Love*, p. 21.
72. King, *Stride Toward Freedom*, in *A Testament of Hope*, p. 419.
73. Kristeva, *New Maladies of the Soul*, p. 3.
74. Ibid., p. 8.
75. Ibid., p. 5.
76. Kristeva, *In the Beginning Was Love*, p. 23.
77. Kristeva, *New Maladies*, p. 7.
78. Ibid., p. 7.
79. A similar point is made in Graham Ward, *Theology and Contemporary Critical Theory*, 2nd edn (London: Macmillan, 2000), p. 94.
80. Kristeva, *New Maladies*, p. 128.
81. Kristeva, *In the Beginning*, p. 24.
82. Kristeva, *New Maladies*, p. 119.
83. Kristeva, *Revolution in Poetic Language*, p. 25.
84. Kristeva, *Black Sun: Depression and Melancholia*, p. 109.
85. For a sympathetic critique of the perceived essentialism in the work of Kristeva and other French feminists see Ann Rosalind Jones, 'Writing the Body: Toward an Understanding of *l'Écriture Féminine*', in *The New Feminist Criticism*, ed. Elaine Showalter (London: Virago, 1986), pp. 371–5.
86. Kristeva, *Tales of Love*, pp. 234–63.
87. Clément and Kristeva, *The Feminine and the Sacred*, p. 13.
88. Ibid., p. 26.
89. Ibid., p. 27.
90. Ibid., p. 27.
91. Ibid., p. 27.
92. Kristeva, *New Maladies*, p. 8.
93. Clément and Kristeva, *The Feminine and the Sacred*, p. 141.
94. For a discussion of Kristeva's overcoming of oppositions between absence and presence, emptiness and fullness see Philippa Berry, 'Woman and Space According to Kristeva and Irigaray', in *Shadow of Spirit*, ed. Berry and Wernick, pp. 256–9.
95. Clément and Kristeva, *The Feminine and the Sacred*, p. 141.
96. For further discussion of Kristeva's feminising of religion see Grace Jantzen, *Becoming Divine: Towards a Feminist Philosophy of Religion* (Manchester: Manchester University Press, 1998), pp. 193–203.

Chapter 6 Pagan Humanism

1. Shakespeare, *King Lear*, IV, i, 36–7.
2. John Ford, *'Tis Pity She's a Whore and Other Plays*, ed. Marion Lomax (Oxford: Oxford University Press, 1995), V, v, 79–81.
3. Ibid., V, ix, 10.
4. Ibid., V, v, 70.
5. Nietzsche, *On the Genealogy of Morals*, p. 67.
6. Lyotard, 'Lessons in Paganism', trans. David Macey, in *The Lyotard Reader*, ed. Andrew Benjamin (Oxford: Blackwell, 1989), pp. 135–6.
7. Ibid., pp. 136–7.
8. Ibid., p. 135.
9. Ibid., p. 134.
10. Ford, *'Tis Pity She's a Whore*, I, iii, 34.
11. Alice Walker, *Meridian* (London: The Women's Press, [1976] 1982), p. 50. Walker discusses her pagan impulses in 'The Only Reason You Want to Go to Heaven Is That You Have Been Driven Out of Your Mind' (1997), reprinted in *By These Hands*, ed. Pinn, pp. 287–98.
12. Walker, *Meridian*, p. 52.
13. Benjamin, *Charles Baudelaire*, p. 171.
14. Nietzsche, *The Birth of Tragedy*, p. 110.
15. Ibid., p. 17.
16. Ibid., p. 17.
17. Nietzsche, *On the Genealogy of Morals and Ecce Homo*, p. 85.
18. Nietzsche, *Beyond Good and Evil*, p. 53.
19. Ibid., p. 36; p. 35.
20. Nietzsche, *On the Genealogy of Morals*, p. 119.
21. Nietzsche, *Human, All Too Human*, p. 66.
22. Nietzsche, *Beyond Good and Evil*, p. 31; pp. 104–5.
23. Ibid., p. 105.
24. Nietzsche, *On the Genealogy of Morals*, p. 85.
25. Nietzsche, *Human, All Too Human*, p. 14.
26. Ibid., p. 14.
27. Nietzsche, *Beyond Good and Evil*, p. 35.
28. Ibid., p. 138.
29. Ibid., p. 199.
30. Nietzsche, *Twilight of the Idols*, p. 73.
31. Nietzsche, *Beyond Good and Evil*, p. 26.
32. Ibid., p. 23.
33. Ibid., p. 33.
34. Ibid., p. 115.
35. Ibid., pp. 114–15.
36. Bakhtin, *Rabelais and his World*, p. 10.
37. Ibid., p. 10.
38. Ibid., p. 147.
39. Ibid., p. 148.
40. Ibid., p. 149.
41. Bakhtin, 'Discourse in the Novel', in *The Dialogic Imagination*, p. 280.
42. Bakhtin, *Rabelais and his World*, p. 150.
43. Ibid., pp. 61–2.

44. Ibid., p. 62.
45. Ibid., pp. 98–101; p. 367.
46. Ibid., p. 364.
47. Simon Dentith, *Bakhtinian Thought: An Introductory Reader* (London: Routledge, 1995), pp. 74–6. See also Peter Stallybrass and Allon White, *The Politics and Poetics of Transgression* (London: Methuen, 1986).
48. Bakhtin, *Rabelais and his World*, p. 37.
49. Kobena Mercer, '1969', in *Cultural Studies*, ed. Lawrence Grossberg et al. (New York: Routledge, 1992), p. 441.
50. Joseph Conrad, *Heart of Darkness* (London: Penguin, 1973), p. 97.
51. Marianna Torgovnick, *Gone Primitive: Savage Intellects, Modern Lives* (Chicago: University of Chicago Press, 1990), p. 153; p. 142. Torgovnick also discusses the fascination of Bataille and Conrad with decapitation, pp. 148–50.
52. Bataille, *Eroticism*, p. 34.
53. Ibid., pp. 33–4.
54. Ibid., pp. 254–5.
55. Paul Hegarty, *Georges Bataille* (London: Sage, 2000), p. 7.
56. Bataille, *Eroticism*, p. 15.
57. Bataille, 'The Practice of Joy before Death', in *Visions of Excess*, pp. 236–7.
58. Bataille, *Eroticism*, p. 22.
59. Allan Stoekl, 'Introduction', in *Visions of Excess*, p. xiv; p. xiii.
60. Georges Bataille, *The Accursed Share*, Volume 1, p. 56.
61. Ibid., p. 20.
62. Ibid., pp. 55–6.
63. Bataille, *Eroticism*, p. 90.
64. For further discussion of Bataille and capitalism see Jean-Joseph Goux, 'General Economics and Postmodern Capitalism', in *Bataille: A Critical Reader*, ed. Fred Botting and Scott Wilson (Oxford: Blackwell, 1988), pp. 196–213.

Chapter 7 Pragmatic Humanism

1. The confusion between instrumental reason and what Cornel West calls the 'future-oriented instrumentalism' of pragmatism is understandable given John Dewey's liking for the term 'instrumentalism': Cornel West, *The American Evasion of Philosophy* (Madison, WI: University of Wisconsin Press, 1989), p. 5.
2. Peter Augustine Lawler, *Postmodernism Rightly Understood: The Return to Realism in American Thought* (Lanham, MD: Rowman & Littlefield, 1999), p. 5.
3. Theodore Adorno and Max Horkheimer, *Dialectic of Enlightenment* (London: Verso, [1944] 1979), p. 25.
4. Quoted in Daniel Wilson, 'Science and American Philosophy, 1870–1930', *Transactions of the Charles S. Peirce Society*, 23(2) (1987), 242.
5. Bertrand Russell, *History of Western Philosophy* (London: Routledge, [1946] 1961), p. 770.
6. For discussion of this brand of 'new humanism' see, for example, J. David Hoeveler Jr, *The New Humanism: A Critique of Modern America, 1900–1940* (Charlottesville, VA: University of Virginia Press, 1977).
7. John Patrick Diggins, *The Promise of Pragmatism: Modernism and the Crisis of Knowledge and Authority* (Chicago: University of Chicago Press, 1994), pp. 3–4.
8. West, *The American Evasion of Philosophy*, pp. 3–4.
9. Rorty, *The Consequences of Pragmatism: Essays 1972–1980*, p. xvii.

10. Morris Dickstein (ed.), *The Revival of Pragmatism: New Essays on Social Thought, Law, and Culture* (Durham, NC: Duke University Press, 1998), p. 17.

11. West, *The American Evasion of Philosophy*, p. 5.

12. James Sully, 'Review of *The Principles of Psychology*', *Mind* 16(63) (1891), 393. George Cotkin, 'William James and the "Weightless" Nature of Modern Existence', *San Jose Studies*, 12(2) (Spring 1986), 7.

13. William James, *The Principles of Psychology* (New York: Dover, [1890] 1950), Volume 1, p. 125.

14. William Wordsworth, *The Prelude*, ed. J. C. Maxwell (Harmondsworth: Penguin, [1805] 1971), p. 36.

15. Ralph Waldo Emerson, *Essays and Poems* (London: Dent, 1986), p. 147.

16. James, *The Will to Believe*, p. 22.

17. James, *Essays in Radical Empiricism*, p. 190.

18. Ibid., p. 193.

19. Ibid., p. 194.

20. Ibid., p. 247.

21. James, *Pragmatism*, p. 38; p. 110.

22. Ibid., p. 31.

23. Ibid., p. 32.

24. Ibid., p. 32; p.114.

25. Ibid., p. 28.

26. Ibid., p. 10.

27. Ibid., p. 11.

28. Ralph Barton Perry, *The Thought and Character of William James* (Boston: Little, Brown, 1935), Volume 2, p. 327.

29. James, *Varieties of Religious Experience*, p. 166.

30. James, *The Moral Equivalent of War and Other Essays*, p. 38.

31. Ibid., p. 47.

32. Randolph Bourne, *The Radical Will*, ed. Olaf Hansen (New York: Urizen, 1977), p. 331.

33. Sidney Hook, *Pragmatism and the Tragic Sense of Life* (New York: Basic Books, 1974), p. 101.

34. Dewey wrote two essays on James in *Problems of Men* (New York: Philosophical Library, 1946), pp. 379–409.

35. Bourne, *The Radical Will*, p. 333.

36. Dewey, 'The Scholastic and the Speculator', *Inlander*, 2 (December 1891), 145.

37. Kenneth Burke, 'Intelligence as a Good', *The New Republic*, 64 (1930), 77.

38. Dewey, *Reconstruction in Philosophy* (New York: Mentor Books, [1920] 1950), p. 59.

39. George P. Adams and William Pepperell Montague (eds), *Contemporary American Philosophy* (London: George Allen & Unwin, 1930), Volume 2, p. 16.

40. Dewey, *The Early Works of John Dewey, 1882–1898*, ed. Jo Ann Boydston (Carbondale, IL: South Illinois University Press, 1967–72), Volume 3, p. 320.

41. Dewey, *The Public and Its Problems*, p. 154.

42. Neil Coughlan, *Young John Dewey: An Essay in American Intellectual History* (Chicago: University of Chicago Press, 1973), p. 112.

43. See Dewey, 'The School and the Life of The Child', in *The School and Society* (Chicago: University of Chicago Press, 1915), pp. 47–73.

44. Dewey thought Roosevelt dealt only in half-measures, that his politics were too experimental and based on shaky premises. Critics are divided on this issue: Arthur Schlesinger Jr and Kenneth Thompson argue that Roosevelt was a pragmatic democrat, while Paul Conkin and James McGregor share Dewey's perspective that Roosevelt's

'haphazard, theoretically attenuated programs' were 'the very antithesis of the pragmatic': Paul Conkin, *The New Deal* (London: Routledge & Kegan Paul, 1968), p. 12.

45. Dewey, 'The Need for a New Party', *New Republic*, 66 (1931), 178. Dewey, 'Social
    Science and Social Control', *New Republic*, 67 (1931), 277.

46. Dewey, *John Dewey: The Political Writings*, ed. Debra Morris and Ian Shapiro
    (Indianapolis, IN: Hackett, 1993), p. 225.

47. Ibid., p. 226.

48. Ibid., p. 229.

49. Ibid., p. 227; p. 228.

50. Alan Ryan, *John Dewey and the High Tide of American Liberalism* (New York: Norton,
    1995), p. 349.

51. Dewey, *John Dewey: The Political Writings*, p. 229.

52. Dewey, *A Common Faith*, p. 2.

53. Ibid., pp. 14–15.

54. Ibid., p. 8.

55. *Humanist Manifestos I and II* (Buffalo, NY: Prometheus Books, 1973), p. 7. The second
    American *Humanist Manifesto* (1973) established a clearer system of ethics than the first.

56. Ibid., p. 14.

57. The chair of the World Student Christian Federation, Francis Pickens Miller,
    responded violently to *A Common Faith*, claiming that Dewey's liberal humanism was
    the American version of Nazi religion in his stress on imagination over conscience:
    Martin E. Marty, *Modern American Religion, The Noise of Conflict, 1919–1941* (Chicago:
    University of Chicago Press, 1991), p. 313. Another prominent American theologian,
    Helmut Richard Niebuhr, did not attack Dewey explicitly, but argued that 'liberalism
    glibly identified human values with the divine' and liberals used religious language as a
    bulwark for the crisis of faith in secular progress: ibid, p. 320.

58. Rorty, *Philosophy and Social Hope*, p. 17.

59. Ibid., p. 20.

60. Ibid., p. 14.

61. Ibid., pp. 19–20.

62. Ibid., p. 19.

63. It is possible to divide Rorty's work into three phases: (1) language and epistemology;
    (2) aesthetics and Romanticism; (3) social and political theory; but there is also a sense
    that he is casting wider his discursive net rather than progressing developmentally.

64. Richard Rorty, *Philosophy and the Mirror of Nature* (London: Blackwell, [1979] 1990),
    p. 359.

65. Ibid., p. 315. To understand how Rorty has inherited the mirror metaphor from the
    early phase of pragmatism, it is worth quoting Randolph Bourne on Dewey: 'The mind
    is not a looking-glass, reflecting the world for its private contemplation, not a logic-
    machine for building up truth, but a tool by which we adjust ourselves to the situations
    in which life puts us': Bourne, *The Radical Will*, p. 332.

66. Rorty, *Philosophy and the Mirror of Nature*, p. 315.

67. Ibid., pp. 316–17.

68. Ibid., p. 317.

69. Ibid., p. 316; p. 318.

70. Ibid., p. 359. Rorty claims that James and Dewey should have 'dropped the term
    "experience", not redefined it', suggesting that certain kinds of redescription do not
    always prove useful: Rorty, *Truth and Progress*, p. 297.

71. Rorty, *Philosophy and the Mirror of Nature*, p. 362.

72. Ibid., p. 377.

73. Ibid., p. 358.
74. Rorty, *Consequences of Pragmatism*, p. xviii.
75. Ibid., p. xlii.
76. Rorty, *Objectivity, Relativism, and Truth*, p. 199.
77. Ibid., p. 189.
78. Ibid., p. 182.
79. Rorty, *Achieving Our Country* (Cambridge, MA: Harvard University Press, 1998), p. 18.
80. Rorty, *Objectivity, Relativism, and Truth*, p. 194.
81. Rorty, 'Le Cosmopolitanisme sans emancipation: En réponse à Jean-François Lyotard', *Critique* 41 (1985), 570.
82. Rorty, *Contingency, Irony, and Solidarity*, p. 74.
83. Ibid., p. 73.
84. Ibid., p. 86.
85. Ibid., p. 87.
86. Ibid., p. 88; pp. 92–3. See Simon Critchley's essay 'Deconstruction and Pragmatism: Is Derrida a Private Ironist or a Public Liberal?' for a discussion of Rorty's skewed reading of Derrida and a general comparison of pragmatic and poststructuralist ideas: Critchley, *Ethics–Politics–Subjectivity*, pp. 83–105.
87. Rorty, *Philosophy and Social Hope*, p. 14.
88. Ibid., p. 127.
89. Ibid., p. 128; p. 127.
90. Ibid., p. 129; p. 130.
91. Ibid., p. 234.
92. Ibid., p. 239.
93. Ibid., p. 248.
94. Ibid., p. 248; p. 250. For a similar analysis of tensions between individualism and community in America, see Robert Bellah et al., *Habits of the Heart: Individualism and Commitment in American Life* (New York: Harper & Row, 1986).

Chapter 8 Technological Humanism

1. Bryan Appleyard, *Understanding the Present: Science and the Soul of Modern Man* (London: Picador, 1992), p. 2.
2. Haraway, *Modest_Witness@Second_Millennium*, p. 24.
3. Joseph Needham (ed.), *Science, Religion and Reality* (New York: George Braziller, 1955), pp. 3–4.
4. David Harvey, *The Condition of Postmodernity* (Oxford: Blackwell, 1990), p. 12.
5. Norman Mailer, *Advertisements for Myself* (London: HarperCollins, [1961] 1994), p. 292.
6. Peter Brooker (ed.), *Modernism/Postmodernism* (London: Longman, 1992), p. 132.
7. Auguste Lumière, *La recherche scientifique* (Paris: Société d'Edition d'Enseignement Superieur, 1948), p. 5.
8. Catherine Waldby, *The Visible Human Project: Informatic Bodies and Posthuman Medicine* (London: Routledge, 2000), p. 7.
9. Martin Heidegger, *Basic Writings*, ed. David Farrell Krell (London: Routledge, 1993), p. 311.
10. Ibid., p. 312.
11. Ibid., p. 323.
12. The acceleration of technology has been always been a central feature of modernity,

but the inventor Ray Kurzweil has argued that that it is speeding up exponentially. In 2002 Kurzweil claimed that 'the twenty-first century, because of the explosive power of exponential growth, will be equivalent to twenty thousand years of progress at today's rate of progress, which is far greater than all of recorded history': *Partisan Review*, 69(4) (Fall 2002), 543.

13. Richard Wise, *Multimedia: A Critical Introduction* (London: Routledge, 2000), p. 185. Philip Marchand and Marshall McLuhan, *The Medium and the Message* (New York: Ticknor & Fields, 1989), p. 205. See also Gary Genosko, *McLuhan and Baudrillard: The Masters of Implosion* (London: Routledge, 1999).

14. Waldby, *The Visible Human Project*, p. 46.

15. Haraway, *Simians, Cyborgs and Women*, p. 150.

16. Haraway, *Modest_Witness@Second_Millennium*, p. 14. Haraway, *Simians, Cyborgs and Women*, p. 181.

17. Hayden White, *The Content of the Form: Narrative Discourse and Historical Representation* (Baltimore, MD: Johns Hopkins University Press, 1992), p. 35.

18. Foucault, *The Order of Things*, p. 342.

19. Foucault, *Ethics: Subjectivity and Truth*, p. 309; p. 306.

20. Foucault, *The Order of Things*, p. 344.

21. Ibid., p. 342; p. 343.

22. Foucault, *Ethics: Subjectivity and Truth*, p. 313.

23. Ibid., pp. 313–14.

24. Foucault, *The Archaeology of Knowledge*, trans A. M. Sheridan Smith (London: Routledge, [1969] 1992), p. 13.

25. See Jürgen Habermas, 'Modernity versus Postmodernity', *New German Critique*, 22 (Winter 1981), 3–14. For a discussion of Habermas and Foucault on humanist issues, see Nancy Fraser, 'Michel Foucault: A "Young Conservative"?', *Ethics*, 96(1) (1985), 165–84, reprinted in *Feminist Interpretations of Michel Foucault*, ed. Susan J. Hekman (University Park, PA: The Pennsylvania State University Press, 1996), pp. 15–38.

26. Jon Simons, *Foucault and the Political* (London: Routledge, 1995), p. 17.

27. Foucault, *Madness and Civilization*, trans. Richard Howard (New York: Pantheon, [1961] 1965), p. 206. For Foucault 'governmentality' arose from a potent mixture of power, knowledge and discipline in the eighteenth century and is geared to controlling individuals through the implementation of procedures and legitimating certain forms of behaviour.

28. Alan Petersen and Robin Bunton (eds), *Foucault: Health and Medicine* (London: Routledge, 1997), p. 181.

29. Haraway, *Modest_Witness@Second_Millennium*, p. 11.

30. Foucault, *Ethics: Subjectivity and Truth*, p. 24.

31. Ibid., p. 35.

32. Ibid., pp. 40–1.

33. Foucault, *Technologies of the Self*, p. 15.

34. Foucault, *Ethics: Subjectivity and Truth*, p. 315

35. Michel Foucault, *The History of Sexuality*, 2: *The Use of Pleasure*, trans. Robert Hurley (London: Penguin, 1985), p. 9.

36. Foucault, *Technologies of the Self*, p. 21.

37. Ibid., p. 35.

38. Foucault, *The Foucault Reader*, p. 94.

39. Steve Best and Douglas Kellner, *Postmodern Theory* (London: Guilford Press, 1988), p. 18. Foucault, *The Foucault Reader*, p. 351.

40. Simons, *Foucault and the Political*, pp. 78–80.

41. Lois McNay, *Foucault: A Critical Introduction* (New York: Continuum, 1994), p. 154.
42. Foucault, *Technologies of the Self*, p. 15.
43. Graham Coulter-Smith, 'Between Marx and Derrida: Baudrillard, Art and Technology', in *Jean Baudrillard: Art and Artefact*, ed. Zurbrugg, p. 92.
44. Ibid., p. 93.
45. Foucault, *The Use of Pleasure*, p. 8. For a discussion of Baudrillard's strategies see 'Baudrillard's List' (1994), in *Jean Baudrillard: Art and Artefact*, ed. Zurbrugg, pp. 43–50.
46. Don DeLillo, *White Noise* (London: Picador, [1984] 1986), p. 16.
47. Baudrillard, *Selected Writings*, ed. Mark Poster (Cambridge: Polity Press, 1988), p. 170.
48. Baudrillard, *Simulations*, p. 152.
49. Ibid., pp. 52–3.
50. Ibid., p. 53.
51. Ibid., pp. 53–4.
52. Don DeLillo, *Players* (London: Vintage, [1977] 1991), p. 16.
53. William Gibson, *Neuromancer* (London: Grafton, [1984] 1986), p. 68.
54. Baudrillard, *Simulations*, p. 58.
55. Baudrillard, *The System of Objects*, p. 112.
56. Ibid., p. 111.
57. Ibid., p. 120.
58. Ibid., p. 123.
59. Stanley Aronowitz, 'The Production of Scientific Knowledge: Science, Ideology, and Marxism', in *Marxism and the Interpretation of Culture*, ed. Cary Nelson and Lawrence Grossberg (Basingstoke: Macmillan, 1988), p. 519.
60. Ibid., pp. 185–6.
61. Baudrillard, *Revenge of the Crystal: Selected Writings on the Modern Object and its Destiny, 1968–1983*, ed. Paul Foss and Julian Pefanis (London: Pluto, 1990), pp. 15–17.
62. Baudrillard, *The Ecstasy of Communication*, p. 16.
63. Ibid., p. 27.
64. Ibid., p. 27; p. 38.
65. Ibid., pp. 38–9.
66. Zurbrugg (ed.), *Jean Baudrillard: Art and Artefact*, p. 19.
67. Ibid., p. 19. See William Bogard, *The Simulacra of Surveillance: Hypercontrol in Telematic Societies* (Cambridge: Cambridge University Press, 1996).
68. Zurbrugg (ed.), *Jean Baudrillard: Art and Artefact*, p. 20.
69. Ibid., p. 23.
70. Ibid., p. 24.
71. Ibid., p. 37.
72. Ibid., p. 34.
73. Ibid., p. 38.
74. Ibid., p. 40.
75. Haraway, *Simians, Cyborgs and Women*, p. 149.
76. Haraway, *How Like a Leaf*, p. 23. Haraway does not deny the influence of Heidegger, but finds his propositions in 'The Question Concerning Technology' dogmatically narrow.
77. Haraway, *Simians, Cyborgs and Women*, p. 150.
78. Ibid., p. 151.
79. Haraway, *How Like a Leaf*, p. 23.
80. Craig M. Klugman, 'From Cyborg Fiction to Medical Reality', *Literature and Medicine*, 20(1) (Spring 2001), 44.

81. Haraway, *Modest_Witness@Second_Millennium*, p. 50.
82. Haraway, *Primate Visions*, p. 54.
83. Ibid., p. 55.
84. Haraway, *Modest_Witness@Second_Millennium*, p. 51.
85. Haraway, *Primate Visions*, p. 5.
86. Haraway, *How Like a Leaf*, p. 88.
87. Haraway, *Modest_Witness@Second_Millennium*, p. 240; p. 238.
88. Ibid., p. 239.
89. *The Family of Man* (New York: Simon and Schuster, [1955] 1983), pp. 2–4.
90. Haraway, *Modest_Witness@Second_Millennium*, p. 243.
91. Haraway, *Primate Visions*, p. 110.
92. Ibid., p. 228.
93. Jana Sawicki, 'Feminism, Foucault, and "Subjects" of Power and Freedom', in *Feminist Interpretations of Michel Foucault*, ed. Hekman, p. 169.
94. Baudrillard, *Forget Foucault*, trans. Nicole Dufresne (New York: Semiotext(e), [1977] 1987), p. 25.
95. Sadie Plant, 'On the Matrix: Cyberfeminist Simulations' (1996), in *The Gendered Cyborg: A Reader*, ed. Gill Kirkup et al. (London: Routledge, 2000), p. 265.
96. Ibid., pp. 265–6.
97. Haraway, *Primate Visions*, p. 287.
98. Monique Wittig, *The Straight Mind and Other Essays* (Boston, MA: Beacon Press, 1992), p. 8.
99. Haraway, *Modest_Witness@Second_Millennium*, pp. 49–118. Haraway, *How Like a Leaf*, pp. 139–48.
100. Ibid., p. 106.
101. Haraway, *Modest_Witness@Second_Millennium*, p. 33.
102. Godfrey Reggio displays his humanist sensibility in describing the aims of the *qatsi* project: 'What I tried to show is that the main event today is not seen by those that live in it … the transiting of old nature as our host of life for human habitation into a technological milieu, into mass technology as the environment of life': *Essence of Life* (dir. Greg Carson, 2002). Although he is keen to distance his filmmaking from cultural critique, Reggio's trilogy is a clear example of cinematic and digital technology being used to explore a culture of technoscience, which he argues has become so ubiquitous that 'we are no longer conscious of its presence'.

Conclusion: Inhuman, Posthuman, Transhuman, Human

1. All the images discussed here are included in Zurbrugg (ed.), *Jean Baudrillard: Art and Artefact*, between pp. 48 and 49.
2. Fredric Jameson, *Postmodernism, or, The Cultural Logic of Late Capitalism* (London: Verso, 1991), p. 6; p. 10.
3. Ibid., p. 8.
4. Heidegger, *Basic Writings*, p. 159.
5. Jameson, *Postmodernism*, p. 9. Derrida is more questioning about this kind of humanist reading of Van Gogh's picture in *The Truth in Painting*, trans. Geoff Bennington and Ian McLeod (Chicago: University of Chicago Press, [1978] 1987), pp. 257–382.
6. Jean-François Lyotard, *The Postmodern Explained to Children: Correspondence 1982–1985*, ed. Julian Pefanis and Morgan Thomas (London: Turnaround, [1986] 1992), p. 17.
7. Fanon, *The Wretched of the Earth*, p. 76.
8. Lyotard, *The Postmodern Explained to Children*, p. 19.

9. Ibid., p. 20.

10. Noam Chomsky, *The New Military Humanism: Lessons from Kosovo* (London: Pluto, 1999), p. 13. William V. Spanos, *The End of Education: Toward Posthumanism* (Minneapolis, MN: University of Minnesota Press, 1993), p. xiii.

11. David Barsamian and Noam Chomsky, *Propaganda and the Public Mind: Conversations with Noam Chomsky* (London: Pluto, 2001), p. 147.

12. Chomsky, *Chronicles of Dissent: Interviews with David Barsamian* (Monroe, ME: Common Courage Press, 1992), p. 247; p. 339. See also Barsamian and Chomsky, *Propaganda and the Public Mind*, p. 153.

13. Michael Ignatieff, *Virtual War: Kosovo and Beyond* (London: Chatto & Windus, 2000), p. 72.

14. Said, *The World, the Text, and the Critic*, p. 172.

15. Chomsky, *Chronicles of Dissent*, p. 163. David Rieff also worries about the rhetoric of humanitarianism, given that the Serb massacre in Srebrenicia and the Rwandan genocide of 1994 were given little media attention compared to the bombing of the World Trade Center in 2001. Rieff argues that one of the consequences of September 11 has been to reinforce 'the same moral hierarchy among victims of the world's horrors ... the difference, even when speaking of the dead, between the West and the rest': David Rieff, *A Bed for the Night: Humanitarianism in Crisis* (New York: Simon and Schuster, 2002), p. 5. For a critical reading of the United Nations, see Rosemary Righter, *Utopia Lost: The United Nations and the World Order* (New York: Twentieth Century Fund Press, 1995) and for a wider-ranging discussion of human rights, see Costas Douzinas, 'Human Rights, Humanism and Desire', *Angelaki*, 6(3) (December 2001), 183–206.

16. Ignatieff, *Virtual War*, p. 163.

17. Chomsky, *The New Military Humanism*, p. 1. David Rieff argues that Ignatieff is too optimistic about the potential of the 'international community' to intervene for humane ends, claiming that this phrase is often used as a more palatable version of a US-dominated 'international order': 'the reality is that the moment one taps on the idea of the international community it falls apart like a child's broken toy': Rieff, *A Bed for the Night*, p. 9.

18. Lyotard, *The Inhuman: Reflections on Time*, p. 1.

19. Ibid., p. 2.

20. Kristeva, *New Maladies of the Soul*, p. 7.

21. Paul Harris, 'Thinking @ the Speed of Time: Globalization and its Dis-contents or, Can Lyotard's Thought Go On Without a Body?', *Yale French Studies*, 99 (2001), 141.

22. Ibid., p. 130.

23. Lyotard, *Political Writings*, trans. Bill Readings and Kevin Paul Geiman (London: UCL Press, 1993), p. 150.

24. Lyotard, *The Inhuman*, p. 4.

25. Lyotard, *Political Writings*, p. 152.

26. Lyotard, *The Inhuman*, p. 7. Lyotard claims the 'debt to childhood is one which we never pay off. But it is enough not to forget it in order to resist it and perhaps, not to be unjust. It is the task of writing, thinking, literature, arts, to venture to bear witness to it': ibid., p. 7. See also Lyotard's 'Foreword: Spaceship' to *Education and the Postmodern Condition*, ed. Michael Peters (Westport, CT: Bergin & Garvey, 1995), pp. xix–xx.

27. Lyotard, *The Postmodern Explained to Children*, p. 90.

28. Ernesto Laclau, 'Politics and the Limits of Modernity', in *Universal Abandon*, ed. Andrew Ross (Edinburgh: Edinburgh University Press, 1988), pp. 63–82.

29. Ibid., p. 92.

30. Gregory Stock, *Redesigning Humans: Choosing Our Children's Genes* (London: Profile, 2002), p. 1.

31. Ibid., p. 3.

32. Ibid., p. 17.

33. Ibid., p. 170.

34. Francis Fukuyama, *Our Posthuman Future: Consequences of the Biotechnology Revolution* (London: Profile, 2002), p. 7.

35. Stock, *Redesigning Humans*, p. 151.

36. Fukuyama, *Our Posthuman Future*, p. 218.

37. Lyotard, *The Inhuman*, p. 10.

38. Badmington (ed.), *Posthumanism*, p. 9.

39. Ibid., p. 10.

40. Waldby, *The Visible Human Project*, p. 48.

41. Keith Ansell Pearson, *Viroid Life: Perspectives on Nietzsche and the Transhuman Condition* (London: Routledge, 1997), p. 1.

42. Gilles Deleuze and Félix Guattari, *A Thousand Plateaus: Capitalism & Schizophrenia*, trans. Brian Massumi (London: Athlone, 1992), p. 136.

43. Ibid., p. 251; p. 259.

44. Ibid., p. 167.

45. Ibid., p. 187.

46. Ibid., p. 252.

47. From the Vision Statement of The Buffalo Trust: 'a non-profit foundation for the preservation and return of their cultural heritage to Native Americans'.

48. Waldby, *The Visible Human Project*, p. 44.

49. Ibid., p. 45.

50. George Slusser and Tom Shippey (eds), *Fiction 2000: Cyberpunk and the Future of Narrative* (Athens, GA: University of Georgia Press, 1992), pp. 1–2.

51. Martha C. Nussbaum, *Cultivating Humanity: A Classical Defense of Reform in Liberal Education* (Cambridge, MA: Harvard University Press, 1997), p. 6.

52. Bill Clinton, 'The Struggle for the Soul of the Twenty-First Century', The 2001 Richard Dimbleby Lecture, London, 14 December 2001; transcript available on www.bbc.co.uk/arts/news-comment/dimbleby/clinton.shtml. Roger Scruton, *The West and the Rest: Globalization and the Terrorist Threat* (London: Continuum, 2002), p. 159.

53. Naomi Klein, *No Logo* (London: HarperCollins, 2000), p. xviii.

54. Naomi Klein, *Fences and Windows: Dispatches from the Frontline of the Globalization Debate* (London: HarperCollins, 2002), pp. xiii–xiv.

55. Lyotard, *The Postmodern Explained to Children*, p. 17. Klein, *Fences and Windows*, p. xv.

56. Mark Poster draws attention to the fact that interfacing with the Internet 'draws the human into technology' by turning the user into a form of cyborg. He also offers some cautionary warnings about placing too much faith in the Internet as a 'free' transhuman technology: Poster, 'Postmodern Virtualities', in *FutureNatural: Nature, Science, Culture*, ed. George Robertson et al. (London: Routledge, 1996), pp. 183–202.

General Bibliography

Allen, Norm R. (ed.), *African–American Humanism: An Anthology* (Buffalo, NY: Prometheus, 1991).

Angelaki, Special Issue: Impurity, Authenticity and Humanity, 3(1) (April 1998).

Ansell Pearson, Keith, *Viroid Life: Perspectives on Nietzsche and the Transhuman Condition* (London: Routledge, 1997).

Arac, Jonathan (ed.), *After Foucault: Humanistic Knowledge, Postmodern Challenges* (New Brunswick: Rutgers University Press, 1988).

Arendt, Hannah, *The Human Condition* (Chicago: University of Chicago Press, [1958] 1998).

Badmington, Neil (ed.), *Posthumanism* (London: Palgrave, 2000).

Barsamian, David and Noam Chomsky, *Propaganda and the Public Mind: Conversations with Noam Chomsky* (London: Pluto, 2001).

Bauman, Zygmunt, *Mortality, Immortality and other Life Strategies* (Oxford: Blackwell, 1992).

Belsey, Catherine, *Critical Practice* (London: Methuen, 1980).

Benhabib, Seyla, *Situating the Self: Gender, Community and Postmodernism in Contemporary Ethics* (Cambridge: Polity Press, 1992).

Blackham, H. J. et al., *Objections to Humanism* (London: Penguin, [1963] 1965).

——, *Humanism* (Harmondsworth: Penguin, 1968).

Blair, Brook Montgomery, 'Post-metaphysical and Radical Humanist Thought in the Writings of Machiavelli and Nietzsche', *History of European Ideas*, 27 (2001), 199–238.

Bookchin, Murray, *Re-enchanting Humanity: A Defense of the Human Spirit Against Antihumanism, Misanthropy, Mysticism, and Primitivism* (London: Cassell, 1995).

Brewster, Scott et al. (eds), *Inhuman Reflections: Rethinking the Limits of the Human* (Manchester: Manchester University Press, 2000).

Bullock, Alan, *The Humanist Tradition in the West* (New York: Thames and Hudson, 1985).

Canclini, N. G., *Hybrid Cultures: Strategies for Entering and Leaving Modernity* (Minneapolis, MN: University of Minnesota Press, 1995).

Carroll, John, *Humanism: The Wreck of Western Culture* (London: Fontana, 1993).

Chambers, Iain, *Culture After Humanism: History, Culture, Subjectivity* (London: Routledge, 2001).

Chomsky, Noam, *The New Military Humanism: Lessons from Kosovo* (London: Pluto, 1999).

Cohen, Tom (ed.), *Jacques Derrida and the Humanities* (Cambridge: Cambridge University Press, 2001).

Copjec, Joan and Michael Sorkin (eds), *Giving Ground: The Politics of Propinquity* (London: Verso, 1999).

Critchley, Simon, *Ethics–Politics–Subjectivity* (London: Verso, 1999).

Cunningham, Valentine, *Reading After Theory* (Oxford: Blackwell, 2002).

Davies, Tony, *Humanism* (London: Routledge, 1997).

Derrida, Jacques, *Margins of Philosophy*, trans. Alan Bass (London: Harvester, 1982).

Dollimore, Jonathan, *Death, Desire and Loss in Western Culture* (London: Penguin, 1998).

Eaglestone, Roger, *Ethical Criticism: Reading After Levinas* (Edinburgh: Edinburgh University Press, 1997).

Ehrenfeld, David, *The Arrogance of Humanism* (New York: Oxford University Press, 1981).

Finkielkraut, Alain, *In the Name of Humanity* (London: Pimlico, [1996] 2001).

Foucault, Michel, *The Foucault Reader*, ed. Paul Rabinow (London: Penguin, 1991).

——, *Ethics: Subjectivity and Truth*, ed. Paul Rabinow, trans. Robert Hurley et al. (London: Penguin, 1994).

Fraser, Nancy, 'Foucault's Body-Language: A Post-Humanist Political Rhetoric', *Salmagundi*, 61 (Fall 1983), 61–3.

Fukuyama, Francis, *Our Posthuman Future: Consequences of the Biotechnology Revolution* (London: Profile, 2002).

Fuss, Diana, *Essentially Speaking: Feminism, Nature, and Difference* (London: Routledge, 1989).

Glover, Jonathan, *Humanity: A Moral History of the Twentieth Century* (London: Jonathan Cape, 1999).

Good, Graham, *Humanism Betrayed: Theory, Ideology and Culture in the Contemporary Universe* (Montreal: McGill-Queen's University Press, 2001).

Grafton, Anthony and Lisa Jardine, *From Humanism to the Humanities: Education and the Liberal Arts in Fifteenth- and Sixteenth-Century Europe* (London: Duckworth, 1986).

Gray, John, *Straw Dogs: Thoughts on Humans and Other Animals* (London: Granta, 2002).

Grayling, A. C., *The Meaning of Things: Applying Philosophy to Life* (London: Weidenfeld and Nicolson, 2001).

Halliwell, Martin, *Modernism and Morality: Ethical Devices in European and American Fiction* (Basingstoke: Palgrave, 2001).

Harris, Paul, 'Thinking @ the Speed of Time: Globalization and its Dis-contents or, Can Lyotard's Thought Go On Without a Body?', *Yale French Studies*, 99 (2001), 129–48.

Heidegger, Martin, *Basic Writings*, ed. David Farrell Krell (London: Routledge, 1993).

Hoeveler, J. David, Jr, *The New Humanism: A Critique of Modern America, 1900–1940* (Charlottesville, VA: University of Virginia Press, 1977).

Huxley, Julian, *Essays of a Humanist* (London: Penguin, 1964).

Ignatieff, Michael, *Virtual War: Kosovo and Beyond* (London: Chatto & Windus, 2000).

Jacoby, Russell, *The End of Utopia: Politics and Culture in an Age of Apathy* (New York: Basic Books, 1999).

James, William, *Essays in Radical Empiricism* (Lincoln, NB: University of Nebraska Press, [1912] 1996).

Johnson, Pauline, *Feminism as Radical Humanism* (Boulder, CO: Westview Press, 1994).

Kearney, Richard, *Dialogues with Contemporary Continental Thinkers* (Manchester: Manchester University Press, 1984).

Klein, Naomi, *Fences and Windows: Dispatches from the Frontline of the Globalization Debate* (London: HarperCollins, 2002).

Kraye, Jill (ed.), *The Cambridge Companion to Renaissance Humanism* (Cambridge: Cambridge University Press, 1996).

Kurtz, Paul, *Forbidden Fruit: The Ethics of Humanism* (Buffalo, NY: Prometheus, 1988).

——, *Skepticism and Humanism: The New Paradigm* (New Brunswick: Transaction Books, 2001).

Levinas, Emmanuel, *Humanisme de l'autre homme* (Montpellier: Fata Morgana, 1972).

Lippman, Walter, *A Preface to Morals* (New Brunswick: Transaction Books, [1929] 1982).

Lyotard, Jean-François, *The Inhuman: Reflections on Time*, trans. Geoffrey Bennington and Rachel Bowlby (Cambridge: Polity, [1988] 1991).

——, *The Postmodern Explained to Children: Correspondence 1982–1985*, ed. Julian Pefanis and Morgan Thomas (London: Turnaround, [1986] 1992).

Mansfield, Nick, *Subjectivity: Theories of the Self from Freud to Haraway* (New York: New York University Press, 2000).

Maritain, Jacques, *Integral Humanism, Freedom in the Modern World, and A Letter on Independence*, ed. and trans. Otto Bird (Notre Dame, IN: University of Notre Dame Press, 1996).

Mousley, Andy, *Renaissance Drama and Contemporary Literary Theory* (Basingstoke: Macmillan, 2000).

——, 'Humanising Contemporary Theory, Re-Humanising Literature', *Working Papers on the Web: The Value of Literature*, 2 (2000), www.shu.ac.uk/wpw/wpw.htm

——, 'Post-Theory, Literature, Marxism', *Keywords*, 3 (2000), 59–73.

Nussbaum, Martha C., 'Human Functioning and Social Justice: In Defense of Aristotelian Essentialism', *Political Theory*, 20 (1992), 202–46.

——, *Cultivating Humanity: A Classical Defense of Reform in Liberal Education* (Cambridge, MA: Harvard University Press, 1997).

Osborne, Peter, *A Critical Sense: Interviews with Intellectuals* (London: Routledge, 1996).

Peltonen, Markku, *Classical Humanism and Republicanism in English Political Thought: 1570–1640* (Cambridge: Cambridge University Press, 1995).

Peters, Michael (ed.), *Education and the Postmodern Condition* (Westport, CT: Bergin & Garvey, 1995).

Pincombe, Mike, *Elizabethan Humanism: Literature and Learning in the Later Sixteenth Century* (Harlow: Pearson, 2001).

Pinn, Anthony B. (ed.), *By These Hands: A Documentary History of African American Humanism* (New York: New York University Press, 2001).

Plowright, Bernard, *Humanism: Pagan or Christian?* (London: Independent Press, 1932).

Porter, Roy (ed.), *Rewriting the Self: Histories from the Renaissance to the Present* (London: Routledge, 1997).

Rieff, David, *A Bed for the Night: Humanitarianism in Crisis* (New York: Simon and Schuster, 2002).

Robertson, George et al. (eds), *FutureNatural: Nature, Science, Culture* (London: Routledge, 1996).

Rorty, Richard, *Philosophy and Social Hope* (London: Penguin, 1999).

Sartre, Jean-Paul, *Existentialism and Humanism*, trans. Philip Mairet (London: Methuen, [1946] 1973).

Soper, Kate, *Humanism and Anti-Humanism* (London: Hutchinson, 1986).

——, 'Feminism, Humanism and Postmodernism', *Radical Philosophy*, 55 (Summer 1990), 11–17.

Spanos, William V., *The End of Education: Toward Posthumanism* (Minneapolis, MN: University of Minnesota Press, 1993).

Taylor, Charles, *Sources of the Self* (Cambridge: Cambridge University Press, 1989).

Todorov, Tzvetan, *On Human Diversity*, trans. Catherine Porter (Cambridge, MA: Harvard University Press, 1993).

——, *Imperfect Garden: The Legacy of Humanism* (Princeton, NJ: Princeton University Press, 2002).

Waldby, Catherine, *The Visible Human Project: Informatic Bodies and Posthuman Medicine* (London: Routledge, 2000).

Young, Iris Marion, 'Humanism, Gynocentrism, and Feminist Politics', *Women's Studies International Forum*, 8(3) (1985), 173–85.

Zeldin, Theodore, *An Intimate History of Humanity* (London: Vintage, 1998).

Index